THE HEBREW BIBLE AND ITS INTERPRETERS

BIBLICAL AND JUDAIC STUDIES FROM THE UNIVERSITY OF CALIFORNIA, SAN DIEGO

Volume 1

THE HEBREW BIBLE AND ITS INTERPRETERS

edited by
William Henry Propp
Baruch Halpern
David Noel Freedman

EISENBRAUNS
Winona Lake, Indiana
1990

Published for Biblical and Judaic Studies,
The University of California, San Diego

by

Eisenbrauns
Winona Lake, Indiana

Printed in the United States of America.

Library of Congress Cataloging-in-Publication Data

The Hebrew Bible and its interpreters / edited by William Propp, Baruch Halpern, and David Noel Freedman.

p. cm. — (Biblical and Judaic studies ; 1)

Some of the papers are based on presentations at the Fourth Conversation in Biblical Studies held at the University of California, San Diego, on May 18–19, 1986.

ISBN 0-931464-52-8

1. Bible. O.T.—Criticism, interpretation, etc. 2. Propp, William Henry. 3. Halpern, Baruch. 4. Freedman, David Noel, 1922– . I. Series.

BS1192.H43 1990

221.6—dc20 89-23372

CONTENTS

PREFACE

Six of the following papers were originally presented at the Fourth Conversation in Biblical Studies held at the University of California, San Diego, on May 18–19, 1986; to these each editor has added a piece of his own. The scope of the collection reflects the multifarious interests of contemporary interpreters of the Bible, which range from old-fashioned exegesis to linguistics, archaeology, theology, historiography, history of interpretation and pedagogy.

The proceedings of prior UCSD Conversations have been published as *The Creation of Sacred Literature* (ed. R. E. Friedman; Near Eastern Studies 22; Berkeley/Los Angeles: University of California Press, 1981), *The Poet and the Historian* (ed. R. E. Friedman; Harvard Semitic Studies 26; Chico: Scholars Press, 1983), and *The Future of Biblical Studies* (ed. R. E. Friedman and H. G. M. Williamson; Semeia Studies; Atlanta: Scholars Press, 1987).

The year 1989 marks the thirteenth year of the UCSD Judaic Studies Program, which now enters full adulthood with the inauguration of a series of scholarly publications. Biblical and Judaic Studies from the University of California, San Diego, will produce monographs and books treating all phases of Jewish civilization, from the Iron Age to the Atomic.

The publication of *The Hebrew Bible and Its Interpreters* has been made possible by the University of California, San Diego, and the Jerome and Miriam Katzin Publication Fund of the UCSD Judaic Studies Endowment.

The Editors

Is a Critical Biblical Theology Possible?

John J. Collins
University of Notre Dame

Biblical theology is a subject in decline. The evidence of this decline is not so much the permanent state of crisis in which it seems to have settled, or the lack of a new consensus to replace the great works of Eichrodt or von Rad. Rather the decline is evident in the fact that an increasing number of scholars no longer regard theology as the ultimate focus of biblical studies, or even as a necessary dimension of those studies at all. The cutting edges of contemporary biblical scholarship are in literary criticism on the one hand and sociological criticism on the other. Not only is theology no longer queen of the sciences in general, its place even among the biblical sciences is in doubt.

The reasons for the decline of biblical theology are manifold, but one of the most deep-rooted is the perennial tension between biblical theology and the historical critical method, with which its history has been closely intertwined. The distinction of biblical theology as an independent discipline is usually ascribed to the inaugural address of Johann Philipp Gabler at the University of Altdorf in 1787, almost exactly two hundred years ago. His subject was "The Proper Distinction between Biblical and Dogmatic Theology and the Specific Objectives of Each" (Sandys-Wunsch and Eldredge 1980). The main thrust of his address was to establish the necessity of making this distinction. Biblical theology was conceived as a descriptive, historical discipline, in contrast to dogmatic theology, which derived its knowledge not only from scripture but also from other sources such as philosophy. The theological character of this enterprise was not a problem for Gabler, since he was convinced that the Bible contained "pure notions which divine providence wished to be characteristic of all times and places" as well as ideas that were historically relative (Hays and Prussner 1985: 3). Biblical theology in the stricter sense was constituted by the collection and arrangement of these universal ideas. Nonetheless, Gabler's insistence on the historical, descriptive nature of the discipline contained from the outset the seeds of later tension between biblical theology and the history of Israelite and early Christian religion.

The Principles of Historical Criticism

The difficulty of conceiving biblical theology as a descriptive historical discipline became evident in the work of the "history of religions" school approximately one hundred years later. Critical historiography, as it developed in the nineteenth century, had its own principles, without deference to the expectations of theologians. Among theologians these principles received their classic formulation from Ernst Troeltsch in 1898. Troeltsch set out three principles (1913: 729–53): (1) The principle of criticism or methodological doubt: since any conclusion is subject to revision, historical inquiry can never attain absolute certainty but only relative degrees of probability. (2) The principle of analogy: historical knowledge is possible because all events are similar in principle. We must assume that the laws of nature in biblical times were the same as now. Troeltsch referred to this as "the almighty power of analogy." (3) The principle of correlation: the phenomena of history are inter-related and inter-dependent and no event can be isolated from the sequence of historical cause and effect. To these should be added the principle of autonomy, which is indispensable for any critical study. Neither church nor state can prescribe for the scholar which conclusions should be reached (Harvey 1966: 39–42).

The problem posed by these principles for biblical theology was most sharply formulated by Wilhelm Wrede in his essay on "The Task and Methods of New Testament Theology." Wrede found that, in theory, most people would grant that biblical theology is an historical discipline. In practice, however, it was still subordinated to dogmatics so that biblical material was pressed for answers to dogmatic questions and distorted to fit dogmatic categories. Consequently, unorthodox biblical ideas were suppressed, and the Bible was not heard in its own right. For Wrede,

> Biblical Theology has to investigate something from given documents . . . it tries to grasp it as objectively, correctly, and sharply as possible. That is all. How the systematic theologian gets on with its results and deals with them—that is his own affair. Like every other real science, New Testament theology has its goal simply in itself and is totally indifferent to all dogma and systematic theology. What could dogmatics offer it? Could dogmatics teach New Testament theology to see the facts correctly? At most, it could color them. Could it correct the facts that were found? To correct facts is absurd. Could it legitimize them? Facts need no legitimation (1973: 69–70).

Wrede's confidence that historical criticism could establish "the facts" sounds naïve, even arrogant a century later, but he had correctly perceived a fundamental opposition between historical method and dogmatics. Criticism cannot offer assured facts, but it offers degrees of probability, based on evidence. The evidence, whatever its strength or weakness, cannot be cast aside or overruled for dogmatic, *a priori* reasons.

Wrede's view of biblical theology was, in effect, indistinguishable from the history of the religion. He made no apology for that fact: "But in what should the specifically theological type of treatment consist? . . . can a specifically theological understanding of the discipline guarantee some kind of knowledge that goes beyond the knowledge of the historical fact that such and such was taught and believed . . ." (1973: 70)?

The "specifically theological understanding" against which Wrede polemicized consisted of a faith perspective derived from dogmatic theology. This entailed the profession that the biblical writings were inspired or revealed and should be regarded as normative. Invariably, it also implied agreement between the Bible and the postulates of dogmatic theology. Wrede's basic complaint was that dogmatic concerns led to historical distortions. He was not, however, only calling for a separation of the historical and dogmatic tasks, as Gabler had done. In his view, historical criticism undercut some of the postulates of traditional theology. So: "For logical thinking there can be no middle position between inspired writings and historical documents" (Wrede 1973: 69). Equally: "It is impossible to continue to maintain the dogmatic conception of the canon," since canonical status is not intrinsic to the biblical writings but only represents the judgment of the church fathers (Wrede 1973: 70). The tension here is not a matter of specific doctrines or conclusions, but, as Van Harvey has put it (1966: 103), a clash between two conflicting moralities, one of which celebrated faith and belief as virtues and regarded doubt as sin, whereas the other celebrated methodological skepticism and was distrustful of prior commitments.

The Neoorthodox Phase

The revival of biblical theology in the decades after World War I corroborated Wrede's judgment that theological commitment lends itself to historical distortion. The dominant neoorthodox theology sought to reconcile historical criticism with dogmatic views of the Bible as an inspired document. Walter Eichrodt conceded that "OT theology presupposes the history of Israel" and that one should "have the historical principle operating side by side with the systematic in a complementary role" (1961: 1.32).

He also declared his rejection of "any arrangement of the whole body of the material which derives not from the laws of its own nature but from some dogmatic scheme" (1961: 1.32) and professed his intention to "avoid all schemes which derive from Christian dogmatics" (1961: 1.33). Yet he conceived his task as "to understand the realm of OT belief in its structural unity and . . . by examining on the one hand its religious environment and on the other its essential coherence with the NT, to illuminate its profoundest meaning" (1961: 1.31). The view that the profoundest meaning of the Hebrew Bible is disclosed by its relation to the New Testament is, however, plainly a matter of Christian dogmatics and was accompanied by a highly distorted view of Judaism, as Jon Levenson has pointed out (1987). The discovery of structural unity in a tradition that spans a millennium has also proven endlessly problematic from a historical point of view and, here again, Eichrodt was more dependent on dogmatic considerations than he seems to have realized.

Again, the internal contradictions of the so-called Biblical Theology Movement in America have often been rehearsed (Childs 1970). G. E. Wright insisted that biblical theology must start from the descriptive work of the historian. Yet he saw its task as the "recital" of the acts of God, which were not simply the results of historical research but "history interpreted by faith" (1952: 128) that involves a "projection of faith into facts that is then considered as the true meaning of the facts" (1952: 117). In typical neoorthodox fashion Wright was attempting to combine the contradictory moralities of modern scientific method and traditional, confessional faith. Even apart from the question as to whether Wright's reconstruction of the history was unduly colored by his conviction that "in Biblical faith everything depends on whether the central events actually occurred" (1952: 126), it is clear that his understanding of these events depended on dogmatic rather than strictly historical considerations (Gilkey 1961). Even Gerhard von Rad, who tried harder than most to respect the historical variety of the Hebrew Bible, argued that any attempt to interpret the Old Testament without reference to the New Testament must "turn out to be fictitious from a Christian point of view" (1962–65: 2.321). His critics may be pardoned for suspecting that this conviction colored his detection of a tension between law and gospel already in the pentateuchal traditions. More fundamentally, von Rad's position was undermined by the tension between his view that the theologian's task was to testify to the biblical salvation history and his acceptance, as a historian, of the quite different reconstruction of that history by critical scholarship (Barr 1980: 11). Biblical theology, then, in the second and third quarters of this century, has been vulnerable to the charge of inconsistency: of allowing dogmatic convictions to undercut its avowedly historical method. The problem is not that the theologians brought presuppositions to the text, since this is also true of even the most "objective" historians, but that their theological presuppositions were inconsistent with the historical method on which they otherwise relied. This was true even of the most radical of biblical theologians, Rudolf Bultmann, in his insistence on the unique significance of Jesus Christ (Harvey 1966: 139–46; Ogden 1961).

Throughout the neoorthodox period of biblical theology, the theological component was seen as confessional faith, which was understood to require some measure of *a priori* belief and conviction. The specific requirements might vary greatly in scope, from the historicity of the "acts of God" to the nature of the relation between the Testaments or the uniqueness of Israel or of Christ, but they affirmed some certainty that was independent of historical research and was more specific than a general commitment of loyalty to a religious tradition. There does, in fact, seem to be an inherent contradiction between theology so conceived and historical criticism, as understood by Wrede and Troeltsch. One of the basic principles formulated by Troeltsch was the principle of criticism, by which any conclusion or conviction must be subject to revision in the light of new evidence. Historical criticism, unlike traditional faith, does not provide for certainty but only for relative degrees of probability. Many of the convictions most dearly cherished by biblical theologians were challenged by historical criticism: the historicity of crucial events, the unity of the Old Testament, the uniqueness of Israel (or some conceptions thereof), or the view that the Old Testament is best understood as a process leading to Christ. A biblical theology that takes historical criticism seriously will have to forego any claim of certainty on these matters.

If, then, there is an inherent contradiction between historical criticism and theology conceived as confessional faith in the neoorthodox manner, biblical theology can only proceed in one or other of two ways: by abandoning historical criticism, at least in theological matters, or by reconceiving the theological aspect of the discipline. The issue is no longer the quest for a unifying center within the Old Testament or the Bible, but the context within which biblical theology should be pursued and the nature of the pursuit itself.

Childs's Approach

There have always been attempts by religious conservatives to evade the consequences of historical criticism for biblical theology. In recent years, however, a more substantial challenge has been mounted by Brevard Childs, in his "canonical approach" to biblical theology (Childs 1970, 1979, 1984, 1985). Childs does not reject historical criticism or dispute its results, but he grants it no theological importance. For theological purposes the text is not to be read in its historical context but can confront the reader directly as the word of God. Childs rightly objects to the label "canon criticism," since his view of the Bible is not a criticism at all (1979: 56–60, 74–75). He explicitly rejects the principle of analogy between biblical and modern situations, which has been a cornerstone of critical method since Troeltsch (1970: 100–101). He also resolutely distinguishes his theological approach from literary and hermeneutical methods with which it has some affinities, but which construe the text as a human product (1979: 77).

Childs's work has been widely reviewed and the main criticisms are by now well-known (Barr 1983: 49–104; Barton 1984: 77–103). His explicitly confessional approach cannot be faulted for consistency, but it has grave liabilities, nonetheless. Chief of these is the apodictic way in which the approach is presented. For Childs, "the status of canonicity is not an objectively demonstrable claim but a statement of Christian belief" (1970: 99). It is not clear, however, that Childs's view of the canon has ever been normative, even in Protestant Christianity, not to mention Catholicism or Judaism. Childs fails to give reasons why anyone should adopt this approach to the text unless they happen to share his view of Christian faith. The canonical approach then fails to provide a context for dialogue with anyone who does not accept it as a matter of faith.

A further liability of Childs's approach is its lack of explanatory power. We are repeatedly told that the scripture shapes and enlivens the church or mediates the revelation of God, but we are not told *how*. Childs is convinced, as Bultmann was, that the text has something to say to the present, but he has no hermeneutic, as Bultmann had, that might provide the common ground necessary for intelligibility. Again, his rejection of sociological approaches excludes a potentially fruitful source of analogies that might permit us to relate the biblical situations to our own. Some of the most suggestive biblical scholarship in recent years has been in the areas of sociology and feminism, and its power has lain in the perception that biblical texts, like any other, serve and legitimate specific human interests. Childs's refusal to reckon with the ideological aspects of biblical texts as human products seems naïve and superficial and weakens the credibility of his theological affirmations.

The effect of Childs's proposal is to isolate biblical theology from much of what is vital and interesting in biblical studies today. Such a strategy, it seems to me, must ultimately be self-defeating. If biblical theology is to retain a place in serious scholarship, it must be able to accommodate the best insights of other branches of biblical scholarship and must be conceived broadly enough to provide a context for debate between different viewpoints. Otherwise it is likely to become a sectarian reservation, of interest only to those who hold certain confessional tenets that are not shared by the discipline at large. Childs's dogmatic conception of the canon provides no basis for advancing dialogue. In my opinion historical criticism still provides the most satisfactory framework for discussion.

Critiques of Historical Criticism

Historical criticism has often come under attack in recent years, not always for valid reasons. The most telling of these critiques have been directed against the pretence of value-free objectivity. Philosophers such as H. G. Gadamer (1982) and Paul Ricoeur (1980) have repeatedly made the point that there is no strictly autonomous reason. Without a tradition (a "text" in Ricoeur's terms) no understanding is possible. George Lindbeck has recently made the same point in somewhat different terms:

> It seems, as the case of Helen Keller and of supposed wolf children vividly illustrate, that unless we acquire language of some kind we cannot actualize our specifically human capacities for thought, action and feeling. Similarly, so the argument goes, to become religious involves becoming skilled in the language, the symbol system of a given religion (1984: 34).

The critical ideal of autonomy, then, must be severely qualified. We can no longer claim with Wrede that historical criticism gives us objective facts. It too is a tradition, with its own values and presuppositions, derived in large part from the Enlightenment and western humanism.

If there is no interpretation without presuppositions, and if the presuppositions of critical scholarship differ from those of traditional Christianity, then some biblical theologians suggest that we should refashion the presuppositions of scholarly method and replace the "hermeneutic of suspicion" with a "hermeneutic of consent" that would be "open to transcendence" (Stuhlmacher 1977: 84). However, the inevitability of presuppositions should not be taken as an invitation to excel in bias (Stendahl 1984: 22). Some presuppositions are better or more adequate than others. One criterion for the adequacy of presuppositions is the degree to which they allow dialogue between differing viewpoints and accommodate new insights. The great strength of historical criticism lies in Troeltsch's principle of criticism. All conclusions are subject to revision in the light of new evidence and arguments. This openness to revision is the trademark that distinguishes critical method from dogmatism of any sort. Consequently, historical criticism has proven itself highly adaptable in accommodating the new insights of form criticism, redaction criticism, etc. Even the recent sociological and feminist critics, who are highly critical of the claims of objectivity (Gottwald 1979;

Fiorenza 1983), have nonetheless relied on the standard critical methods to argue for their revisionist reconstructions. Perhaps the outstanding achievement of historical criticism in this century is that it has provided a framework within which scholars of different prejudices and commitments have been able to debate in a constructive manner.

Where the principle of criticism is consistently applied, there is no basis for the common objection that the principle of analogy dogmatically disallows real novelty in history (see Harvey 1966: 16; Thiselton 1980: 78–79). No possibility is excluded in principle, but the critic endorses the Enlightenment ideal that the assurance with which we entertain a proposition be proportional to the evidence that supports it (Harvey 1966: 123, citing John Locke). The demand for evidence and reasoned calculation of probability is precisely what enables the critical method to serve as a forum for dialogue between people of different views. So while historical criticism does not enjoy the degree of autonomy or of objectivity that has often been claimed for it, it still has many advantages to commend it.

The modification of the claim of autonomy is significant for biblical theology. Critical method is incompatible with confessional faith insofar as the latter requires us to accept specific conclusions on dogmatic grounds. It does not, and cannot, preclude a commitment to working within specific traditions, and biblical theology is inevitably confessional in this looser sense. For biblical theology, the biblical tradition is a given and it is assumed to be meaningful and to have continuing value, although the meaning and value can be subject to critical examination (Tracy 1981: 237–46). Parenthetically, the biblical theologian inevitably works with some canon of scripture (*pace* Wrede), although this does not necessarily imply a qualitative difference over against other ancient literature but only a recognition of the historical importance of these texts within the tradition.

The modern theologian, however, is heir to more than one tradition. We are shaped by the rational humanism that underlies our technological culture and political institutions, no less than by the Bible (usually far more so). It is possible to have critical dialogue between our modern world view and the Bible, but we cannot simply abandon the twentieth century for the ancient world. Rather than a "hermeneutic of consent," then, we need a model of theology that provides for critical correlation between the various traditions in which we stand. It has been said that "the heart of any hermeneutical position is the recognition that all interpretation is a mediation of past and present" (Tracy 1981: 99). It cannot be a mere recital of sacred history or submission to a canonical text. The point here is not just that the theologians *should* be informed by sources other than the Bible or the Christian tradition, but that they cannot avoid it. Biblical fundamentalism is influenced by nineteenth-century rationalism (Barr 1978). Biblical archaism, as advocated by Wright and others, is a product of twentieth-century positivism (Miles 1976). Childs's focus on the canonical shape of the text has affinities with the twentieth-century literary theory of "new criticism," which cannot be dismissed as coincidental, whether he acknowledges them or not (Barton 1984).

The Task of a Critical Theology

The principles of critical method identified by Troeltsch are deeply ingrained in modern consciousness and their relevance is not confined to purely historical criticism. The new developments of literary and sociological criticism are often critical of the more antiquarian kind of historical research, with its obsession with sources, but they too abide by the principles of analogy and criticism. As Troeltsch already observed, "The historical method, once it is applied to biblical science . . . is a leaven which transforms everything and finally explodes the whole form of theological methods" (1913: 730). The crucial methodological shift is a matter of epistemology. Traditional theology started, so to speak, from the side of God, and relied on the postulate of revelation to guarantee theological truth. Historical method starts from the human side and insists on the epistemological questions: how do we control our evidence, and what warrants do we have for the assertions we make? Obviously these questions become acute when we are dealing with assertions about God.

If biblical theology is to be based on critical methodology, then its task is the critical evaluation of biblical speech about God. It is an area of historical theology, and as such is one source among others for contemporary theology (Ogden 1976: 243–45). It necessarily overlaps with the history of religion. It is the specialization of that discipline that deals with the portrayal of God in one specific corpus of texts. Biblical theology should not, however, be reduced to "the historical fact that such and such was thought and believed" (Wrede 1973: 70), but should clarify the meaning and truth-claims of what was thought and believed from a modern critical perspective (I have attempted to do this in various writings on apocalypticism; see my essay "Apocalyptic Eschatology as the Transcendence of Death" [1974]).

The Question of Genre

The primary contribution of historical criticism to biblical theology, in my opinion, lies in its clarification of the various genres in the biblical text and the different expectations appropriate to them. The basic point is simple and obvious. The truth claims that can be made for a biblical passage vary according to the kind of writing involved (Barton 1984: 8–29; Koch 1969:

3–16). The point was raised forcefully in Gunkel's classic discussion of the legends of Genesis, where he made a sweeping distinction between history and legend: "History, which claims to inform us of what actually happened, is in its very nature prose, while legend is by nature poetry, its aim being to please, to elevate, to inspire and to move" (1964: 10). This statement would certainly have to be reformulated now, perhaps in terms of a contrast between referential, informative language and expressive, evocative language (Caird 1980: 7–36), but Gunkel's work marked an important shift away from the attempt to interpret the text as a record of objective reality, toward an appreciation of it as a medium of human expression.

The implications of Gunkel's linguistic turn for biblical theology were largely obscured in the heyday of the Biblical Theology Movement, at least in North America. In recent years the issue has again come to the fore in the much-heralded paradigm shift from history to "story" in biblical theology (Stendahl 1977: 4–5; Frei 1974). James Barr was among the first to proclaim this shift: "the long narrative corpus of the Old Testament seems to me, as a body of literature, to merit the title of story rather than that of history. Or, to put it another way it seems to merit entirely the title of story but only in part the title history . . ." (1980: 5). Elsewhere Barr has distinguished two sorts of writing: "The first is intended as informational; its value can be assessed from the accuracy of its reports about entities ('referents,' things referred to) in the outside world. The second has a different kind of meaning and value. Its meaning lies rather in the structure and shape of the story, and in the images used within it. It is valued as literature, aesthetically, rather than as information" (1973: 55). He adds that "much of literature, to put it bluntly, is fiction." Barr's reformulation of biblical theology parallels the proposal of literary critic Robert Alter that biblical "sacred history" should be read as "prose fiction" (1980: 23–46).

This shift, of course, has not gone unchallenged. Meir Sternberg accuses Alter and his admirers of "a category mistake of the first order" (1985: 25), of mixing "truth value and truth claim, source (the nature of the materials) and discourse (their working in context), standards of literariness, especially literary excellence, and marks of fictionality" (1985: 30). His point is well taken. The genre of a text is determined by its intention, or truth claim, rather than by its success or value. However, Sternberg's objection does not seriously affect the paradigm shift in biblical theology. For Sternberg "history-writing is not a record of fact—'of what really happened'—but a discourse that claims to be a record of fact. Nor is fiction-writing a tissue of free inventions but a discourse that claims freedom of invention" (1985: 25). History writing too is a form of human expression, of *poiesis*, of imagination, and that is the main point at issue in the introduction of the category story in biblical theology.

Moreover, the truth-claims of the biblical narratives are more complex than Sternberg allows. Ancient writers did not distinguish fact and fiction as sharply as we do. The biblical narratives include enough discrepancies and make enough use of folkloric and mythic themes to qualify the common assumption that "their religious intent involves an absolute claim to historical truth" (Auerbach 1953: 14). Moreover, the teleology of a text like Exodus is not exhausted by one intention. We may grant that the story in Exodus 1–15 was assumed, in ancient Israel, to be historically reliable. Nonetheless, it also served, and was intended to serve other functions. It served as the basis for the covenantal law and as the motivation for ethical conduct. It also served as a paradigm by which later historical events could be interpreted, notably the Babylonian exile in Second Isaiah (Isa 40:3–5, 51:9–11). Ultimately, it served as a formulation of Jewish identity in the festival of the Passover, so that everyone must think of themselves as having been slaves in the land of Egypt (Neusner 1970: 13–18). In all of these functions the historicity of the Exodus is scarcely a consideration—indeed, in Second Isaiah the crossing of the sea is mentioned in parallelism with the mythical piercing of the dragon. The value of the story, then, cannot be adequately assessed if it is judged only as historiography.

It may well be objected that the real problem here is that biblical theology has worked with a deficient notion of history and historiography. In effect, both terms have been understood primarily as "a factually reliable account of the past" and it is this oversimplified understanding that has been undermined in the recent discussion. If history is understood more adequately, with due allowance for the blend of fact and fiction that it necessarily entails, it may well be the better genre designation for much of biblical narrative. In the context of biblical theology, however, the shift in terminology from history to story has served a useful purpose, in making the point that the biblical narratives are imaginative constructs and not necessarily factual. They do, of course, provide valuable historical information, but they do not provide the bedrock of certainty that theologians have often sought. Their value for theology lies in their functions as myth or story rather than in their historical accuracy.

The significance of the paradigm shift from history to story is that it abandons the last claim of biblical theology to certain knowledge of objective reality. A story is a work of the human imagination, drawing on the ingredients of human experience. It does not lay claim to logical necessity in the manner of a philosophical system—a point already emphasized in the biblical theology movement. Neither does it rely on the factual verifiability of historical records. We recognize stories as "true" or as valid expressions of reality in so far as they fit our experience, although the fit cannot be scientifically verified and the view of reality is necessarily partial and perspectival. Stories can also be read as proposals that open up new ways of viewing life, though again, there is no guarantee of their value or validity. They may provide insight or inspiration but not the reassuring certainty that has so often been sought by biblical theologians.

The same point can be made with reference to other biblical genres besides narrative—the poetic genres of prophecy and psalms or the inductive, pragmatic formulations of wisdom. Biblical theology is not only narrative theology, but more broadly it is an experiential, symbolic theology, which can find expression in several genres.

It seems to me, then, that Paul Ricoeur has correctly identified the first step in a critical biblical theology when he speaks of "a return to the origin of theological discourse" (1980: 75) by analyzing the various genres of biblical speech; he invites us "to place the originary expressions of biblical faith under the sign of the poetic function of language" (1980: 103), which addresses our imagination rather than our obedience (1980: 117).

This way of viewing the biblical text also seems, in principle, compatible with a process hermeneutic that "regards Biblical texts precisely in their function as *proposed* ways of understanding (aspects of) objective reality," with the provision that "the truth of a text's proposal, however, cannot be taken for granted" (Lull 1983: 193).

The Portrayal of God

The polemical thrust of Barr's distinction between story and history was directed against biblical theologians such as G. E. Wright, who read the Bible as a source of historical information from which the nature and attributes of God can be inferred. The paradigm shift, however, is no less damaging to some other biblical theologians that are ostensibly more attuned to the literary character of the text. David Kelsey contrasted Wright with Karl Barth's construal of scripture as "rendering an agent." In Barth's usage, "Narrative is taken to be the authoritative aspect of scripture"; it "is taken to have the logical force of stories that render a character, that offer an identity description of an agent . . ."; and it is "like the patterns in a realistic novel or short story to which a literary critic might draw attention when he tries to analyze characterization. Indeed it is as though Barth took scripture to be one vast loosely-structured, non-fictional novel—at least, Barth takes it to be non-fiction" (Kelsey 1975: 48). Therein, of course, lies the rub, for a nonfictional novel is a contradiction in terms. Many Christians of conservative leanings have welcomed the category "story" as a means of evading the possibility of disconfirmation to which history is subject. The freedom from disconfirmation, however, is bought at a price, since it necessarily excludes the possibility of confirmation, too.

If we recognize that much biblical "history" is fiction, in the sense of Ricoeur's poetic language, then we must also recognize that statements about God must be interpreted in the context of that fiction. Sternberg objects that "were the narrative written or read as fiction, then God would turn from the lord of history into a creature of the imagination, with the most disastrous results" (Sternberg 1985: 32). The modern reader, however, who can no longer accept the historical truth value of Genesis or Exodus, can only choose between inaccurate historiography and imaginative fiction. It is not clear why fiction should appear the more disastrous of these alternatives, if we free ourselves of the prejudice that equates fiction with falsehood and accept it as a fundamental way of apprehending reality.

If we regard biblical texts as fictions, or proposals whose truth or adequacy remains to be assessed, we must admit the possibility of a distinction between God the character in a biblical story and "the living god" or the power that moves the universe (Wismer 1983: 187–253). This distinction is not especially novel: virtually all strands of biblical theology have emphasized the transcendence of God in the Hebrew Bible and the inadequacy of any portrayal, iconic or verbal. Ricoeur, for example, refers to "God's trace in the event" and goes on to insist that the God who reveals himself is still a hidden God (1980: 93–95). A consistent critical approach, however, goes further. God the character must be understood in terms of his function within the story and of the human experiences and concerns from which it arises. Biblical assertions about God are not necessarily always pointers to transcendence but can also serve various functions of a more mundane nature.

The radical implications of historical criticism for biblical theology can be seen most clearly in recent sociological and feminist scholarship. Norman Gottwald's thesis that Yahweh was the symbol for the social ideal of early, tribal Israel is a case in point (1979: 667–709). Whether or not we regard such a definition as reductionistic, there is no doubt that religious language often functions to legitimate social power structures (Berger 1969). When we are told that the conquest of Canaan was justified by divine command or that God gave his unconditional support to the king, we may suspect that we are dealing with ideological rhetoric rather than theological truth, however tentative. God-language is no less ideological when it is used in more "liberal" causes, to authorize the Sinai covenant or to support prophetic preaching of social justice.

Historical criticism lends itself most readily to a view of biblical religion as a functional system where myth and cult are supporting devices to regulate the conduct that is at the heart of the religion. We can understand how the accounts of creation fostered respect for humanity as the image of God or led to the subordination of women, or how the expectation of reward after death strengthened the Maccabean martyrs. We cannot establish whether those beliefs were well founded. Consequently, assertions about God or the supernatural are most easily explained as rhetorical devices to motivate behavior. Such an analysis of biblical God-language is in itself a theological exercise, since it clarifies our use of theological language. It also has some warrant in the Hebrew Bible, where *miṣwôt* are the end of history (Levenson 1985: 42) and ethical performance is more important than belief.

A biblical theology that ignores the ideological uses of God-language must appear naïve in the modern culture, which is permeated with the hermeneutic of suspicion. Nonetheless, a biblical theology that adverts *only* to sociological and historical functions is reductionistic. The biblical texts must also be recognized as proposals about metaphysical truth, as attempts to explain the workings of reality. This aspect of the Bible is perhaps most obvious in the Wisdom Literature, but is also a factor throughout the Bible, from the creation stories to the apocalypse. The proposals are diverse. The God of Job is appreciably different from the God of the Deuteronomist, and either from the God of Daniel. The question here is whether any of these biblical accounts can now be accorded any explanatory value; whether any of the biblical world views can be said to be true as well as useful. The problem is that we lack any acceptable yardstick by which to assess metaphysical truth. It is possible to compare and contrast biblical world views with a modern system, such as process philosophy, but philosophical systems too are traditions of discourse and there is no consensus on their validity in contemporary culture. It is not within the competence of biblical theologians as such to adjudicate the relative adequacy of metaphysical systems. Their task is to clarify what claims are being made, the basis on which they are made, and the various functions they serve.

Conclusion

We return, finally, to our initial question as to whether a critical biblical theology is possible. The answer evidently depends on the model of theology we are willing to accept. Historical criticism, consistently understood, is not compatible with a confessional theology that is committed to specific doctrines on the basis of faith. It is, however, quite compatible with theology, understood as an open-ended and critical inquiry into the meaning and function of God-language. Biblical theology on this model is not a self-sufficient discipline, but is a subdiscipline that has a contribution to make to the broader subject of theology. The main contribution of the biblical theologian is to clarify the genre of the biblical material in the broad sense of the way in which it should be read and the expectations that are appropriate to it.

Despite the critiques to which it has been subject, historical criticism remains the most satisfactory context for biblical theology. Some of the claims for the objectivity of that method are now recognized to be exaggerated. It has its presuppositions. Nonetheless, it still commands the allegiance of the great majority of biblical scholars, including most of those who work in biblical theology, and with good reason, since it provides a broad framework for scholarly dialogue. My purpose here has been to explore the implications of accepting historical criticism as a basis for biblical theology. It is my thesis that there is a legitimate enterprise that goes beyond the simple description of what was thought and believed (*à la* Wrede), while stopping short of the "projection of faith into facts" that was characteristic of neoorthodoxy. Theological language is an integral part of the biblical material, and should not be simply bypassed in the interests of secular interpretation. We can only ask that the methods we endorse in historical and literary research be applied consistently also to the theological problems.

Bibliography

Alter, R.
1980 *The Art of Biblical Narrative*. New York: Basic.

Auerbach, E.
1953 *Mimesis: The Representation of Reality in Western Literature*. Princeton: Princeton University.

Barr, J.
1973 *The Bible in the Modern World*. New York: Harper.
1978 *Fundamentalism*. Philadelphia: Westminster.
1980 *The Scope and Authority of the Bible*. Philadelphia: Westminster.
1983 *Holy Scripture: Canon, Authority, Criticism*. Philadelphia: Westminster.

Barton, J.
1984 *Reading the Old Testament: Method in Biblical Study*. Philadelphia: Westminster.

Berger, P. L.
1969 *The Sacred Canopy*. Garden City: Doubleday.

Caird, G. B.
1980 *The Language and Imagery of the Bible*. Philadelphia: Westminster.

Childs, B. S.
1970 *Biblical Theology in Crisis*. Philadelphia: Westminster.
1979 *Introduction to the Old Testament as Scripture*. Philadelphia: Fortress.
1984 *The New Testament as Canon*. Philadelphia: Fortress.
1985 *Old Testament Theology in a Canonical Context*. Philadelphia: Fortress.

Collins, J. J.
1974 Apocalyptic Eschatology as the Transcendence of Death. *Catholic Biblical*

Quarterly 36: 21–43; reprinted in P. D. Hanson, ed., *Visionaries and Their Apocalypses*, 61–84 (Philadelphia: Fortress, 1983).

Eichrodt, W.
1961 *Theology of the Old Testament*. 2 vols. Philadelphia: Westminster.

Fiorenza, E. S.
1983 *In Memory of Her*. New York: Crossroad.

Frei, H.
1974 *The Eclipse of Biblical Narrative*. New Haven: Yale University.

Gadamer, H. G.
1982 *Truth and Method*. New York: Crossroad.

Gilkey, L.
1961 Cosmology, Ontology, and the Travail of Biblical Language. *Journal of Religion* 41: 194–205.

Gottwald, N. K.
1979 *The Tribes of Yahweh*. Maryknoll: Orbis.

Gunkel, H.
1964 *The Legends of Genesis*. New York: Schocken.

Harvey, V. A.
1966 *The Historian and the Believer*. New York: Macmillan.

Hayes, J. H., and F. Prussner
1985 *Old Testament Theology: Its History and Development*. Atlanta: John Knox.

Kelsey, D. H.
1975 *The Uses of Scripture in Recent Theology*. Philadelphia: Fortress.

Koch, K.
1969 *The Growth of the Biblical Tradition*. New York: Scribners.

Levenson, J. D.
1985 *Sinai and Zion: An Entry into the Jewish Bible*. Minneapolis: Winston.
1987 The Hebrew Bible, the Old Testament, and Historical Criticism. Pp. 19–59 in *The Future of Biblical Studies*, ed. R. E. Friedman and H. G. M. Williamson. Atlanta: Scholars Press.

Lindbeck, G.
1984 *The Nature of Doctrine: Religion and Theology in a Postliberal Age*. Philadelphia: Westminster.

Lull, D. J.
1983 What is Process Hermeneutics? *Process Studies* 13: 189–200.

Miles, J. A.
1976 Understanding Albright: A Revolutionary Etude. *Harvard Theological Review* 69: 151–75.

Neusner, J.
1970 *The Way of the Torah: An Introduction to Judaism*. Belmont, CA: Dickenson.

Ogden, S. M.
1961 *Christ without Myth*. New York: Harper.
1976 The Authority of Scripture for Theology. *Interpretation* 30: 242–61.

Rad, G. von
1962–65 *Old Testament Theology*. 2 vols. New York: Harper and Row.

Ricoeur, P.
1980 *Essays on Biblical Interpretation*. Ed. L. Mudge. Philadelphia: Fortress.

Sandys-Wunsch, J., and L. Eldredge.
1980 J. P. Gabler and the Distinction between Biblical and Dogmatic Theology: Translation, Commentary and Discussion of His Originality. *Scottish Journal of Theology* 33: 133–58.
Stendahl, K.
1984 *Meanings: The Bible as Document and as Guide.* Philadelphia: Fortress.
Sternberg, M.
1985 *The Poetics of Biblical Narrative.* Bloomington: Indiana University.
Stuhlmacher, P.
1977 *Historical Criticism and Theological Interpretation of Scripture.* Philadelphia: Fortress.
Thiselton, A. C.
1980 *The Two Horizons: New Testament Hermeneutics and Philosophical Description.* Grand Rapids: Eerdmans.
Tracy, D.
1981 *The Analogical Imagination: Christian Theology and the Culture of Pluralism.* New York: Crossroad.
Troeltsch, E.
1913 Über historische und dogmatische Methode in der Theologie. Pp. 729–53 in *Gesammelte Schriften, Vol. 2.* Tübingen: Mohr.
Wismer, P. L.
1983 The Myth of Original Sin: A Hermeneutic Theology Based on Genesis 2–3. Ph. D. diss., University of Chicago.
Wrede, W.
1973 The Task and Methods of New Testament Theology. Pp. 68–116 in *The Nature of New Testament Theology.* Ed. R. Morgan. London: SCM.
Wright, G. E.
1952 *God Who Acts.* London: SCM.

Archaeology and Biblical Studies: The Book of Joshua

Michael David Coogan
Stonehill College

In preparing a short commentary on the book of Joshua, as well as in some recent articles (Coogan 1987a, 1987b), I have been preoccupied with the relationship between archaeology and biblical studies. I prefer this designation to something like "archaeology and the Bible," since archaeology is, etymologically, also a study; its text, as it were, is material culture. The relationship between archaeological evidence and the Bible is thus analogous to that between extrabiblical texts and the Bible; in each case we have two bodies of evidence that need to be critically examined, and it is from the informed comparison of the various sources that history in the broadest sense, the reconstruction of the past from all available data, develops.

In this general context the focus for this essay will be the book of Joshua, to be dealt with under several geographical headings.

Jericho and Its Walls

Until the excavations of Kathleen Kenyon in the 1950s, for most historically minded commentators archaeological evidence of the destruction of the walls of Tell es-Sultan, walls variously dated from the sixteenth to the thirteenth centuries B.C., provided dramatic confirmation of the essential historicity of the story in Joshua 6.

Let me begin with a review of the biblical traditions about Jericho outside the book of Joshua. In narratives about the Mosaic period Jericho is simply a reference point for the "plains of Moab"[1] and Mount Nebo (Deut 32:49; 34:1). During the period of the monarchy it figures briefly in 2 Sam

1. Note the different formulae: *bĕᶜarbôt môʾāb mēᶜēber lĕyardēn yĕrēḥô* (Num 22:1; 34:15) and *bĕᶜarbōt môʾāb ᶜal-yardēn yĕrēḥô* (Num 26:3, 63; 31:12; 33:48, 50; 35:1; 36:13).

10:5, in the context of the Ammonite war; its (re)construction is mentioned in 1 Kgs 16:34; in 2 Kings 2, part of the Elijah–Elisha cycle, it is a residence of the "sons of the prophets"; and at the end of the monarchic period Zedekiah is captured in its vicinity (*bĕᶜarbôt yĕrēḥô* [2 Kgs 25:5; Jer 39:5 (= 52:8)]). In the postexilic period Jericho figures in the lists of returnees (Ezra 2:34 [= Neh 7:36]) and of the rebuilders of the fortifications of Jerusalem (Neh 3:2).

As for Jericho in Joshua, in the MT Jericho is the city in which Rahab lives (Josh 2:2, 3), opposite which the Israelites cross the Jordan (3:16), west of Gilgal (4:19) and in its vicinity (5:10), at which Joshua has his vision of the commander of the heavenly army (5:13), the first city captured by the Israelites (6:1, 2, 25, 26; and subsequent references to that event [7:2; 8:2; 9:3; 10:1, 28, 30; 12:9; 24:11]), a city in Benjamin (18:21) near its border with Ephraim (16:1–7), and also a reference point for Transjordan, as in Numbers and Deuteronomy (13:32; 20:8).[2]

But the fate of Jericho in Joshua is not a simple matter. There appear to be at least two independent traditions, one, the more famous, in which the walls "came a-tumblin' down" on the seventh day, and another in which Jericho was first besieged (6:1) and, after a battle (24:11), its king killed. The references to the king of Jericho may be the key to distinguishing between the traditions. He is mentioned in 2:2–3; 6:2; 8:2; 10:1, 28, 30; 12:9. Including the *baᶜălê yĕrîḥô* (24:11) as a variant for *melek*, we have a fairly complete episode, to which the Rahab episode belongs, so that this narrative in chap. 2, with its sequel in 6:17, 22–25, may plausibly be interpreted as a story of betrayal from within the city (see Soggin 1972: 38; de Vaux 1978: 597). Notably, in the other tradition, found only in 6:3–21, there is no mention of resistance by the inhabitants of Jericho, nor of its king, nor of Rahab, nor even of Jericho by name. This may indicate not just a separate Jericho tradition, but perhaps even an originally independent tradition only secondarily attached to Jericho. Notable also is the lack of reference to the event in

2. The vocalization of Jericho in different traditions may be chronologically significant. In P (Num 22:1; 26:3, 63; 31:12; 33:48, 50; 34:15; 35:1; 36:13; Deut 32:49; 34:1, 3) and in traditions after 587/586 B.C. (2 Kgs 25:5; Jer 39:5 [= 52:8]; Ezr 2:34; Neh 3:2; 7:36; 1 Chr 6:63; 19:5; 2 Chr 28:15) the city's name is consistently spelled *yĕrēḥô*; elsewhere regularly *yĕrîḥô* (Joshua; 2 Kings 2), except for *yĕrēḥô* (2 Sam 10:5) and the archaic spelling *yĕrîḥôh* in 1 Kgs 16:34. It is difficult to know how much to make of this, especially given the apparent variations among the manuscript traditions (note the differences in vocalization from *BHS* [followed here] given by BDB, *HALAT*, and Mandelkern 1959), but the patterning may be significant. There is clearly a distinction between priestly and post-587/586 sources on the one hand, and deuteronom(ist)ic sources (Dtr^1?) on the other. The sole archaic form (cf. the regular spelling *šĕlōmōh*) is in 1 Kgs 16:34, which is arguably the oldest tradition about Jericho preserved in its original form (see further below).

either form outside Joshua, suggesting that it was a local tradition incorporated only at a fairly late date into the biblical recital.

Any interpretation of the archaeological evidence from Jericho (Tell es-Sultan [*pace* Franken 1976: 6–7]) must begin with Kenyon's excavations, now fully published with the appearance of the final volume in the Jericho series (Kenyon and Holland 1983). The latest Late Bronze Age occupation uncovered in her work is a section of a house and some tombs, both to be dated to the late fourteenth century B.C. (Kenyon 1957: 262). As she noted in her popular summary, "this is a date which suits neither the school of scholars which would date the entry of the Israelites into Palestine to *c*. 1400 B.C. nor the school which prefers a date of *c*. 1260 B.C." (1957: 263). Undaunted, as elsewhere in her writings, by the weight of biblical and historical scholarship, Kenyon nevertheless suggested that what she found was "part of the kitchen of a Canaanite woman, who may have dropped the juglet beside the oven and fled at the sound of the trumpets of Joshua's men"! (1957: 265).

A late-fourteenth century date for the events described in Joshua, however, is unlikely, as are recent attempts to revive an even higher chronology (e.g., Bimson 1981). Was there subsequent Late Bronze Age occupation at Jericho? Here the interpretation of the archaeological record has been misleading. No evidence for it has been found, but it is often asserted, from what I can only characterize as *parti pris*, that the city that was there has been eroded. There is not a shred, or a sherd, of evidence for subsequent Late Bronze Age settlement. H. J. Franken, a member of the excavation team, speaks of "a complete lack of stray pottery from this particular period on all the surface and immediate surroundings of the tell" (1965: 182). The argument from silence, then, is untenable, but despite its weakness it still has adherents, who desperately try to construct in the void the walls of Joshua 6, much as Victor Hugo created the reaction of Jericho's inhabitants to the march of the Hebrews around their town in his "Sonnez, sonnez toujours."

As for Jericho in the early Iron Age, the evidence is fragmentary at best. The recent study by the Weipperts (1976) of the artifacts of the Sellin and Garstang expeditions is not entirely convincing; at best there are some hints of occupation in the eleventh century. There is a greater probability that the site was occupied in the ninth century; this would fit the dating of the city's reconstruction in 1 Kings 16 to the reign of Ahab. It should be noted, however, that the Kenyon expedition found no evidence of substantial occupation before the seventh century B.C.

So, unless we drastically redate Joshua's campaign, the archaeological record shows no evidence of occupation during the more than three centuries from the middle of the Late Bronze Age to the end of Iron I; in short, no one lived there. Why then is the story of Jericho so prominent in Joshua? Why Jericho? I have two proposals.

1. Like the rest of the accounts of capture and destruction in Joshua, the story of Jericho's conquest is a construction, a retroversion to the time of origins of a political fact of the monarchy: Israel controlled Jericho, as indeed it controlled the land. But why especially Jericho? Here the deuteronomistic historians give us a clue. Why Jericho?—because it was rebuilt in the reign of Ahab. The account of the reconstruction of the city under (A)Hiel is unparalleled. In the first place, the narrative contains a poetic tricolon (*bānâ* [*ʾa*]*ḥîʾēl bêt-hāʾĕlî yĕrîḥōh* / *bāʾăbîrām bĕkōrô yissĕdāh* / *baśĕgûb ṣĕʿîrô hiṣṣîb dĕlātêhā* [12/10/12] [1 Kgs 16:34]), indicating that the historians were using an established tradition, one that in written form preserved the archaic spelling *yĕrîḥōh*; and second, the attribution of the (re)construction of a city to someone other than the reigning king is highly unusual. At the risk of piling up hypotheses, I suggest that Ahiel's activity was a kind of rebellious secession, disapproved of by the deuteronomistic historians, and that this event was the motivation both for the inclusion of the curse pronounced by Joshua in Kings and even for the central position of Jericho in the Joshua narrative. In other words, what the authors of Joshua are saying is that Jericho is doomed unless it is Israelite. I further suggest, with some diffidence, that the separate traditions about Jericho's destruction, incorporated into Joshua, originate in the ninth century, with Jericho's reestablishment as a major fortified settlement.[3]

2. A contributing element to the centrality of Jericho may be its defenses. As far back as the Neolithic period Jericho was well fortified, and in that period especially its fortifications were anomalous. Is it possible that there was an ancient folk-tradition about Jericho's walls, a tradition that was the basis both for the Ahiel fragment and the miraculous event of Joshua 6?

Lachish, Ai, and Hazor

At intervals in the book of Joshua there are lists of conquered kings and cities (notably 10:23, 28–39; and 12:9–24). Some of the cities mentioned cannot be identified with certainty, and some of those that can be identified seem not to have been either inhabited or destroyed at the appropriate period. The list in 12:9–24 is especially suspect, since inner biblical evidence alone contradicts its statements. We may take Lachish as a representative illustration, since its archaeological history has often been cited as a confirmation of the at least partial historicity of the Joshua material. But in his

3. Admittedly the mention of Jericho in 2 Sam 10:5 is chronologically problematic.

meticulous excavations at Tell ed-Duweir David Ussishkin (1985) has shown that Stratum VI was destroyed in the mid-twelfth century B.C., at least a century after the destruction of Late Bronze Age Hazor (and was not resettled for a century or more). Whatever the origin of the lists and short notices, it is impossible, I think, to assume their essential historicity, since what archaeological evidence there is contradicts the plain sense of the biblical narrative in Joshua, namely that the cities, or at least their populations, were destroyed within a generation.

Furthermore, the formulaic character of the accounts makes them even more suspect. I wonder if the authors of the book of Joshua were not aware of the difficulty; this may account for the absence of references to the destruction of the cities themselves, but only to that of their rulers and inhabitants.

Apart from Jericho, only two cities are described as having been destroyed and burned by Joshua and the Israelites, Ai (chap. 8) and Hazor (chap. 11). In the case of Ai, again the archaeological record is deafening in its silence: there is no evidence of occupation at et-Tell from the late-third millennium to the early Iron Age. J. A. Callaway's earlier attempt to preserve "the essential historicity of the conquest" by attributing to "people . . . who may very well have been Israelites" (1968: 319) the burning of one building of the first of his two Iron I strata implies a loose definition of historicity. To be fair, Callaway noted discrepancies between the biblical and archaeological evidence: in opposition to Josh 7:5; 8:29, there were no gates or fortifications in the small village at Ai (L. E. Stager's [1985: 21] estimate is no more than 328 total population). And more recently, Callaway has abandoned this reconstruction (1985).

Then why does Ai figure so prominently in Joshua? The etiological explanation still seems best: it was "the ruin" par excellence;[4] in fact, a most impressive ruin, one of the few large tells in the region not settled in the Iron II period. How did it become a ruin? Joshua did it!

As Zevit (1983) has shown, the narrative tradition is late, and was a kind of historical fiction that incorporated topographic elements of the unoccupied city's remains. One can imagine travelers passing by, pointing to the ruins as Joshua's handiwork. On the common in Cambridge, Massachusetts, there is a small elm surrounded by a metal picket fence; beside it is a stela on which is inscribed: "Under this tree Washington first took command of the American Army July 3, 1775." Day after day tourists stop and photograph the tree, which by my estimate cannot be more than 25

4. Despite Z. Zevit's (1983) argument against this etymology, based on transliteration, I wonder if we don't have at least paronomasia here. In other words, an ancient audience may have understood the name to mean "ruin" whatever its actual etymology.

years old. It may be a shoot of the original "Washington elm," or it may not be; but for the tourists that is irrelevant: the tree is part of American history, even if it was not there. Washington, and the Revolution, are made more real by being associated with the tree. Similarly, I suspect, for Ai: the process of historicizing, originating in theological reflection, is not primarily concerned with what actually happened; what is important is the story, and its meaning.

The literary source for the story of the capture of Ai is the account of the attack on Gibeah in Judg 20:19–48 (de Vaux 1978: 618–19). This is another example of the technique of the authors of Joshua: their primary source was not authentic historical memory, but already existing literary traditions, much as the Septuagintal Old Testament was a source for the gospel narratives of the life and especially the death of Jesus.

Finally I turn to Hazor. Here, it has seemed, is one unequivocal correspondence between biblical tradition and archaeological fact. A flourishing Late Bronze Age metropolis, Hazor (Strata XIII of the "Upper City" and IA of the "Lower City") was violently destroyed in the mid-thirteenth century B.C., and, apparently after an interlude, was succeeded by a small unfortified village (Yadin 1972: 108, 126). But, as I will argue in more detail presently, archaeological data are anonymous; an extensive layer of ashes indicates the destruction of the city but not the cause of that event. Of the destruction of Hazor in the mid-thirteenth century there is no doubt, but of its destruction by Joshua and/or the Israelites there is no evidence, apart from the book of Joshua.

The primary source, however, for the narrative in Josh 11:1–15 is not actual events involving Joshua but rather preexisting literary traditions, related to those now found in Judges 4–5. The key to this analysis is the name of Hazor's king, Jabin. Unless it is supposed (Boling 1982: 311), without any real evidence, that the monarchy of Hazor used papponomy, it appears that there is only one event described in these two texts, the defeat of a Canaanite (non-Israelite) coalition. The tradition-history is complex. For example, the "waters of Merom" (Josh 11:5, 7) may be a variant for the "waters of Megiddo" (Judg 5:19), and the phrase *ʿal mĕrômê śādeh* (Judg 5:18; of Naphtali) may be a wordplay alluding to the waters of Merom (de Vaux 1978: 665). The cumulative evidence suggests that the primary account is that in Judges, and that the Joshua narrative is based on it. (See further Maisler [Mazar] 1953: 83–84; Aharoni 1979: 221–23.)

Shechem, the Mount Ebal Sanctuary, and the Problem of Ethnic and Political Identifications

Josh 8:30–35 describes the construction of an altar by Joshua on Mount Ebal, in fulfillment of the command of Moses in Deut 27:5–6. The pericope is a kind of floating narrative, placed in the LXX after 9:2, and with no apparent connection with what precedes or follows: Joshua's base of operations both before and after the episode is Gilgal, and no mention is made of a journey to or from the Shechem vicinity; some have suggested that it has been displaced from its original association with Joshua 24 (Soggin 1972: 226–29). In any case, apart from its inclusion in the border description of Manasseh (17:7), and among the cities of asylum (20:7) and the Levitical cities (21:21), Shechem and its vicinity figure only in these two passages in Joshua.

It is generally acknowledged that Josh 8:30–35 and 24 are dependent on Deuteronomy 27 (see, e.g., Soggin 1972: 241). But there is another literary allusion here: the tree at Shechem, *hāʾallâ* '*the* oak' (24:26), the well-known tree mentioned in one form or another in Gen 12:6; 35:4; Deut 11:30; Judg 9:6 (and 6:11?). It is especially the tree of Gen 35:4 (*hāʾēlâ* 'the terebinth') that is alluded to here (cf. Gen 35:2 and Josh 24:23), and the unique vocalization in Josh 24:26 may be a Masoretic effort to dissociate Joshua from that repository of heterodox cult objects. Despite the different vocalization, then, the mention of the familiar tree connects Joshua not just with Moses, one of the dominant literary devices throughout the book, but with ancestral tradition as well.

In 1980, in the course of an intensive survey of the tribal territory of Manasseh, Adam Zertal discovered not far from Shechem the remains of an installation that he has interpreted as an altar, and has suggested that it is in fact the altar described in Joshua 8 and 24 and Deuteronomy 27 (Zertal 1983, 1984, 1985, 1986). In the absence of full publication it is hazardous to discuss the structure and its interpretation, but since it continues to attract attention some comments are appropriate.

The site, el-Barnat, is securely dated to the Iron I period, and has at least two major architectural phases. The primary installation, the "altar," is situated in the northeast quadrant of a large enclosure. It is rectangular in plan, ca. 7.5 × 9 m, with walls ca. 1.4 m thick, which surround a center divided by two incomplete crosswalls and in the earlier phase containing a number of stone installations amid ashy debris. In the succeeding phase this core is filled with layers of soil, stones, and ashes containing animal bones. Attached to the structure are two rectangular courtyards divided by a wall that Zertal interprets as a ramp leading to the top of the filled chamber in its final phase. Within the larger enclosure are further stone installations, some containing more ashes and animal bones and others pottery. The ceramic repertoire consists mainly of collared-rim store jars (accounting for 70% of the total), jugs and chalices (20%), and some miniature vessels; few cooking pots have been found.

The site is unlike others of the period. In view of the unusually proportioned ceramic repertoire and the miniature vessels and the site's isolation, I concur with Zertal's cultic interpretation.[5] But I cannot agree with Zertal's fairly definite identification of the altar as that built by Joshua, or even as Israelite. Such a suggestion may be comforting, since so little in Joshua can be proven to be historical in the sense that what it says actually happened. But, as I have noted, archaeological remains are almost always anonymous. Even though the altar dates from the early Iron Age and is found in a region that was under Israelite control at a later period, nothing in the material remains requires that the installation, even if cultic, was Israelite, let alone built by Joshua; in fact, there are serious problems with such an identification. (See further Coogan 1987a: 7 n. 1.)

Indeed, I must strenuously protest the tendency by many archaeologists, and especially Israeli archaeologists, to identify as Israelite various sites, features, and destruction layers dating from the early Iron Age. (For recent examples of this tendency see A. Mazar 1985; M. Dothan 1985.) As I have recently argued, since the division of the land in Joshua is an ideal picture, often a retroversion of later geopolitical realities, the mere presence of a premonarchic remains within the ideal tribal boundaries does not require their construction or use by the members of that tribe.

What differentiated the Israelites from their non-Israelite contemporaries was metaphysical, not physical: acceptance of Yahweh, the god of Israel, and concomitant allegiance to fellow Yahwists. The biblical record taken as a whole indicates that as Israel developed, or, to use Baruch Halpern's apt terminology (1983), "emerged," in Canaan its membership was augmented by the inclusion of individuals and groups who had not been part of the original nucleus, whether defined by kinship or shared experience or both. Examples include Rahab and her family (Joshua 2; 6:25), the Gibeonites (Joshua 9; 18:25), Hepher (cf. Josh 12:17 and 17:2), and Ruth the Moabite. As a result, I strongly doubt that the material culture of settlements known from textual sources to have been Israelite can at present be distinguished from that of settlements known to have been Canaanite (i.e., non-Israelite) in the absence of determinative written evidence. (See further Coogan 1987a: 5–6.)

It is possible that as methodological sophistication increases it may be possible to develop criteria for isolating distinct political and ethnic features. Later periods may provide models for the testing of such distinctions, for example, between Judean and Philistine cultures in the later Iron Age and Persian period. We know from biblical and extrabiblical sources that the Philistines retained distinctive cultural features, including personal names, dialect (Neh 13:24), and political institutions. We also have presumed that

5. The criteria implicit in this interpretation are discussed at length in Coogan 1987a, where I suggest that four useful criteria in determining whether or not a site has a cultic (i.e., public ritual) function are isolation, exotic materials, continuity, and parallels.

on a broad scale the Philistines' material culture largely assimilated to that of their Israelite contemporaries and occasional overlords during the monarchy. This presumption needs to be examined. Are there distinctive elements of material culture that are more than just regional variants and that can be identified as Philistine? There is already a large body of data from sites such as Ashdod, although much of it is not adequately published. The current work at Tel Miqne (Ekron) and Ashkelon will provide much more, tightly controlled from a stratigraphic point of view. These sites should be compared with each other and with others that are not Philistine to see if there are significant patterns in the distribution, frequency, form, and use of artifacts; then, perhaps, it will be possible to develop models for correlating material culture and ethnic, political, and religious designations.

Concluding Observations

Much of the above is negative in conclusion, for the integration of archaeological and biblical data has all too often been based on the presupposition that the book of Joshua is an historical account that more or less accurately depicts the events it narrates. To put it somewhat differently, biblical scholars, especially of the Albright school, have not fully assimilated the results of literary and form criticism. In my understanding, the book of Joshua is historico-theological fiction. The primary purpose of its authors was to present a theological construct. This is evident, to take one example, in its representation of the character of Joshua, who is presented as a carbon copy of Moses, whose law he keeps fully and precisely; as such he is a prototype of the ideal deuteronomistic king (see Nelson 1981) and the model against which failed leaders are implicitly measured; in contrast, for example, to Saul, Joshua enforces the rules of holy war (Joshua 7; cf. 1 Samuel 13–15) and keeps the oath made with the Gibeonites (Joshua 9; cf. 2 Sam 21:1–14). The resulting character depiction is simplistic: Joshua is a "good guy" beyond reproach, in contrast with the presentation of other national figures in other traditions, traditions to be sure also preserved by the deuteronomistic historians.

In the development of this construct the authors make use of explicit quotations (e.g., *nēd* in Josh 3:13, 16; cf. Exod 15:8) and of indirect references (as in the Jericho, Ai, Hazor, and Shechem material discussed above). The historical, or factual, element, as elsewhere in biblical narrative, is subordinated to the theological. Anachronism, inconsistency, formalistic patterning, and literary allusion are common and were apparently untroubling to ancient authors and audiences.

But, it may be objected, if the book of Joshua is a work of historical fiction, is it not possible that there is historical verisimilitude, that is, that the authors of Joshua wished at least implicitly to make it appear authentic, and to that extent relied upon earlier traditions about premonarchic Israel? Yet Joshua is also remarkable for its lack of the stuff of poetry, of concrete detail, and the few examples that can be gleaned from its pages are consistently unspecific. L. E. Stager's recent essay on "The Archaeology of the Family in Ancient Israel" (1985) is a brilliant synthesis of textual and artifactual data on the topic, and in it there are repeated illuminations (despite his disclaimer) of biblical texts and ancient Israelite institutions. But none of the material he adduces in connection with Joshua is chronologically specific: no detail of domestic architecture, whether of the nuclear or extended family; of social organization, from the *bêt ʾāb* to the tribe; or of land-use, from local terracing to regional deforestation, can be dated exclusively to the Iron I period; both texts and excavated remains make it clear that they continue well into the first millennium and beyond.

The same is true of other elements in Joshua, be they geographical (e.g., the Valley of Achor or Lebo-Hamath), artifactual (the iron vessels that were part of the booty from Jericho), or geopolitical (the episode of the Transjordanian tribes in chap. 22, or the reference to the Hittites in the MT of 1:4); none is datable solely to the late-second millennium and most are much more at home in the first. Thus, an archaeological commentary on Joshua would find little if anything to illustrate genuine and exclusively premonarchic traditions.

On the other hand, as a work of the deuteronomistic historians, the book of Joshua reflects to some extent the realities of its time of composition. Without entering upon the vexed problem of the history of the deuteronomistic history, let me suggest that archaeological data by way of illustration and by way of confirmation of the results of critical investigation do support a date for the book of Joshua late in the Iron II period.[6] This applies, for example, to the division of the land. A good illustration is the list of Levitical cities in Joshua 21; as John L. Peterson's survey (1977) has shown, in its present form this list cannot have been compiled before the eighth century B.C. (see Boling 1982: 492–94). The same is true of the "province list" of Judah (chap. 15), although in this case a slightly earlier date may be possible (Cross and Wright 1956).

To some extent I may seem to have reinvented the wheel. Have I added anything to the results of earlier literary-critical scholarship? Perhaps not, but I have attempted to apply the results of excavation to the text in a serious and consistent way, recognizing the limitations of both kinds of evidence. My conclusion is that the archaeological data when rigorously

6. The book itself has a much longer history, as is shown by the substantial differences between the Masoretic and 4QJos[b] traditions on the one hand and the shorter, more original, LXX and 4QJos[a] traditions on the other.

interpreted support the literary-critical analysis of the book of Joshua as a composition of the deuteronomistic historians. When reexamined, then, the archaeological evidence has required a reconsideration of the text.

This has been the general effect of archaeological discoveries: they have raised many more problems about the Bible than they have solved. From the second half of the nineteenth century, with the decipherment of ancient Mesopotamian literature and the discovery in the Epic of Gilgamesh of a story of a flood similar even in specific details to that found in Genesis, a major effect of archaeological investigation has been to challenge prevailing biblical interpretations. The cumulative evidence of sherds and strata, of texts and tesserae, has contributed to the erosion of biblical authority as traditionally understood, for it has forced us to reconsider our sacred texts.

In the course of such a reconsideration I have come to the conclusion that the book of Joshua is a literary creation, a historico-theological fiction whose primary sources were the already existing literature of Israel. In this literary work the emergence of Israel was indeed a conquest, and it is only in the context of a discussion of Joshua that I think this term appropriate. From the hindsight of its creators, this conquest was a historical event. If we disagree, that may be because our definition of history is too narrow. Let me close by quoting from another story of battles and conquest, the Song of Roland:

> There were only three French barons left alive. One was Gualter of Hum, who had fought all day on the mountains. Now, a sole survivor, he rode down toward the plain to Rollanz. "Where are you, gentle count? Where are you, Rollanz? I was never afraid when I could fight beside you!" Side by side, Rollanz, Gualter, and the Archbishop Turpins of Rheims faced the Sarrazin host. None of them would abandon the others. Forty thousand mounted Sarrazins face them, and one thousand on foot. No pagan stirs a foot to meet them. Instead, they shower volleys of spears, lances, arrows, and darts; Gualter falls. The archbishop's horse falls. The archbishop's body is pierced through with four spears!
>
> Yet the gallant archbishop still struggled to his feet. His eyes sought Rollanz. He gasped, "I am not defeated! I do not surrender!" Then the huge Turpins advanced boldly toward the enemy, swinging his sword about his head in a frenzy of anger and will to defy them. The Book says he injured four hundred more, and so says the eyewitness, the Baron Gilie who built the monastery at Laon. Anyone who doesn't know this, understands nothing about History![7]

7. Laisses 153–55 (lines 2056–98), translated by Goodrich 1977: 86. Interestingly, since there were no survivors to the battle, the Baron Gilie is not an ordinary eyewitness; see further Brault 1978: 1.233–35.

Bibliography

Aharoni, Y.

1979 *The Land of the Bible: A Historical Geography*. Rev. ed. Philadelphia: Westminster.

BDB F. Brown, S. R. Driver, and C. A. Briggs (eds.), *A Hebrew and English Lexicon of the Old Testament*. Oxford: Clarendon, 1907 (repr. 1953 with corrections).

BHS K. Elliger and W. Rudolph (eds.), *Biblia Hebraica Stuttgartensia*. Stuttgart: Deutsche Bibelstiftung, 1967/77.

Bimson, J.

1981 *Redating the Exodus and Conquest*. Sheffield: Almond.

Boling, R. G.

1982 *Joshua*. Anchor Bible 6. Garden City: Doubleday.

Brault, G. J.

1978 *The Song of Roland: An Analytical Edition*. 2 vols. University Park: Pennsylvania State University.

Callaway, J. A.

1968 New Evidence on the Conquest of Ai. *Journal of Biblical Literature* 87: 312–20.

1985 Was My Excavation of Ai Worthwhile? *Biblical Archaeology Review* 9: 68–69.

Coogan, M. D.

1987a Of Cults and Cultures: Reflections on the Interpretation of Archaeological Evidence. *Palestine Exploration Quarterly* 119: 1–8.

1987b Canaanite Origins and Lineage: Reflections on the Religion of Ancient Israel. Pp. 115–124 in *Ancient Israelite Religion: Essays in Honor of Frank Moore Cross*, ed. P. D. Miller, Jr., P. D. Hanson, and S. D. McBride. Philadelphia: Fortress.

Cross, F. M., Jr., and G. E. Wright

1956 The Boundary and Province Lists of the Kingdom of Judah. *Journal of Biblical Literature* 75: 202–26.

Dothan, M.

1985 Terminology for the Archaeology of the Biblical Periods. Pp. 136–41 in *Biblical Archaeology Today: Proceedings of the International Congress on Biblical Archaeology, Jerusalem, April 1984*. Jerusalem: Israel Exploration Society.

Franken, H. J.

1965 Tell es-Sultan and Old Testament Jericho. *Oudtestamentische Studien*: 189–200.

1976 The Problem of Identification in Biblical Archaeology. *Palestine Exploration Quarterly* 108: 3–11.

Goodrich, N. L.

1977 *Medieval Myths*. 2d ed. New York: New American Library.

HALAT W. Baumgartner et al., *Hebräisches und aramäisches Lexikon zum Alten Testament*. Leiden: Brill, 1967 –.

Halpern, B.
1983 *The Emergence of Israel in Canaan.* Society of Biblical Literature Monograph Series 29. Chico, CA: Scholars Press.
Kenyon, K. M.
1957 *Digging Up Jericho.* London: Ernest Benn.
Kenyon, K. M., and T. A. Holland
1983 *Excavations at Jericho V: The Pottery Phases of the Tell and Other Finds.* Jerusalem: British School of Archaeology.
Mandelkern
1959 *Veteris Testamenti concordantiae Hebraicae atque Chaldaicae.* 4th ed. Tel-Aviv: Schocken.
Maisler [Mazar], B.
1953 Beth She^{c}arim, Gaba, and Harosheth of the Peoples. *Hebrew Union College Annual* 24: 75–84.
Mazar, A.
1985 The Israelite Settlement in Canaan in the Light of Archaeological Excavations. Pp. 61–71 in *Biblical Archaeology Today: Proceedings of the International Congress on Biblical Archaeology, Jerusalem, April 1984.* Jerusalem: Israel Exploration Society.
Nelson, R. D.
1981 Josiah in the Book of Joshua. *Journal of Biblical Literature* 100: 531–40.
Peterson, J. L.
1977 A Topographical Surface Survey of the Levitical "Cities" of Joshua 21 and 1 Chronicles 6: Studies on the Levites in Israelite Life and Religion. Th.D. diss., Seabury-Western Theological Seminary.
Soggin, J. A.
1972 *Joshua: A Commentary.* Trans. R. A. Wilson. London: SCM.
Stager, L. E.
1985 The Archaeology of the Family in Ancient Israel. *Bulletin of the American Schools of Oriental Research* 260: 1–35.
Ussishkin, D.
1985 Levels VII and VI at Tel Lachish and the End of the Late Bronze Age in Canaan. Pp. 213–30 in *Palestine in the Bronze and Iron Ages: Papers in Honor of Olga Tufnell,* ed. J. N. Tubb. London: Institute of Archaeology, University of London.
de Vaux, R.
1978 *The Early History of Israel.* Trans. David Smith. Philadelphia: Westminster.
Weippert, H., and M. Weippert
1976 Jericho in der Eisenzeit. *Zeitschrift des deutschen Palästina-Vereins* 92: 104–48.
Yadin, Y.
1972 *Hazor: The Head of All Those Kingdoms.* London: Oxford University.
Zertal, A.
1983 Mount Ebal. *Excavations and Surveys in Israel* 2: 72.
1984 Mount Ebal. *Israel Exploration Journal* 34: 55.
1985 Has Joshua's Altar Been Found on Mt. Ebal? *Biblical Archaeology Review* 11: 26–43.

1986 How Can Kempinski Be So Wrong? *Biblical Archaeology Review* 12: 43, 49–53.

Zevit, Z.

1983 Archaeological and Literary Stratigraphy in Joshua 7–8. *Bulletin of the American Schools of Oriental Research* 251: 23–35.

The Book of Job

David Noel Freedman
The University of Michigan and University of California, San Diego

The Book as a Whole

The book of Job is one of the world's great literary works—of ancient times or any time. Its grandeur lies not only in its literary excellence but in its profound examination of foundational and perennial, agonizing and ultimate questions of human experience: the problem of suffering, especially on the part of the innocent; the general question of theodicy; the way of the world; and the boundaries of human existence, knowledge, and experience.

In scholarly tradition, the book of Job is at least as well known for the problems it has posed and the issues spawned and ultimately left unresolved, as for the lessons it teaches. While to the untutored eye, Job (at least in translation) reads smoothly from the beginning to end and exhibits a cohesion amid diversities, more critical investigation uncovers seams in the fabric if not rents, and divergences leading to opposition if not contradiction. Remaining issues confront the serious reader: what is the relationship between the prose sections, principally the Prologue (chaps. 1–2) and the Epilogue (chap. 42), and the poetry (mostly chaps. 3–41)? How does the story, with its neat, satisfying denouement, conform with a dialogue that begins on the ragged edge of heresy and lurches and sags in a variety of directions increasingly distant from the central biblical tradition, with its absolutes and its historical certainties and commitments, and alien to traditional affirmations about God, his universe and humankind, and the relationship between them. The story is not a simple folk tale, though perhaps there was one once, behind the present subtle and multiple presentation of parallel and disjunctive developments on at least two levels, the heavenly and the earthly. One drama is being played out on earth with misfortunate Job and his household or what is left of it (only his wife), a story that provides the framework for the dialogue as well, while the other is played out in heaven

A shorter version of this essay appeared in *Bible Review* 4 (1988).

by an entirely different cast of characters, including an all-powerful and willful deity, surrounded by servitors, who nevertheless are not merely echoes or sycophants of the Almighty, but intelligent if not guileful actors whose participation in heavenly decision making is both impressive and alarming. Chief among these "offspring of the deity" (Heb. *bĕnê ʾĕlōhîm*) is the adversary (*haśśāṭān*, in later tradition none other than Satan himself, the onetime leader of the heavenly host) cast in the role of the accuser of human beings and troublemaker of cosmic dimensions.

While these two stories intertwine and produce palpable effects one on the other, nevertheless, the levels are kept separate by a tinted glass that permits vision and knowledge in one direction only. The heavenly participants alone know what is happening to whom and why, while the earthly counterparts wander in a vast confusion, their confident assumptions and assertions playing against the contrary realities revealed in the heavenly scenes. The reader is carefully positioned by the author/editor so as to be fully aware of both scenes and the carefully calculated ironies and paradoxes—under compulsion to remain a permanent outsider, knowing but unable to intervene, to warn or persuade, and at the same time pushed to the limits of patience as the drama of misperception and misdirection unfolds. As much as anything, suspense builds as the audience, within and without the story, wonders not only what will happen to Job and his interlocutors, but whether any of them will ever find out the real truth—unwind the onion to its core—or instead have to be content with conventional wisdom, pious platitudes, and the pervasive subterfuge that dominates the dealings of the heavenly sphere with that of humans.

In the end, all outstanding issues are resolved, but only at the level at which they began: Job, innocent and righteous sufferer through no fault of his own, is restored to health and happiness, recovers his family and his fortune, but in the end is no wiser than he was before. His testing has satisfied his testers and he has passed with flying colors and great rewards. But he may well be more perplexed than satisfied, more disturbed than complacent—and certainly he is ignorant of the true workings of the heavenly court. That confusion may well pervade the heavenly scene where conflict and confrontation between deity and divine agent are narrowly averted, and while the particular issue between God and the adversary is apparently settled in favor of the deity, it is also clear that the issue of independent human righteousness and the possibility of an entirely altruistic love of God will arise again and again.

So the story is itself an intricate account of divine and human transactions on two planes, each independent and yet with impact on the other. The reader has the benefit of 360° vision, hindsight, and suprahuman knowledge, like a novelist who controls all of his characters, who knows what is happening above and below and among all of his characters. At the same time, the reader must respect the autonomy of the participants and their right as well as their obligation to play their role without the benefit of such universal knowledge. Even God does not know how matters will turn out, since at the heart of the story is the question of Job's integrity—will he stand fast and hold to it or will he succumb to the inexorable pressures of his undeserved suffering and finally the temptation to curse his maker? If there is uncertainty for God, how much more for the other actors, especially the human ones, who are never privy to the central secret of the story: the wager between God and the Satan. If Job, ignorant of the truth, is deeply disturbed by the course of events, how would he behave and react if he had an inkling of the truth? In the end we can take comfort in the knowledge that the author knows not only everything, but also what is best, and all ends well, as we must have suspected from the beginning.

If the story in the prose Prologue and Epilogue is not as simple as it seems, the case with the poetic Dialogue is much more complicated and difficult. In the first place, the Dialogue is written in an unusual idiom very hard to understand. Second, the cast of characters is varied, and ultimately the parts do not join smoothly (for details see Pope 1965: xxiii–xxx). The main section consists of a round of speeches by Job and the three friends introduced in the Prologue, in which, after Job announces the problem and his predicament, each friend in turn offers both an explanation of Job's dire distress and a prescription for curing his mental anguish and his physical suffering (in that order). There are, in all, three cycles of these talks in which Job responds to each of the friends, thereby dominating the discussion. There is very little motion from one round to another, although the level of elaboration on both sides rises until everything that could be said on the subject of theodicy has been said twice or three times or more. No one's mind is changed, although the word "friend" progressively loses content and meaning for these four oldtimers as their irritation increases. All remain obdurately convinced of their starting positions and remarks to the contrary by Job or this or that friend only tend to freeze the opposition. The futility of debate except to solidify one's own resolve was never more dramatically demonstrated. The author only wishes to raise the level of dramatic fury, thus focusing all attention on the beleaguered Job to whom the friends address their remarks. They never speak to one another, they never question each other or discuss strategy. Their only interaction is with Job, who himself is entirely impartial, responding in the same vein and spirit to each of them. In the end, as the Dialogue winds down, the speeches become shorter and the orderly sequence seems to wobble and then fragment and fall apart as though they had finally worn themselves out, and Job closes off debate, just as he had opened it, with an eloquent appeal to the deity himself. He, Job, not only asserts by oath his innocence—that he is not and has never been guilty of any of the crimes posited by his single-minded, now hostile friends—but he challenges the deity to come to court and defend himself against Job's highly charged accusations of ungodly behavior and mistreatment of a faithful servant. With this climactic address, Job rests his case, and the author rests the friends (permanently) and gives the reader a chance to reflect.

It should be pointed out that there is a pause before the great speech by Job (chaps. 29–31) provided by a digressive allocution on the subject of wisdom, clearly aimed at the reader—a kind of intermezzo on its scarcity and extraordinary value, as though to advise the audience that the preliminaries are now over. The discussion to come will require of the reader the most serious exercise of that prized faculty to grasp the points at issue and the proposed resolutions. While chap. 28 is incorporated into a series of speeches by Job beginning at chap. 26, it is an independent composition having little connection with what precedes or with what follows.

When Job has concluded his final speech of self-defense and thrown down a legal challenge to the deity, then, before Yahweh finally responds in the closing speeches of the Dialogue, there is another interlude. A fourth friend appears on the scene, previously unannounced and unaccounted for. He is Elihu, a comparative youngster, brash at that, who speaks to and at everybody, criticizing the friends for inferior debating, but at the same time attacking Job for his behavior. He lays about himself vigorously, brooking neither interruption nor rejoinder. After four speeches filling six chapters of the Book of Job (chaps. 32–37) he finally stops. While these consecutive addresses by the same speaker may reflect the strategy of the author in depicting and then conveying the impetuosity and breathless pursuit of his quarry by this young savant, the fact that neither Job nor his friends respond in any way suggests that all contact among the human parties has now ended and the last one in particular is speaking for the record and possibly the reader. The alienation of man from man has reached an ultimate point. They are all talking, but no one is responding, probably because they are no longer listening. As it happens, while Elihu is highly critical of all who have preceded him and scornful in his politely prolix fashion, he does not add much to the sum of human knowledge, and in spite of his insistence on being heard and his rapid-fire, nonstop loquaciousness, he earns an ultimate reward. He is totally ignored, not only by those whom he addresses but by the Almighty as well. At least the presence of the three friends, and their misguided zeal for the deity, bordering on insolence and presumption, is acknowledged and they are included at the end of the story, but not Elihu, who enters suddenly and departs as abruptly when he has had his say. Perhaps he tried the patience of the author, or editor, or perhaps there were larger plans for him that were never fulfilled. My theory (described in some detail in Freedman 1968) is that the original author of Job (at least the poetry) planned to add a fourth friend to the colloquy, the young and brash intruder, Elihu, who would speak after each round of speeches, and thus contribute his observations and opinions in sequence as is the case with the others. Thus, instead of being lumped together after the Dialogue had ended, Elihu's allocutions would have been distributed through the book and integrated into the argument. It can be shown that Elihu quotes from the speeches of the others and that his own talks can be arranged in sequence with them. Presumably this plan was never carried out and only the speeches survived to be attached to the Dialogue at the most reasonable place. In any case, when youth has spoken its piece, Job, the other friends, and the readers are now ready for the climax of the Dialogue, the denouement of the story.

Beginning in chap. 38, Yahweh himself speaks to the group, addressing Job in particular, in a speech of great power and brilliance. Here at last Job has a worthy antagonist, and as Job himself concedes, he indeed is overmatched. The first speech (chaps. 38–39) is followed by a brief interchange between Yahweh and Job, and then Yahweh launches into a second major address (chaps. 40–41). Job in turn makes a final response, in which he confesses his fault—failure to understand, lack of wisdom and knowledge—and repents on dust and ashes (42:1–6). While Yahweh's speeches hardly dealt with Job's grievances, a genuine dialogue has been established, and Job is content with the fact that Yahweh, while basically professing to be thoroughly occupied with responsibility for running the universe and with some of its more spectacular components and denizens, nevertheless has responded to the urgent appeals, or rather demands of Job, and hence has demonstrated that he is aware of the human predicament and intervenes when there is a compelling reason. With this partial reconciliation—Job has withdrawn his grievance and charges and has finally done what the friends had insisted on arrogantly and insultingly from the beginning, namely, to repent on dust and ashes (i.e., fully and with a heavy heart)—the way is then cleared for the final resolution of the predicament in which Job has been placed.

At this point the prose story resumes. All the loose ends are tied up, the tragedy is reversed, and everything that was wrong is made right. Not only does Job recover family and double his fortune, but even the friends, who are condemned for their contribution and are restored to favor through the intercession of Job, a remarkable extension of the righteousness of an upright person. The power to intervene successfully for blood relations was acknowledged in the case of men of integrity such as Noah and Job, but to extend that power beyond family limits was extraordinary. It adds a touch to the final picture of Job, not only restored to his former prosperity and enjoyment of his life of serenity and piety, but going beyond the former life to something better.

As this brief survey of the Book of Job has shown, there is an overall unity, while at the same time, it must be conceded there are rough passages and transitions, and the possibility of intrusive elements must also be considered. There are significant differences in approach and attitude between the prose framework and the poetic Dialogue. Within each part there are inconsistencies and unanswered questions. There is widespread agreement among scholars that the Elihu speeches, let alone his person, are intrusive and were not part of the original work. There is argument as well about the cohesiveness of the dialogue, with or without Elihu, the relevance of the speech from the whirlwind as a response to the preceding dialogue, especially Job's challenging address in chaps. 29–31. Other questions have been raised about the sequence of speeches and the integrity of some of them, especially in the later rounds of the Dialogue between Job and his three friends (see Pope 1965: xx). Nevertheless, we must also respect the final editor of the Book of Job as we have it. It is not an accidental assemblage of disparate materials. Whatever the origin of the several parts, they have been worked into a whole, and if seams and gaps are still visible, that is hardly different from other great works of literature and art. It is as legitimate to deal with the whole as to analyze the parts separately and in detail. In the end, the Dialogue requires a frame, and the one we have does as well as or better than any we might reconstruct. In the same way, the story, while not requiring the Dialogue to form a bridge between beginning and ending (Prologue and Epilogue), is nonetheless greatly enriched thereby. While on the surface the test is posed at the beginning, and Job passes it and is properly restored and rewarded, there is much more beneath the surface that is brought out in the Dialogue. While from one perspective the issue is the test of Job's integrity and faithfulness, from earth—on the dust and ashes—it looks very different. It is a test of God's righteousness and faithfulness. Is there a moral law of the universe, does God have any ethical integrity, or is the universe run in a totally amoral fashion? The reader is shown two very different sides of the same human situation, and perhaps the intention was not to resolve issues but to explore and exploit them. The explanation and solution offered in the Prologue and Epilogue suffice to provide a framework and a way of starting and stopping, but long after the fate of Job himself is resolved, the issues raised in the Dialogue persist, and the speeches of all the participants express deep concern about the fundamental religious issues of all times: the nature of God, his relationship to the created universe, including humanity, the problem of suffering, and the responsibility and obligation of humans toward God and toward each other. Then, when we are ready to embrace the Dialogue and the Speech from the

Whirlwind as the most profound word on the subject, perhaps we should ask whether it is proper to jettison the narrative as trivial or juvenile and the account of the wager between God and Satan as a joke rather than a serious description of the heavenly scene, if metaphoric or literary rather than scientific and theological. In the end we may gain wisdom from both parts of the book and the interweaving of themes and ideas from both the story framework and the Dialogue. The author/editor operates at several levels of discourse simultaneously and in sequence, and perhaps we should try to do the same.

Finally, the question must be raised about the issue between God and Satan. Why does God accept Satan's challenge about Job's righteousness? Satan questions Job's integrity and sincerity. His devotion, according to Satan, is merely a device to gain Yahweh's blessing. Satan is confident that if Job's faithfulness is tested, he will break under pressure and the malign truth about his inner feelings will be revealed. Satan can't know this in advance, and ultimately he is proved wrong. But what about God? Doesn't he know? In advance? Doesn't he know everything and especially what goes on inside a man's heart and mind? It is axiomatic in Christianity and Judaism and other theistic religions that God is omniscient, omnipotent, and has a monopoly of all the other attributes reflecting his absolute divinity. So how can there be question as to whether he knows in advance or whether he is entering into the test in good faith? There are actually two problems. If God knows everything and in particular that Job is truly faithful, as God avers, then why should he allow Job's faithfulness to be tested? First of all, it is a terrible thing to subject Job to trials and outright suffering, especially when there is no point except to show up Satan's pretensions. But second, it isn't fair to the Satan either. If God knows it is a sure thing, then he shouldn't enter into a wager with the Satan.

The proper position, however, is that in spite of theological statements or claims about divine omniscience, and assumptions by most believers, the God of the Hebrew Bible is not omniscient, although he certainly has a great deal of knowledge about most things that count. There is, apparently, a self-imposed limitation when it comes to the inner workings of the human soul. To determine finally what makes human beings decide ultimate questions and offer ultimate commitments requires scrutiny and testing. That seems inescapable, as several examples from the Bible will show. In spite of efforts by the great exegetes and theologians to show that the story of Abraham's near sacrifice of Isaac does not imply any limitation in God's knowledge of Abraham's fidelity, the story clearly says otherwise: the purpose of the test (so stated in the first verse of Genesis 22) is so that God can determine whether Abraham is willing to obey the divine command and surrender his only son, whom he loves, to God's demand for such a sacrifice.

The implication is clearly that God imposes the test in order to find out something he did not know before: note vv. 11–12 where God says, "*Now* I know. . . ."

The same is true in Deut 8:2–3, in which God explains that he kept the Israelites for forty years in the wilderness to test them (among other things), to find out what was in their hearts, whether they would prove loyal and faithful or false. The same is true in the case of Job. The test is imposed so that God as well as the Satan can find out whose contention about Job is correct—is he faithful and loyal to God for God's sake or for his own? The essential determination cannot be made without testing. God might have created human beings differently, so that they could be known and understood without testing, but it was essential to his purpose that human beings be responsible for their decisions and actions, and to be answerable for what they decide and do they must be free even of divine control and foreknowledge. It is a highly debated issue in both Judaism and Christianity and theism generally, but for the Hebrew Bible the evidence points to a mystery at the center of the human person, a mystery that even God respects so that the ultimate truth of human commitment can only be decided by time and testing.

The Story of Job: Prologue and Epilogue

This is the story of an upright, God-fearing man, Job of the land of Uz, who endured terrible suffering, but who nevertheless persevered in his integrity and fidelity and ultimately was rewarded by being restored to his former estate and compensated for his losses, pain, and suffering. It is one of the most familiar of all the biblical narratives, and may be compared with similar prose works such as Ruth and Jonah. The main difference is that the story of Job is told in two parts (Prologue, chaps. 1–2, and Epilogue, 42:7–17) separated by a lengthy Dialogue involving six different speakers (3:1–42:6), whereas Ruth and Jonah, approximately the same length as the story of Job, are told consecutively. The narrative of Jonah is also interrupted by a poem (chap. 2), but it is brief.

From the start it is established that Job is a righteous person. In fact, God himself asserts to the Satan that there is no one on earth to be compared with Job in his integrity and loyalty to his God. Only one other person in the Hebrew Bible is similarly described, and that is Noah, also a paragon of integrity and fidelity. These two heroes of faith and doers of good deeds are linked in tradition and piety by the prophet Ezekiel, who depicts them as men of surpassing righteousness, whose meritorious lives served to rescue not only themselves but their families from perdition. Ezekiel's tradition concerning Noah corresponds to the account of Noah and the flood that overwhelmed the earth and wiped out most living things. Not only was Noah spared but his family was rescued with him. In the Book of Job there is at least a hint of a similar situation, in which Job's goodness and merit serve to protect his family, and ultimately Job is responsible for the return and restoration of his family. Ezekiel also mentions a third hero of faith, a man named Daniel, who is not, however, the Daniel known to us from the book of that name in the Bible. Rather, the Daniel referred to by Ezekiel is another ancient worthy, like Noah and Job, and also a non-Israelite like them. Among the poetic epics discovered at Ras Shamra (ancient Ugarit) in North Syria is a text whose central figure is a pious king named Dan(i)el, a righteous person. The legend reported in the Ugaritic poem does not relate directly the circumstances that justify Ezekiel's categorization of Daniel alongside the other two, but there is little doubt that it is Ugaritic Daniel that the prophet had in mind, for, like Job, Daniel loses a child and perhaps gets him back.

The divine assertion concerning Job arouses the opposition of the Satan, who is apparently an officer of the divine court, and a very important one at that. Using modern language, we would call him the attorney general of the divine court, that is, the prosecutor of the divine realm. He seems to have a standing assignment to accuse human beings who have broken the divine rules and regulations. In the case of Job, it is clear that Satan has no valid charge to bring against that upright man. But he invents one nevertheless and thereby raises a serious theological question for which there is no easy answer. What Satan says is that Job's righteousness is not a matter of undiluted faith, but rather it is a calculated piety rooted in the relationship between the two of them. In other words, God cannot claim that Job serves and fears God for the latter's self alone, which is the true test of faith and faithfulness, but rather Job is responding to the care, protection, and prosperity that God has provided for Job. It is a very good deal for both parties, but it by no means establishes that Job is inwardly righteous, only that he knows how to respond to divine grace and thereby reap a rich and continuing reward. In so doing he has successfully hoodwinked the deity, who thinks that Job is objectively just and disinterestedly righteous. According to the Satan, nothing could be further from the truth, and if God would only take away from Job what he has given him in the way of material possessions and blessings, he would quickly discover what Job really thinks of him, and how superficial Job's piety and righteousness in fact are.

God is intrigued by the proposal, and since he is convinced that Job is truly faithful and righteous, namely that he reveres God for himself alone and will adhere to him regardless of personal fortunes, he permits Satan to follow out his proposal. As a result, Satan inflicts a series of devastating blows on Job's possessions including not only his material goods, but his servants and children as well (only his wife is spared, an interesting point, but not discussed or explained in the story). All is lost—nevertheless, Job commits no sin, utters no blasphemy, and does not condemn the deity who brought these disasters upon him. No one in the entire book ever questions that God is responsible for what happens to Job. Just as Job's righteousness is a given, so is Yahweh's ultimate responsibility for what transpires. In the present instance it is clear that the Satan acts only as agent. True, it was his idea, and Yahweh only granted him permission to proceed, but in the end it doesn't matter. The notion that things can get out of hand or that responsibility can be diverted from the deity is simply unacceptable in biblical thought. The buck stops at God himself.

The Satan is not satisfied that Job's behavior has vindicated the divine position against his own attitude concerning human beings generally and this one in particular. He contends that the test thus far has been insufficient and that Job must himself be attacked. Then, according to the Satan, Job will abandon his faith and his integrity and curse God openly, thereby vindicating the Satan's view against that of God. God accepts the possibility that the Satan may be right and grants that the whole protective structure that God has built around Job be removed and Job be exposed to all the malignancies that the Satan can muster against him. That will be a true test of Job's loyalty. So it happens that Satan, armed with divine permission, inflicts a terrible disease on Job, with the result that Job must finally feel that he has been abandoned by God. Even in that dire strait, he refuses to reject the God who may have rejected him, or to utter the blasphemy that might be regarded as appropriate or understandable under the circumstances.

At this point, the heavenly debate is suspended while the drama continues on earth. Job, having rebuked his wife, goes outside the village to suffer in solitude. He is joined by three companions, and then the lengthy dialogue about Job's condition—physical and spiritual—commences. The central problem is this: Can a human being ultimately face the question of disinterested devotion to God and meet this requirement, or are both the deity and the worshiper to be permanently frustrated in that quest for the ideal relationship of grace and compassion on the part of God, and love and loyalty on the part of humans? Since from the beginning and for as long as he/she lives, the human partner is inescapably dependent for life and sustenance on the deity, is it possible ever to separate the circumstances from the act or state of devotion? Isn't the Satan always correct in saying that the circumstances condition the relationship and that it is inevitable and natural that the creature should praise the creator and thank him for his surpassing grace and goodness? The only way to determine whether disinterested devotion is possible is by rejecting the framework on which the relationship between humanity and divinity depends. And even in the extreme case in which Job is deprived of family, possessions, and finally his own well-being, there is something left—life. Surviving itself is a sign that God still sustains the sufferer, and to that extent Satan's question about human faithfulness remains unanswered. But the answer is obvious. If you deprive the person of life, the test is automatically ended, so that can't be done. But that is itself the point. Separation from God is death and the debate has to end. Human beings can show a loyalty up to point of death because their living is itself a sign of divine care. Beyond that point it is impossible to go. So far as a human can, he can remain committed, and that is the case with Job.

The transition from the Dialogue to the Epilogue comes in the aftermath of the voice of Yahweh from the whirlwind (chaps. 38–41). Job, who has been complaining bitterly about his plight, about his friends, and indeed about what he perceives to be the inequity of the deity, is abashed by the divine intervention and ashamed of his words. This repentance on Job's part leads then to the conclusion of the story. God judges that Job has vindicated the deity's faith in him, and therefore Job can be restored and compensated for his suffering. First, however, the case of the friends must be settled, since they had defended God in the disputation with Job by impugning Job's behavior as well as his intemperate words aimed at or about the deity. They thereby fell into guilt themselves by impeaching the divine word (admittedly unheard by them) that Job is righteous. Even the Satan cannot challenge the truth of that statement. He can only shift the ground by saying that Job's righteous behavior is not so great an achievement considering the way in which God surrounds him with security and prosperity and pampers him and his family. But underneath the nice superficialities, Job is probably no better than anybody else, indeed he may be worse, because he has come to expect all these things as his due and will resent deeply their removal. The friends in effect bear the burden of the Satan's argument—that at heart Job is guilty and wicked. Understandably God is put out by these so-called defenders of orthodoxy and makes his point against them by requiring sacrifices of repentance and atonement for their foolishness, while indicating that he will only accept their peace-offering if Job also prays for them. Thus the tables are turned; the friends are forgiven because of the intercessory righteousness of the man they have maligned and traduced.

The last act in the drama is to restore Job as he was before, only more so. Yahweh clearly and cheerfully concedes that Job has been wronged and that he has a just cause and claim against the deity (cf. Scholnick 1975). This concession is implicitly confirmed by the compensation over and above simple restoration. With regard to possessions, Job receives double, which is one of the specified damage awards for the victim of unjust confiscation of property. In addition, Job's children are also restored, but here we are dealing with a story-teller who knows how to conclude the story in the best possible way. The miracle confirms the potent goodness of the patriarch and the surpassing grace of the deity, who could not allow the Satan to win even a minor victory against his servant Job, the man of integrity and righteousness.

The Book of Job as a Literary Unity

Whatever the origin of the different parts of Job, especially the story framework (Prologue and Epilogue) and the Dialogue, we must try to deal with the final product that was deliberately assembled. The editor and publisher expected it to be read (aloud) and understood with all its parts. How can this be done?

The answer is to recognize that the Dialogue fills the gap between the conclusion of the second test imposed on Job and his restoration and reward at the end of the story. The Satan plays no further visible role in the story, presumably because Job has vindicated God's faith in his piety and hence the challenge has been met and the wager won by God. This explanation might be satisfactory if there were no Dialogue, and then we would have a short story like Jonah and Ruth. But the huge Dialogue poses a problem, and the best way to deal with it is to recognize it as a continuation of the testing. Whatever the friends may have intended by their coming to condole with Job, the actual visit and subsequent conversation turn out to be another test, perhaps even more trying to Job than his previous experience of suffering. While nothing is said explicitly to that effect, we may suppose that the friends and especially their arguments constitute a third effort on the part of Satan to bring Job down. The friends argue in essence that Job should concede the main point, that he must have been guilty of some breach of the compact with God and that even if he can't identify it he should confess, repent, be forgiven and restored, and that would end the matter. In other words, repentance is a panacea and universal solvent, and even in unclear cases it is better to repent than to be stubborn and compound the hypothetical sin by challenging God and in effect attacking him by a form of self-justification. This sounds reasonable enough but in fact would play into Satan's hands and achieve his objective. Job in so doing would seek cheap grace at the price of his innocence and integrity. In point of fact, the essence of Job's righteousness has subtly shifted. Whereas in the Prologue God and Satan put the issue in terms of whether Job will curse God once his happiness is revoked and thereby compromise his integrity, in the Dialogue the question is reformulated by the friends and Job. The friends maintain that the only solution is for Job to confess and repent for his unknown sin, thus regaining his integrity. Job, on the other hand, decries this as the height of hypocrisy, since he is blameless. Had he followed his friends' advice, Job would have won the bet for Satan by lying to regain his former prosperity, proving that he fears God only toward that end. Hence the strong anger God expresses about the friends who are nothing more than agents of the Satan in trying to get Job to compromise his integrity.

Job, however, withstands the friends in three cycles of speeches. No ground is gained or lost except that the original friendships are badly frayed by the end of the third round. Job's final speech is an explicit and detailed affirmation of the original premise. Job is an upright person whose manner of life always met with divine favor until the sudden and inexplicable change in God's behavior. Job remains adamant that the problem is with God, not with him. And so at the end of the discourse between Job and the three friends, the third failure to budge Job from his integrity is recorded.

While Elihu and his speeches may be intrusive, we must account for their presence in the final form of the book. Clearly, he also is part of the problem rather than the solution. He is better at his presentation than the friends and hence more dangerous to Job's cause. It is possible that where the friends failed, Elihu might succeed, especially with the four consecutive speeches to which Job does not even attempt to reply. But there is a reply from Yahweh.

First, however, as to the identity of Elihu—he comes from nowhere and he disappears from the scene as soon as he is done with his speeches. I suggest that he is not a real person at all. There no doubt was an Elihu, like the other participants, a person with a patronymic and a profession, but the Elihu here is a disguise—as so often in Greek epic. He is the person assumed by Satan to press his case for the last time. The four speeches are like the four attacks on Job's family and possessions in chap. 1. And because Satan has taken a personal hand and a very threatening one, God feels that he too must intervene. Hence the next and last speech is that of Yahweh himself. He cannot risk Job's reply to Elihu since Job may be at the point of resignation. So he makes his own reply to settle the wager and all its associated issues. But just as Satan was tied by the rules, so Yahweh is too. He is constrained by the compact not to offer Job consolation or encouragement. These would produce the same situation that Satan complained about originally and muddy the waters. For the test to be a good one, Yahweh has to stay out of it. But being totally out of the picture doesn't seem fair either. He can make a statement—this God is too busy with important matters to pay much attention to humans, and hence Job should not make such a fuss because things have gone wrong. The difference between happiness and misery for humans is negligible in the larger world of galaxies and supernovae, and Job will only make things worse by complaining. In other words, he has it all wrong.

Not a very helpful speech, as most readers have observed, and if this is the author's point, then he is at odds with most of the Bible. But the editor has a different strategy. This is all that Yahweh can allow himself to say, since otherwise he will violate the terms of the wager. Just as Satan may not finally kill Job, so God is not allowed to reassure Job about his positive and supportive interest in this frail human being. That would spoil everything. But Job gets the right message even from the wrong words. What God denies in his words is affirmed by the fact of his speaking. Job understands that Yahweh's blast from heaven is nevertheless the very word that Job needs to know that Yahweh has his eye on him and has expressed his concern for him. That is enough and Job says, "With hearing of the ear I had heard you. But now my eyes have seen you." Now he knows that God does care for him, and he can freely repent and thus pave the way for the conclusion of the book—his restoration and reward. Thus both Satan and God have pressed their case upon Job, who finally makes the necessary move to end the struggle between the opposing forces.

The Dialogue

The great bulk of the book of Job is given over to the Dialogue between Job and his three friends, with the fifth man Elihu joining in after the others have finished. Then Yahweh himself closes off the discussion with the great speech from the whirlwind. The dialogue may be outlined in the following manner:

Introduction (2:11–13): the three friends come to console Job

I. Job and his three friends (chaps. 3–31)
  - A. First cycle (chaps. 3–14)
    1. Job: first speech (chap. 3)
    2. Eliphaz: first speech (chaps. 4–5)
    3. Job's reply (chaps. 6–7)
    4. Bildad: first speech (chap. 8)
    5. Job's reply (chaps. 9–10)
    6. Zophar: first speech (chap. 11)
    7. Job's reply (chaps. 12–14)
  - B. Second cycle (chaps. 15–21)
    1. Eliphaz: second speech (chap. 15)
    2. Job's reply (chaps. 16–17)
    3. Bildad: second speech (chap. 18)
    4. Job's reply (chap. 19)
    5. Zophar: second speech (chap. 20)
    6. Job's reply (chap. 21)

C. Third cycle* (chaps. 22–28)
  1. Eliphaz: third speech (chap. 22)
  2. Job's reply (chaps. 23–24)
  3. Bildad: third speech (chap. 25)
  4. Job's reply (chap. 26)
  5. Job's reply (chap. 27)
  6. Wisdom (chap. 28)
D. Conclusion—Job's closing speech (chaps. 29–31)

II. Additional speeches (32:1–42:6)
  A. Elihu's speeches (chaps. 32–37)
    1. First speech (chaps. 32–33)
    2. Second speech (chap. 34)
    3. Third speech (chap. 35)
    4. Fourth speech (chaps. 36–37)
  B. The Lord from the Whirlwind (38:1–42:6)
    1. First speech (chaps. 38–39)
    2. Job's reply (40:1–5)
    3. Second speech (40:6–41:34)
    4. Job's reply (42:1–6)

Conclusion (42:7–9)

In spite of Job's pitiable condition and the friends' general air of superiority, if not condescension, Job dominates the Dialogue. He opens the discussion with a general statement (chap. 3) that shapes the rest of the conversation, and he closes off the debate with a final discourse (chaps. 29–31) that is addressed not merely to the friends, but to the universe and in particular to God. Then, as each of the friends speaks and addresses one or more facets of the basic issue, Job responds to each. In fact, Job speaks more than the three friends put together, matching each of their speeches with one of his own, and adding the opening and closing remarks. What was presented as an occasion of consolation and condolement, so that the friends could comfort their stricken companion, turns into a forum for Job to make his case against the Almighty, and also an opportunity to refute the friends' well-meant but positively wrong interpretation of his status with God and the causes of his terrible and tragic suffering. The friends become little more than stick figures representing conventional wisdom and piety in the ancient Near East, not just Israel, but all the neighboring nations that shared a common, all-purpose theodicy (see Pope 1965: lvi–lxxxiv).

Job inaugurates the proceeding by stating his case poetically and passionately. In a word, he curses his day (3:1)—his birthday, of course.

* For a brief discussion of the problems of this section, not relevant to our treatment, see Pope 1965: xx.

Perhaps the author-editor used the word intentionally—to curse—to evoke in the hearer or reader the expected concern over the issue between God and Satan—namely whether Job will finally surrender to the satanic forces and curse his maker. He may come perilously close to this critical point, but he curses his day, not his God. He will challenge God and disturb the peace of the heavenly as well as the earthly realm, but at this point, the curse that is uttered is nevertheless aimed elsewhere. There will be another oath later on, at the end, when he solemnly affirms his innocence and voluntarily takes an oath of acquittal. He pronounces himself not guilty of any and all crimes implied by the divine punishment and imputed to him by the friends.

The other friends offer different responses, but they vary only in detail, and it must be conceded that the three are not sharply differentiated. They are in essential agreement on main points, the chief one being that it is sacrilegious to even hint at or think, much less utter, that God is not just in his dealings with the world and with humanity. From that premise they argue back to the palpable inference about Job's suffering. Since it is axiomatic that God is the source of bane as well as blessing, and since God is by definition just in his dealings, it follows that Job has done something, or said something, or thought something contrary to the law of God. And he only makes things worse by stubbornly insisting on his integrity and righteousness. There is a solution to the dilemma, and that is to repent. If Job will concede that the root of the trouble lies in his stubborn unwillingness to confess his faults, and make amends and truly repent, then the friends are confident that the present agonies will cease and Job will be restored to divine favor with all the appropriate recompense.

Job does not receive either the analysis of what ails him or the prescription for resolving the issue in a kindly way. He cannot go the route recommended by the friends because he cannot repent and seek forgiveness for sins and crimes that were never committed. God and Satan did not discuss the possibility that Job might repent and seek forgiveness and reconciliation with God as a result of the outrageous treatment received from the heavenly source (that is, at God's stipulation as carried out by Satan and his agents). Satan makes sure that Job's experience is so extreme that he will ultimately curse God—even as is so strongly recommended by his wife (who presumably is not taken from Job because she will act, like the friends, as an agent provocateur: serving Satan's purpose to push Job into the final stage of disillusionment and frustration and thus into cursing God). The friends' argument is impeccably drawn from this premise, which is central to biblical religion: the God who created an orderly universe and made laws by which it is run cannot himself violate those laws and act unjustly toward upright human beings, upholders of his law. The reward for good is good, as the punishment for evil is evil. Hence, if Job is being treated badly by the deity, the latter must have adequate evidence against Job in order to justify the treatment received. Job must be guilty of some grave offense, and his denial of that well-nigh certain inference only compounds the original crime and makes the punishment more certain and more severe.

Job rejects the inference, the argument, and ultimately, at least in a sense, the central premise. His starting point is his own innocence or integrity. On this he will not budge, and in fact this is central to the whole argument. The reader is warned by the author-editor from the very beginning of the story that Job's righteousness is not to be questioned. This is the primary given of the story: divine, satanic, and human views agree. That Job himself has no doubts of his righteousness may bother some readers, but self-consciousness of right-doing and avoiding wrongdoing is essential to the fulfillment of the condition. Humility does not entail ignorance of one's virtues. Righteousness is not mysterious at all—living according to the divine stipulation makes the difference.

Job's inference from the premise of his own integrity is that God is unjust in his dealings. As already pointed out, the vicissitudes of Job, his family, and his retainers are by all acknowledged to be the effects of deliberate decisions and executions by God. Job's deduction is that since his sufferings are incompatible with his merits and deserts, it is clear that the proper system of rewards and punishments has broken down and that God is in violation of his own code of ethics. In a word, he has no right to punish Job, and hence the friends are wrong.

Job's argument from premise to conclusion is just as impeccable as that of the friends. If the premises are accepted, the logical inferences would seem to be correct. But inevitably there is doubt and confusion about the basic premise, and there are repeated efforts to reinterpret or misinterpret and to produce more satisfying results.

In the end, both views are rejected as perhaps one-sided and simplistic. The premises may be correct, and the logical reasoning impeccable, and the inferences may still be quite wrong. And that is where the additional speeches come in. In the case of Job and his three friends, nothing much happens. In spite of repeated statements by all four men, no minds are changed, there is hardly any give-and-take, in fact none: all positions are firmly set and the only visible or audible changes seem to be in the irritation between the friends generated by the debate.

The way out of the dilemma is provided by the addenda: the speeches of Elihu (32–37) and Yahweh (38–41). The former criticizes the friends as well as Job, the friends for not presenting the case for God and hence against Job in adequate fashion. The implication is that they only made things worse. Their well-meant defense of God is repudiated by God himself. Elihu attacks Job for drawing his set of inferences from his premise. Elihu offers a different look, which borrows a little from all the friends and also proleptically from the speech of Yahweh and even from Job. The point to be noted is that Job makes no response at all to Elihu, unlike his reaction to his friends. Here roles have been altered, since Elihu is not rebuked by his elders and he dominates his part of the picture as much as Job dominates the earlier rounds. Elihu represents a shift from the Dialogue. Not only is there a new voice, but the ratios and proportions are different. Job does not reply at all, as though Elihu now occupies center stage and dominates the proceedings. However we explain this intrusive person and his monologues, their present position in the text reflects a summation and evaluation of what has preceded: disparagement of all the participants but especially of Job for his unacceptable assumptions and inferences about God and his relationship with humanity.

The next and final entry is the voice from the whirlwind. Just as Elihu directs most of his remarks to Job, although he does acknowledge the presence of the friends, so the voice from the whirlwind addresses Job directly and does not seem to acknowledge even the existence of Elihu. Nevertheless, the divine disputation is designed to shut down any and all arguments, clear up some central points, but not try either to correct or reconcile the other interpretations. The voice from the whirlwind is concerned about Job's conclusions derived from the premise and the supporting data. It is not necessary for Job to condemn God in the process of exonerating himself. There is linkage, but Job hasn't made the right correlations or deductions. He should go back to the drawing board. The case with the friends is even worse. They have seriously compromised their own integrity in their fervor to defend God. More drastic remedies are required in their case. In a dramatic twist (which carries us through the transition to the Epilogue or story ending), the friends are required to make atonement for their grievous misreading of the real situation, and Job himself will have to intercede for them. As to Job, he concludes the Dialogue by responding briefly but with genuine repentance to the speeches of Yahweh. After the first he promises to hold his peace, and at the end of the second he does repent—something urged on him by his friends—but for entirely different reasons and in an entirely different connection. He does not budge on the question of his prior behavior—his oath of innocence stands firmly and forever. It is his faulty reasoning, his logical inferences that he is now willing to modify or repudiate. The linkage between his suffering and divine malevolence is no longer so clear to him, nor presumably is the necessary linkage of his righteousness and the loss of rewards and benefits. In the story everything will be resolved by the restoration of the *status quo ante*, and with compensation, but at the end of the Dialogue there is still some bewilderment. We might call that the beginning of new wisdom on the part of everyone. All the humans have been wrong in greater or lesser measure. The ways of God remain mysterious, but it is possible to maintain faith and integrity in spite of inexplicable and often trying circumstances.

As R. E. Friedman (personal communication) summed up, the lesson is that friends should be friends, not judges. They should not act as apologists for or agents of the deity. Their role (like that of Job in the days of his glory) is to be comrades and comforters to any and all stricken by trouble. Job charges them with this patent failing, and his charge is fully upheld in the Epilogue, one of the few conclusive points in the book.

Bibliography

Freedman, D. N.
1968 The Elihu Speeches in the Book of Job. *Harvard Theological Review* 61: 51–59; reprinted in Freedman, *Pottery, Poetry, and Prophecy* (Winona Lake: Eisenbrauns, 1980) 329–37.

Pope, M. H.
1965 *Job*. Anchor Bible 15. Garden City: Doubleday.

Scholnick, S. H.
1975 Lawsuit Drama in the Book of Job. Ph.D. diss., Brandeis University.

Interpreting Orthography

W. Randall Garr
University of California, Santa Barbara

0. A written language has no sounds. It does not speak, in a conventional sense, but communicates nonverbally. Language is abstracted into a series of signs that themselves relate information. In writing, language becomes a system of signs.

When a language exists only in written form, the audible sounds that the language contains are not readily apparent. Without the testimony of a native speaker, it may be difficult to match the written sign with specific phones. Discovering the sounds native to a written language, then, is indirect. The internal sound patterns of the language, external evidence of transcriptions in other languages and scripts, and notices about speech behavior recorded by contemporary witnesses can compensate for the lack of direct phonetic data. From these sources, the phonetic base of a written language may be recovered.

I thank Laura Kalman, Baruch Halpern, and William Propp for reading earlier drafts of this paper. I also thank Douglas Johnson and Stephen Kaufman for their input.

The following symbols will be used.

[ ]	phonetic realization (spirantization, however, is not indicated)
V̄	long vowel
V̂	lengthened vowel
*	underlying form, phoneme
#	word boundary
+	morphemic, (pro)nominal boundary
=	morphemic, verbal boundary
-	*maqqeph*
>	develops, developing into
<	develops, developing from
~	alternates, alternating with

[A briefer version of this essay was awarded the Mitchell Dahood Memorial Prize in Biblical Hebrew and Northwest Semitic in 1987—Eds.]

0.1. In the case of Biblical Hebrew (BH; herein, used synonymously with Tiberian Hebrew), however, a different kind of reasoning has been applied to phonetic recovery. Some proceed directly from orthography. Since BH has seven orthographically distinct full vowels, the language itself, according to this view, has a seven-way vocalic contrast (Lambert 1972: §34; cf. Sperber 1959: §58). This contrast, is, above all, qualitative.

0.2. Others rely upon medieval grammatical tradition. Since Geiger's discussion (1856: 98), the division of BH vowels into long-short pairs has been traced to Joseph Kimhi (1105–70) (Kimchi 1888: 17) (BL §7e; cf. Brockelmann 1940: 333; Ben-David 1957–58: esp. pp. 8, 125–26). Influenced by both Arabic and his native Spanish (Brockelmann 1940: 334 n. 1), Kimhi distilled the BH vowels into five pairs; qualitatively, BH has, according to him, a five-way vocalic contrast, and its overall distinction lies in quantitative opposition.

0.3. The division between the qualitative and quantitative analyses of BH vowels (summarized in Brockelmann 1940: 334; Ben-David 1957–58), though, is not complete. The two systems agree on certain phonetic interpretations. The quantitative school divides the vowels as follows.

pathaḥ	[ɑ][1]	*qameṣ gadhol*	[ɑ̄]
seghol	[e]	*ṣere*	[ē]
ḥireq	[i]	*ḥireq*	[ī]
qameṣ qaṭon	[o]	*ḥolem*	[ō]
shureq[2]	[u]	*shureq*	[ū]

The qualitative camp divides them as follows.

pathaḥ	[ɑ] / [ɑ̄][3]
seghol	[ɛ] / [ɛ̄]
ṣere	[e] / [ē]
ḥireq	[i] / [ī]
qameṣ	[ɔ] / [ɔ̄]
ḥolem	[o] / [ō]
shureq	[u] / [ū]

If the question of vowel length is disregarded, both schemes interpret several vowels identically. *Pathaḥ* is [ɑ] for both (see n. 1), *ḥireq* is [i], and

1. The conventional phonemic representation as *a* has been adjusted to reflect phonetic reality. See §§2.1.1 and 7.1.2.

2. On the later appellation *qubbuṣ*, see Chomsky 1971: 23 with nn. 7–8.

3. On the possibility of *pathaḥ* as a long vowel, see Lambert 1972: §131. Cf. GKB 1 §10d.

shureq marks [u]. Both analyses also agree that *ṣere* represents [e], and *ḥolem* [o].

They do not agree on the phonetic interpretation of *seghol* and *qameṣ*. According to the quantitative school, *seghol* and *ṣere* are phonetically identical, [e], except for the question of length. The qualitative camp holds that each has a different sound; [ɛ] for *seghol*, and [e] for *ṣere*. Similarly, the Kimhians analyze *qameṣ* and *pathaḥ* as [ɑ] (long vs. short). Non-Kimhians claim that *qameṣ* is [ɔ], and *pathaḥ* is a different sound [ɑ]. The *seghol* and *qameṣ*, then, are the vowels on which the two systems diverge. Thus, if the phonetic interpretation of these two vowels can be determined, the quantity vs. quality controversy can be resolved.

1.1. The Semitic vowel system, as traditionally reconstructed, contains three vowels: **a*, **i*, and **u*.[4] Each of these vowels can be short or long, depending upon morphophonological requirements. The Hebrew reflexes of proto long vowels are straightforward. **ī* becomes *ḥireq*, **ū* changes into *shureq*, and **ā* is largely replaced by *ḥolem*.[5] The reflexes of proto short vowels, however, are not as self-evident. In word-final, singly closed, accented syllables, verbs show one set of reflexes.

**á* > X̱, as in זָכַר 'he remembered', שָׁמַר 'he guarded', יִלְמַד 'he may learn' (Deut 17:19)
**í* > X̤, as in כָּבֵד 'he is heavy' (see KB 418–19), זָקֵן 'he is old', יִתֵּן 'he gives'
**ú* > ˙X, as in יָכֹל 'he is able'

In unbound adjectives and nouns, too, **í* is replaced by *ṣere* and **ú* by *ḥolem*, yet **á* becomes *qameṣ*.

**í* > X̤, as in זָקֵן 'old (age)', כָּבֵד 'heavy', כָּתֵף 'shoulder'
**ú* > ˙X, as in קָטֹן 'small'
**á* > X̞, as in זָכָר 'male', זָקָן 'beard', and זָנָב 'tail'[6]

On the one hand, then, nouns and verbs jointly replace **í* by *ṣere* and **ú* by *ḥolem*. On the other, **á* is replaced by *pathaḥ* in verbs, and by *qameṣ* in nouns.

1.2. While the outcome of **á* differs between nouns and verbs, the reflex of this vowel also differs even within a single noun class. In **qVtl* nouns, the pattern of vowel replacement externally resembles that of verbs.

4. For the background, see Jastrow 1885: 215 n. 1; and Chomsky 1952: 32 n. 12.
5. See §§8.1 and 8.5.2 for greater detail, including examples.
6. For exceptions, see GKB 1 §24c; BL §26n; Aartun 1967; and Blau 1968.

*á > X̱,[7] as in בַּיִת 'house', בַּעַל 'master', נַחַל 'stream'
*í > X̤,[8] as in זֵכֶר 'mention', סֵפֶר 'document', עֵגֶל 'calf'
*ú > ˙X, as in אֹזֶן 'ear', קֹדֶשׁ 'holiness', רֹגֶז 'anger'

In these nouns, *á > *pathaḥ*, and *í and *ú become *ṣere* and *ḥolem*, respectively. Yet when the final radical of this noun-type is *waw*, the vowel replacement is somewhat different: *í and *ú become *ṣere* and *ḥolem*, yet *á > *qameṣ*.

*í > X̤, as in שֵׂכוּ[9] 'Secu' (place name) (1 Sam 19:22)
*ú > ˙X, as in בֹּהוּ 'waste', תֹּהוּ 'waste'
*á > X̩, as in שָׂחוּ 'swimming', and perhaps אָחוּ 'reed' (see Lambdin 1953: 146 with n. 12)

Not only do nouns and verbs treat the *a vowel differently, but nouns too may show a double realization.

1.3. Although the pattern of vowel replacement can be delineated, the underlying phonetic interpretation of these vowels is not clearcut; the replacement of *á by *pathaḥ* and *qameṣ* requires explanation. Either *qameṣ* and *pathaḥ*, at least in open syllables, are qualitatively identical but differ in length (for example, Ewald 1870: §§29c–d; see also Sperber 1941: 453). Or, *qameṣ* and *pathaḥ* are phonetically, that is, qualitatively, dissimilar (for example, Joüon 1923: §§6d, j).[10] Thus, the quality vs. quantity controversy presents itself again.

2.0. An inquiry into the composition of the BH vowels may help resolve this controversy. For, as in all languages, Hebrew vowels are composed of distinctive features (see Hyman 1975: 24–58). A distinctive feature is an articulatory property used to classify sounds (Ladefoged 1975: 238). For example, sounds produced with a lowered velum, allowing air to pass through the nose, are nasal (Chomsky and Halle 1968: 316; cf. Ladefoged 1982: 260); *mem* and *nun* are nasal sounds in Hebrew. Or, sounds that release air over the side of the tongue are lateral (Chomsky and Halle 1968: 317; Ladefoged 1982: 260); *lamedh* and *śin* are lateral Hebrew phones (see Steiner 1977: esp. pp. 137–43). A distinctive feature, then, is a phonetic property that distinguishes groups of sounds in a given language. And by applying

7. Provided that the second radical is *yodh* (see BL §§61o′, v′) or a pharyngeal/glottal fricative (see ibid. §§61k′, t′). The replacement of *a by *seghol* is late. See §2.2 for greater detail.

8. See Revell 1985.

9. Cf. *BHS ad loc.*, whose reading is unlikely because *qitū (or *qatū) never develops into קָטוּ.

10. For background, see Schreiner 1886: 238–39 n. 4; Yalon 1965: 132–34; Weinberg 1968: 152 n. 2; and Chomsky 1971: 23 with n. 12.

these features to Hebrew, it should be possible to divide the Hebrew vowels into phonetic groups, or classes of sounds.

In BH, three[11] features distinguish the vowels one from another. Two of these features reflect the position of the tongue. On a vertical axis, the degree to which the tongue is raised above or lowered below its neutral position characterizes vowel height (Chomsky and Halle 1968: 304). When the tongue is raised, the vowel is high, when lowered it is low; the intermediate zone produces mid vowels (see Wang 1968; Ladefoged 1982: 262–63). On a horizontal axis, the presence or absence of lingual backward movement is also distinctive (Chomsky and Halle 1968: 305). In retracted position, the vowel is back; without retraction, the phone is nonback (see Hyman 1975: 47).

The lips are responsible for the third distinctive vocalic feature. A sound produced by articulating the upper and lower lips (lip rounding) is labial. Without articulation, the sound is nonlabial (Ladefoged 1982: 259). Thus, the articulation of lips, tongue height, and tongue retraction/nonretraction converge to differentiate Hebrew vowels one from another (see also Gleason 1965: 35).

2.1.1. These features suggest a preliminary description, and classification, of BH vowels (see Malone 1978: 148, revised from Malone 1972: 426; cf. Schramm 1964: 29, 31). *Ḥireq*, representing [i] (disregarding length), is a high, front, nonlabial phone. *Shureq*, [u], is also high but is produced with lip rounding and tongue retraction; it is therefore back and labial (cf. Chomsky 1971: 25–26).[12] *Pathaḥ*, however, is both nonlabial and low; and because of the affinity between *ḥaṭaph pathaḥ* and back consonants, for example, the velar in אַשְׁכְּנַז 'Ashkenaz' (Gen 10:3; 1 Chr 1:6; cf. Jer 51:27) (see GKC §10g; cf. GKB 1 §21w) and the emphatic[13] in הוּטֲלוּ 'they are hurled out' (Jer 22:28), *pathaḥ* is also back.[14] Thus, *pathaḥ*, *ḥireq*, and *shureq* are divided into one low and two high phones, and the two high phones are in turn differentiated by lip rounding and backness.

Like *ḥireq* and *shureq*, *ṣere* and *ḥolem* form a pair. Representing [e] and [o], respectively, *ṣere* and *ḥolem* are produced with a slight raising of the tongue; they are not quite high or mid, but they fall into an area between

11. These criteria have also been assigned various weights in classification. For the primacy of the dichotomy high/low, see Lambert 1893: 274–75 (see also BL §7g). For labial/nonlabial, see Schreiner 1886: 236; and, on Aramaic, Boyarin 1978: 153 n. 65. See also Schramm 1964: 6 n. 1.

12. On the possible interchange of these two high phones, see Dalman 1978: 87; Chomsky 1952: 34 n. 16; and Chomsky 1971: 26–27.

13. For qualitative analyses of emphatics see, for example, Malone 1976: 253; and Dolgopolsky 1977.

14. See too the lengthening of *pathaḥ* into *qameṣ* (§8.5.1).

the two, properly mid-high (see Ladefoged 1982: 263 [on Danish], 257). _Ḥolem_, however, is further distinguished by tongue retraction and lip rounding. Just as _ḥireq_ and _shureq_ share vowel height but are distinguished by labiality and backness, so too _ṣere_ and _ḥolem_ are commonly mid-high but differ in labiality and backness (cf. Lambert 1972: 21 n. 2).

2.1.2. These criteria not only describe vowels but also phonological processes. The relation between *_í_ and its Hebrew reflex, _ṣere_, is one of a high to mid-high vowel. In the shift of *_ú_ to _ḥolem_ the correspondence is identical: high to mid-high. A vowel is lowered under the accent, though it does not change in labiality or backness. Further, that *_á_ does not change in זָכַר or נַחַל is consistent with this theory; the vowel does not participate in vowel lowering because *_a_, a proto low phone, cannot lower further. BH, then, exhibits a rule of accent-conditioned vowel lowering (see Joüon 1923: §6i), common to both nouns and verbs (Malone 1974: 399).

2.2. This rule does not account for the contrasting pairs זָכַר ~ זָכָר[15] or נַחַל ~ שָׁחוּ. In one set, *_á_ > _pathaḥ_, while in the other *_á_ > _qameṣ_. This vacillation is particularly interesting in *_qatl_ nouns. When the second radical is a pharyngeal or glottal fricative (_ḥeth_, _ʿayin_, _he_), *_á_ is perpetuated as _pathaḥ_; for example, נַחַל, בַּעַל, and לַהַט 'flame'.[16] When the second radical is the high semivowel _yodh_, *_á_ is also retained: for example, בַּיִת, זַיִת 'olive (-tree)', and חַיִל 'strength'.[17] If, however, the second consonant is _waw_, *_á_ becomes _qameṣ_: מָוֶת 'death', אָוֶן 'evil', and תָּוֶךְ 'midst'.[18]

Where *_a_ is followed by two identical consonants—*_qall_ nouns[19]—the proto phone also splits into _pathaḥ_ and _qameṣ_. *_á_ usually becomes _pathaḥ_, as in גַּן 'garden', טַל 'dew', and צַר 'enemy' (Olshausen 1861: §58g; cf. GKC §20l). Yet when the second, reduplicated radical is _waw_ or _mem_, *_á_ may (Revell 1981: 84–91, 94) be replaced by _qameṣ_ (see Olshausen 1861: §§58g, h):[20] קָו 'line' (especially the bound form קָו in 2 Kgs 21:13[21]); and יָם 'sea' (especially

15. This minimal pair was suggested to me orally by Robert Hetzron.

16. Except לֶחֶם 'bread' and רֶחֶם 'womb' (cf. רַחַם 'womb' [Judg 5:30]).

17. Exceptions include חֵיל 'rampart (?)', חֵיק 'lap', לֵיל 'night', and perhaps אֵיד 'calamity'.

18. Except עֶוֶל 'injustice' and רֶוַח 'interval; relief' (see BL §61w′); cf. monophthongized יוֹם 'day'. צוֹם 'fasting', שׁוֹט 'whip', and שׁוֹר 'bull'. In verbs, however, *_áwC_ > [ɑ́wC], as in שָׁלַוְתִּי 'I had (no) rest' (Job 3:26) (Malone 1984: 77). See also n. 19. For another exception, see n. 51.

19. For verbs, cf. *_aww_ > [ɑw], for example, וַיְצַו 'he commanded' < *-_ṣaww_, צַו 'command!' < *_ṣaww_, as well as וַיְקַו 'he hoped' (Isa 5:2, 7). Also verbal *_amm_ > [ɑm], for example, חַם 'it was in a rage' (Ps 39:4), יֵחַם 'it is in a rage' (Deut 19:6), and תַּם 'it, they ended, finished' (Gen 47:18; Josh 4:11; Jer 6:29 [_qre_] (?); Lam 4:22). See also Revell 1981: 97–99, and n. 51 below.

20. Adverbial שָׁם 'there' (see שָׁמָּה 'thither') may also reflect this change. See Olshausen 1861: §58h. Cf. §9.4.2.

21. Cf. Isa 34:11. קַו/קָו in Isa 18:2, 7 and 28:10, 13 are onomatopoetic (see BDB 875b; cf. Hallo 1958: 337–38).

the bound form יַם־ 'sea of'[22]), as well as חָם 'hot' (Josh 9:12) and תָּם 'complete'.

2.3. The distribution of *á > *pathaḥ* vs. *á > *qameṣ* is complementary. In **qatl* nouns, *á > *pathaḥ* except when adjacent to *waw* or *mem*. These radicals, moreover, share two distinctive features that isolate them as a group: they are the only two nonvowels that are labial and sonorant (on the latter, see Ladefoged 1982: 253, 261). In other words, then, the rule can be recast: *á in a doubly closed syllable is replaced by *pathaḥ*, except before a labial sonorant, where it may be replaced by *qameṣ*. The affinity between *qameṣ* and labial sonorants therefore suggests that, qualitatively, *qameṣ* too is labial.

2.4. The distribution of *ḥaṭaph qameṣ* reveals another quality of this vowel. Usually, reduced *u is neutralized to shewa in BH. For example, **burāš* > בְּרוֹשׁ 'juniper', **gubūl* > גְּבוּל 'border', **yišmurū* > יִשְׁמְרוּ 'they guard', and **yigmulēnī* > יִגְמְלֵנִי 'he rewards, rewarded me' (2 Sam 19:37, 22:21; Ps 18:21). In the presence of a labial, however, *u is not always neutralized but may[23] appear as *ḥaṭaph qameṣ* (see GKB 1 §21bb): for example, צִפֳּרִים 'birds' (Lev 14:4, 49; Ps 104:17), דֳּמִי 'silence', and יֶהְדֳּפֵם 'he will drive them out' (Josh 23:5). This evidence confirms the labial quality of *qameṣ*.

Nonlabial environments also promote *ḥaṭaph qameṣ* < *u (GKB 1 §21bb; cf. GKC §10h).

**qudqudahū*	>	קָדְקֳדוֹ 'his head' (2 Sam 14:25; Ps 7:17; Job 2:7)
**(ha)barqunīm*	>	הַבַּרְקֳנִים 'the threshing sledges (?)' (Judg 8:7, 16) (both in pause)[24]
**murdukay*	>	מָרְדֳּכַי 'Mordecai'
**(ha)guranāt*	>	הַגֳּרָנוֹת 'the threshing floors' (1 Sam 23:1; Joel 2:24)[25]

In these examples, *ḥaṭaph qameṣ* appears in the presence of velars ([g, k]) and uvulars ([q]); that is, one quality of the original *u vowel is retained before back consonants (see also §2.1.1). This pairing of *ḥaṭaph qameṣ* and back consonants suggests, then, that *qameṣ* is also a back phone (see Joüon 1923: 26 n. 1; Chomsky 1971: 24).

3.0. The distribution of *qameṣ* and *ḥaṭaph qameṣ* has revealed that *qameṣ* is both labial and back. Yet the third quality of *qameṣ*, its height, remains to

22. Except in combination with סוּף 'reed', that is, יַם־סוּף 'Red Sea' (BDB 410b).

23. Cf. prelabial **gubūl* > גְּבוּל and postlabial **yigmulēnī* > יִגְמְלֵנִי.

24. On pausal *ḥaṭeph* vowels, see GKB 1 §21w (which can be extended to include *all ḥaṭeph* vowels).

25. For the last example, cf. GKC §10h and GKB 1 §21aa. Cf. Lambert 1972: §40.

be discovered. This latter quality is best determined by reference to *seghol*, the other test case for Hebrew phonetic interpretation.

3.1.1. *Qameṣ* and *seghol* show a certain relationship: **i* : *seghol* as **u* : *qameṣ*. This parallel behavior is especially clear in unaccented syllables. When a word-final **CiC* syllable is attached to a following word and loses its own accent, **i* is replaced by *seghol*:[26] for example, אֶת־ 'with', עֶת־ 'time of' (Lev 15:25; Hag 1:2), and תֶּן־לִי 'give me!' (Gen 14:21) (see BL §14j′). Under identical conditions, a **CuC* syllable becomes XX̣, as in כָּל־ 'all of', חָק־ 'law of', and שְׁמָר־לְךָ 'note!' (Exod 34:11) (see GKC §9u). The two high vowels, then, are jointly replaced.

3.1.2. The same replacement occurs in closed, posttonic syllables. After the contextual accent shift (see BL §12x; Lambert 1972: §137), posttonic **i* (whether < **i* or **ī*)[27] is replaced by *seghol*: וַיֵּלֶךְ 'he went', וַיֵּשֶׁב 'he dwelt', as well as וַיּוֹלֶךְ[28] 'he led' (Exod 14:21; 2 Kgs 6:19, 25:20; Jer 52:26) and וַיָּקֶם 'he established' (BL §14j′). Similarly, posttonic **u* (< **ū* or **u* [see Stade 1879: §93.1]) becomes *qameṣ* in a word-final, closed syllable: for example, וַיָּגָז 'he cut off' (Job 1:20), וַיָּחָן 'he was gracious' (2 Kgs 13:23), as well as וַיָּמָת 'he died', וַיָּנָס 'he fled', and וַיָּקָם 'he arose' (BL §56l).[29] Whether in a proclitic or posttonic syllable, the evidence is the same: the two proto high vowels are jointly replaced in atonic, closed syllables; the nonlabial high vowel becomes *seghol*, and its labial counterpart becomes *qameṣ*.

3.2.1. Not only do *qameṣ* and *seghol* pattern alike when derived from phonologically similar sources, they are also paired when their origins are phonologically dissimilar. Witness, for example, the operation of *athe meraḥiq*.[30] When the first term is paroxytone and ends in *seghol* or *qameṣ*, *and* when the second, unbound term is accent-initial, the two terms are cemented via gemination of the second term's initial consonant (GKC §20f; and, in greater detail, Yeivin 1980: 290–92). For example, when the first term ends in *seghol*, the following change takes place.

*אֵלֶּה לָךְ	>	אֵ֣לֶּה לָּ֑ךְ	'these of yours' (Gen 33:5); and, with accent retraction,[31]
*שָׂדֶה טוֹב	>	שְׂדֵה טּ֥וֹב	'a good field' (Ezek 17:8)
*לֹא־יִנָּקֶה רָע	>	לֹֽא־יִנָּ֣קֶה רָּ֑ע	'the evil man will not escape' (Prov 11:21)

26. Except when the syllable is marked with a *methegh* (GKB 1 §11e).

27. On posttonic vowel shortening, see Grimme 1896: 55–57, in conjunction with GKB 1 §23a. Cf. Joüon 1923: §28d.

28. Where *plene* and defective spellings both occur, as in ויולך and וילך, the *plene* form has been selected as representative.

29. Except וַיָּרֻם 'it became infested' (Exod 16:20).

30. The terminology follows GKC §20f. Cf. Yeivin 1980: 289–90.

31. For discussion and details, see §§7.4 and 7.5.2.

This operation dovetails with *deḥiq*: phrase-internal consonantal gemination occurring when an oxytone word ending in *seghol*[32] is bound to, and merges with, a following accent-initial term (Baer 1885: 147).

וּמִשְׁנֶה־כֶסֶף*	>	וּמִשְׁנֶה־כֶּסֶף	'double the money' (Gen 43:15)
יִהְיֶה־לוֹ*	>	יִהְיֶה־לּוֹ	'it will be' (Exod 28:32)
מַעֲנֶה־רַךְ**	>	מַעֲנֶה־רַּךְ	'a gentle response' (Prov 15:1)

Athe meraḥiq also applies to word-final *qameṣ*:

עָשִׂיתָ זֹּאת	'you did this' (Gen 3:14)
פָּקַדְתָּ לַּיְלָה	'you visited at night' (Ps 17:3); see also
הָיְתָה זֹּאת	'this is' (Ps 118:23)
הִשָּׁבְעָה לִּי	'swear to me' (Gen 21:23)

Thus in *athe meraḥiq* and in *deḥiq*, word-final *seghol* and *qameṣ* alike produce phrase-internal, consonantal gemination (Joüon 1923: §6j).

3.2.2. Further investigation suggests that the conditions governing both gemination processes are developmentally late. Gemination takes place, for example, only when word-final *seghol* and *qameṣ* are atonic. Although the ultima in some forms never carried the accent—as in אלה לך—some forms were originally oxytone. The accent was lost either by hyphenation—as in ומשנה־כסף—or, more strikingly, by *nesiga*—as in שדה טוב. Only in the final stage of the language, and only after Hebrew-specific sound changes, did these word-final *seghol*s and *qameṣ*s have a uniformly atonic outcome.

3.2.3. Gemination also occurs regardless of the vowel pattern underlying the Hebrew vowel. For example, the *seghol* in אלה probably reflects **ay* (Lambert 1972: 121 n. 1; cf. Barth 1913: §48c), the *seghol* in ומשנה **ay+u* (cf. BL §61mζ),[33] and in ינקה **iy=u* (BL §§44a, f). Nevertheless, all three effect gemination.[34] *Qameṣ*, too, may be of heterogeneous origin: in עשית *qameṣ* comes from **ā* (BL §42k), while in היתה it evolved from *=*at* (BL §25i′). And both forms produce gemination. Gemination takes place, then, only after these dissimilar proto phones have developed and merged into

32. Cf. the nonapplication of *deḥiq* with word-final *qameṣ*: for example, צִוָּה־לָנוּ 'he commanded us' (Deut 33:4), נִגְלָה־לָמוֹ 'it was revealed to them' (Isa 23:1), and הִכָּה־צוּר 'he struck the rock' (Ps 78:20). When, however, —X́ הָX́—* does result in gemination, the oxytone accent is secondary, having developed from a (pausal) paroxytone via the contextual accent shift. See, for example, יָלְדָה־לּוֹ 'she had borne for him' (Gen 21:3) < יָלָדָה־לוֹ*. Cf. Baer 1885: 148; and Yeivin 1980: 291.

33. The operation of vowel attenuation on the **ma* prefix suggests that the nominal pattern is **maqtal*. Had it been **maqtil*, attenuation would have been blocked. Cf. GKC §85h.

34. On the merger of **ay*(*u*) and **iy*(*u*), see GKB 1 §17k. Cf. Blake 1953: 10 n. 13.

their Hebrew reflexes. This evidence therefore correlates with the rule of *athe meraḥiq*: the gemination is conditioned by atonic, phrase-internal *seghol* and *qameṣ*.

4.0. Once again, *seghol* and *qameṣ* form a pair. In their development, *seghol* replaces **i* in conditions identical to the replacement of **u* by *qameṣ*. In their outcome, *seghol* and *qameṣ* pattern alike in *athe meraḥiq*. And the *qameṣ*, for its part, can be characterized as a back, labial vowel. Two questions therefore remain: (1) what feature(s) do *seghol* and *qameṣ* share that account for their parallel behavior (§5); and (2) specifically, how should the Hebrew *seghol* be characterized (§4)?

4.1. The *seghol* represents a merger of two phonemes. On the one hand, *seghol* is a reflex of **i* (GKB 1 §§26g, 28o). As aforementioned, in atonic, closed syllables, **i* > *seghol*; in addition to וַיֵּלֶךְ 'he went' and עֶת־ 'time of', examples include וַיֹּאחֶז 'he grasped' (2 Sam 6:6), הוֹלֶם פָּעַם 'who strikes the anvil' (Isa 41:7 [with *nesiga*]), יְהַלֶּל־פִּי 'my mouth gives praise' (Ps 63:6), and probably[35] אֶתֶּנְךָ 'I will give, make you' (Jer 38:16; Ezek 35:9; Hos 11:8). The *seghol*, according to general consensus, corresponds to **i*.

4.2. On the other hand, *seghol* also represents **a* (GKC §§27p–q). This relationship is especially clear with *ḥaṭeph* vowels following the glottal fricative.[36] For example, while *ḥaṭaph pathaḥ* reflects **a* in הֲלַכְתֶּם 'you went' (Deut 1:31; 1 Sam 10:14; Jer 44:23; Ezek 5:7, 11:12) and הֲרָגוּם 'they killed them' (Josh 9:26), in *qal* forms of *hyh* 'to be' this word-initial, propretonic **a* > *ḥaṭaph seghol* (Olshausen 1861: §64c). In contrast to הֲלַכְתֶּם and הֲרָגוּם < **#ha-*, הֱיִיתֶם 'you were' also develops from **#ha-*. A second instance of alternation between *ḥaṭaph pathaḥ* and *ḥaṭaph seghol* lies in the *qal* imperative **qtVl* (Brockelmann 1940: 357); in this form, vowelless *he* > הֲ, as in הֲרֹג 'kill!' (Judg 8:20) (see GKC §22o). Yet in the verb 'to be', *ḥaṭaph seghol* results: for example, הֱיֵה 'be!'[37] (Exod 18:19; 1 Sam 18:17; Isa 33:2; Ps 30:11, 31:3, 71:3; Qoh 7:14) and הֱיוּ 'be, appear!' (Exod 19:15; Num 16:16) (cf. Barth 1894: 6).[38] Thus, word-initial[39] *ḥaṭaph pathaḥ* > *ḥaṭaph seghol* in *hyh*.

The replacement of *ḥaṭaph pathaḥ* by *ḥaṭaph seghol*, however, is not restricted to *hyh*. Yet outside of *hyh* the replacement is never complete.

35. See יִשְׁמָרְךָ 'he will keep you' (Ps 121:7) < **yišmur+i+kā*.

36. Following pharyngeal fricatives, *ḥaṭeph* vowels are regularly neutralized to *ḥaṭaph pathaḥ*. For example, חֲמַדְתֶּם 'you desired' (Isa 1:29) < **a*, חֲמוֹר 'ass' < **i*, and עֲבֹר 'cross!' (Exod 17:5; Josh 1:2; 2 Sam 19:34; Ezek 9:4) < *Ø. The only exception, *ḥaṭaph qameṣ* < **u*, is preserved because of its labial and back qualities (see GKB 1 §28l; and above, §2.4).

37. Cf. הֲיִי 'become!' (Gen 24:60) where, because of the close connection with את, the word boundary is obscured and behaves as the second member of a bound phrase.

38. See also הֱיֵה in Ezek 21:15.

39. See הֱיִיתֶם vs. וִהְיִיתֶם 'you will be', or הֱיוֹת 'to be' vs. לִהְיוֹת 'to be'.

When, for example, a *ḥaṭaph seghol* lies in the antepenult, the vowel is often replaced by *ḥaṭaph pathaḥ* (BL §14n′): for example, אֱדוֹם 'Edom' > אֲדֹמִי 'Edomite' (Deut 23:8), and אֱמֶת 'truth' > אֲמִתּוֹ 'his truth' (Ps 91:4).[40] Similarly, הֵבִיא 'he brought' > הֲבֵאתֶם 'you brought' (Num 20:4; 1 Sam 21:16; Joel 4:5), and הֵכִין 'he prepared' > הֲכִינוֹתָ 'you set' (Ps 74:16; Job 11:13). There are also many instances in which this *ḥaṭaph pathaḥ*, in turn, develops into *ḥaṭaph seghol*. This latter development occurs especially in middle weak *hiphil* perfects (see Olshausen 1861: §64c; Lambert 1972: 47 n. 4). For example, while הֵכִין > הֲכִינוֹתָ, there also occurs הֱטִיבוֹתָ 'you did, do well' (1 Kgs 8:18; 2 Kgs 10:30; 2 Chr 6:8). Or, הֲנִיפוֹתִי 'I waved' (Job 31:21) alternates with הֱקִיצוֹתִי 'I awoke, end' (Jer 31:26; Ps 3:6, 139:18), and הֲסִיתְךָ 'he allures you' (Job 36:16) ~ הֱסִיתְךָ 'he has incited you' (1 Sam 26:19). *Ḥaṭaph pathaḥ* and *ḥaṭaph seghol* may therefore be interchangeable.

Their interchange, though, is not completely random. In the contrasting pair הֲלַכְתֶּם vs. הֱיִיתֶם, the *ḥaṭaph seghol* may be associated with the unique phonological composition of *hyh*. Unlike הֲלַכְתֶּם, הֱיִיתֶם has a high, front thematic vowel and a homoorganic, semivocalic middle radical. הֱיֵה has the same middle radical, *yodh*, although its ultimate vowel is mid-high. In these examples, then, *ḥaṭaph pathaḥ* is replaced by *ḥaṭaph seghol* before a high, front semivowel and (mid-) high vowel.

The remaining examples, however, modify and mollify this preliminary conclusion. Even in the absence of a following *yodh*, *ḥaṭaph seghol* may replace *ḥaṭaph pathaḥ* as in הֱטִיבוֹתָ and הֱקִיצוֹתִי. The *ḥireq* in these *hiphil* verb forms—like that in הֱיִיתֶם—sufficiently conditions the change (Bauer and Leander 1927: §10o). Thus, whether the high element be a following *yodh* or *ḥireq*, *ḥaṭaph pathaḥ* may be replaced by *ḥaṭaph seghol*. Stated generally, *ḥaṭaph pathaḥ*, regardless of origin, may change into *ḥaṭaph seghol* in the presence of a high, front phone.[41]

4.3. This relationship between *ḥaṭaph seghol* and high, front sounds is confirmed by the development of final *yodh* **qatl* nouns. In these nouns, **a* is replaced by *seghol* (GKC §29m; cf. BL §18a): for example, לֶחִי 'jaw (-bone)' (Ps 3:8; Lam 3:30), פֶּרִי 'fruit' (Jer 17:8; Ezek 17:8; Qoh 2:5; see also Jer 12:2; Ezek 17:23), and שֶׁבִי 'captive, captivity' (Num 21:1; Hab 1:9; Ps 68:19; 2 Chr 28:17)—before the onset of the contextual accent shift. Just as **a* > *ḥaṭaph seghol* in הֱקִיצוֹתִי, so too **a* > *seghol* before *ḥireq* in these nouns as well.[42] The development of לֶחִי, הֱקִיצוֹתִי, הֱיִיתֶם, and הֱיֵה reflects the same sound change;

40. On forms like אֱלֹהִים 'gods' and אֱמֹרִי 'Amorite' (Num 21:29; Ezek 16:45)—in which *ḥaṭaph seghol* is retained—see GKC §22o and Lambert 1972: §93.

41. Cf. הֱוֵה 'be, fall!' (Gen 27:29; Job 37:6) and הֱוִי־ 'be!' (Isa 16:4).

42. This sound change is blocked when [ī] is (part of) a suffix. For example, *ʾ*an*+*ī* > אָנִי 'I' and **a*+*nī* > X<u></u>ַנִי 'me' (objective suffix).

in these forms, an open-syllabic low vowel is replaced by (*ḥaṭaph*) *seghol* before a next-right high, front sound.

4.4. This examination suggests that *seghol* represents two vowels in two respects. On the one hand, *seghol* corresponds to phonemic **i*. On the other hand, *seghol* also reflects phonemic **a*. Further, the shift of **a* to *seghol* is interesting in this context, for open-syllabic **a* is replaced by *seghol* before a high, front phone. Thus, *seghol* is not only a merger of **a* and **i* phonemes, it also develops from the contact between *a* and *i* phones.

4.5. *Seghol* thus represents a compromise, or intermediate zone, between low, back, nonlabial [ɑ] and high, front, nonlabial [i]. [ɛ]—as in Northern English 'p*e*n', 'g*e*t', French 'm*e*ttre', and German 'B*e*tt' (IPA 1949: 8)—best fills these requirements. It is a mid vowel, where high and low approximately intersect. Also like [ɑ] and [i], [ɛ] is nonlabial (cf. Blake 1953: 8 n. 9). Yet this phone, in common with [i], is nonback. *Seghol*, then, is the phonetic midpoint between nonlabial, high, front [i] and nonlabial, low, back [ɑ] (see Joüon 1923: §6d).

5.0. This detour into the *seghol* was prompted by an interest in the *qameṣ*. Direct phonetic information from *qameṣ* was twofold: the vowel is both labial and back. From indirect data, it appeared that *qameṣ* and *seghol* patterned alike in two distinct ways. First, there was a proportional relation between *qameṣ* and *seghol*: *qameṣ* stood to the high, back, labial [u] as *seghol* corresponded to the high, front, nonlabial [i]; or, Hebrew *qameṣ* and *seghol* were paired in a way similar to the pairing of **u* and **i*. Second, in certain phrases, word-final *qameṣ* produced consonantal gemination as did word-final *seghol*, despite entirely dissimilar origins. And the *seghol*, for its part, could be characterized as a mid vowel, produced in the front of the vocal tract, without lip articulation.

5.1. The distinctive features of *qameṣ* fall into place. The complementary distribution of *qameṣ* and *seghol*, coupled with the verified labial and back qualities of *qameṣ*, suggest that *qameṣ* is the labial, back counterpart of *seghol*. Further, since both vowels effect phrase-internal consonantal gemination, the third distinctive feature of *qameṣ* must be shared by *seghol*; *qameṣ*, like *seghol*, then, is a mid vowel (see Joüon 1923: §6j). By defining *qameṣ* in this way, the gemination is readily explicable—atonic mid vowels, which are word-final and phrase-internal, effect consonantal gemination (Malone n.d.: 10). *Qameṣ* is therefore a mid, labial, back vowel, [ɔ] (cf. Dalman 1978: 81 n. 3),[43] as in Scottish 'h*o*t', French 'p*o*rte', and German 'S*o*nne' (IPA 1949: 8–9).

43. For other realizations in different communities, see Dalman 1978: 81; Kahle 1966: 159 with n. 2; Lambert 1911: 394–95; GKB 1 §10a; Joüon 1923: §6k; and Chomsky 1971: 22–23.

6. With the definition of *qameṣ*, the investigation into the BH vowel system is complete. According to the evidence of the linguistic system itself, BH has a vowel system of four vowel heights internally differentiated by back vs. nonback and/or labial vs. nonlabial. *Ḥireq* and *shureq* are the high vowels; the former is nonback and nonlabial, while the latter is back and labial. The next tier is occupied by the mid-high vowels, *ṣere* and *ḥolem*; like *ḥireq*, *ṣere* is nonback and nonlabial, whereas *ḥolem* resembles *shureq* in both qualities. In the mid range, *seghol* is nonback and nonlabial; *qameṣ*, like *shureq* and *ḥolem*, is back and labial. And finally, *pathaḥ* is a low, back phone, without labiality. Each vocalic grapheme, then, represents a distinct vowel color: each of the seven vowel signs is phonetically unique. BH has a seven-way, color-distinct vowel system (for example, Joüon 1923: §§6b–c).

7.0. Since the BH vowel system is quality-sensitive, there has been no need to mention vowel length. Length—the duration of sound in time (Malmberg 1963: 74; Abercrombie 1967: 80)—does not differentiate one BH vowel sign from another. Yet there are language-internal clues that BH distinguished at least two lengths: long, those of relatively greater duration; and short, those of relatively lesser duration (see Malmberg 1963: 74–76; cf. Heffner 1937: 130, 134).

7.1.1. One such clue is the different treatment of proto long and proto short vowels. For example, the initial vowel in **qatal* nouns behaves differently from that in **qātal* nouns, when this vowel is propretonic and open-syllabic.

**qatal*:	**ḥadašīm*	>	חֲדָשִׁים	'new' (ms. pl.)
	**ᶜanawīm*	>	עֲנָוִים	'poor, humble' (ms. pl.)
**qātal*:	**ᶜālamīm*	>	עוֹלָמִים	'ages; forever'; see also
			חֹתָמוֹ	'his seal' (1 Kgs 21:8)

The initial vowel in **qilat* and **qīlat* forms also shows different reflexes in an open, propretonic syllable.

**qilat*:	**ḥimatī*	>	חֲמָתִי	'my poison, rage'
	**šinatī*	>	שְׁנָתִי	'my sleep' (Gen 31:40)
**qīlat*:	**bīnatī*	>	בִּינָתִי	'my understanding' (Job 20:3)
	**ṭīratam*	>	טִירָתָם	'their encampments' (Ps 69:26)

In both sets, the preservation or nonpreservation of the open-syllabic, propretonic vowel is dependent on the length of the underlying vowel. In this circumstance, a long vowel is preserved, whereas a short vowel is reduced to (a form of) zero. It would appear, then, that BH perpetuates the proto distinction between long and short vowels.

7.1.2. Further evidence for a quantitative distinction in BH vowels appears in assimilatory vowel lowering. When an underlying short vowel lay in the ultima of verbs[44] closed by a root-final pharyngeal or glottal fricative, the vowel is lowered to *pathaḥ* (BL §§18d–g).[45] For example, in *piel* forms:

*זִבֵּח (בִּקֵּשׁ) > זִבַּח ‘he sacrificed’ (2 Chr 33:22)
*יְפַלֵּח (יְבַקֵּשׁ) > יְפַלַּח ‘it, he pierces’ (Prov 7:23; Job 16:13)
*בִּלֵּע (בִּקֵּשׁ) > בִּלַּע ‘he has destroyed’ (Isa 25:8; Lam 2:2, 5)
*בִּצֵּע (בִּקֵּשׁ) > בִּצַּע ‘he has carried out’ (Lam 2:17)

Yet when the underlying vowel is long, the vowel splits into two parts—the vowel itself + atonic *pathaḥ* (BL §§18f–g, j).[46] In *hiphil* forms:

*הֹכִיח (הוֹלִיד) > הֹכִיחַ ‘he has decreed’ (Gen 24:44)
*יַפְרִיח (יַשְׁמִיד) > יַפְרִיחַ ‘it will flourish, sprout’ (Prov 14:11; Job 14:9)
*הוֹדִיע (הוֹלִיד) > הוֹדִיעַ ‘he has made known’ (Ps 98:2)
*הוֹשִׁיע (הוֹלִיד) > הוֹשִׁיעַ ‘he will give victory’ (Ps 20:7)

Thus, the underlying distinction between long and short vowels is also reflected in the two results of assimilatory vowel lowering.

7.2.0. Not only do BH phonological operations reflect the underlying difference between vowel lengths, they also reflect the existence of vowel length distinction within BH itself. This distinction appears most clearly in the comparison between contextual and pausal forms of verbs. Whereas contextual forms reflect unmarked, connected speech, pausal forms are marked and clause-final. In pause, the speech tempo often decelerates (see Sievers 1901: 245) as much as five times the regular speed (Lehiste 1970: 52). Pause may also be marked by a change of pitch (Bloomfield 1933: 114) or stress conditions producing vowel lengthening (Jones 1967: 123–24).

7.2.1. The effect of pause on vowel length in BH is seen in the distribution of assimilatory vowel lowering in verbs whose final radical is a pharyngeal. When the verb is accented on the ultima containing an underlying short vowel + pharyngeal, the vowel lowers to *pathaḥ* (see §7.1.2). This operation is generally restricted to contextual verbs, that is, those in

44. Expanded below, §7.2.1.

45. See also occasional assimilatory lowering with a preceding pharyngeal/glottal fricative (Joüon 1923: §21e).

46. For an exception, see n. 27.

TABLE 1

	Contextual		Pausal	
yVnqatil:	יִבָּקַע	'it burst' (Isa 58:8)	יִבָּקֵֽעַ	'it is ready to burst' (Job 32:19)
	יִגָּרַע	'it will be cut off' (Num 27:4, 36:4)	יִגָּרֵֽעַ	'it will be cut off' (Num 36:3)
	יִוָּדַע	'it is known; he makes himself known'	יִוָּדֵֽעַ	'he will be found out' (Prov 10:9)
qittil:	גִּדַּע	'he hewed down' (2 Chr 34:7)	גִּדֵּֽעַ	'he hewed down' (Ps 107:16; 2 Chr 34:4 [*ʾathnaḥ*])
	פִּתַּח	'it opened' (Cant 7:13; see also Job 30:11)	פִּתֵּֽחַ	'he loosens' (Job 12:18, 41:6; see also 39:5 [*silluq*])
	אֲבַלַּע	'I destroy' (2 Sam 20:20)	אֲבַלֵּ֑עַ	'I will confound' (Isa 19:3)
	תְּבַקַּע	'you make burst' (Hab 3:9)	תְּבַקֵּֽעַ	'you will rip open' (2 Kgs 8:12)
	יְשַׁלַּח	'he expells, lets go'	יְשַׁלֵּֽחַ	'he incites, will let go' (Prov 6:14; Isa 45:13 [*zaqeph qaṭon*])

connected, phrase-internal speech. In pause, however, the accented short vowel changes into two vowels: a tonic vowel (whose quality depends on that of its underlying phone) + atonic *pathaḥ*. For as Table 1 shows, the pausal accent converts a single short vowel into two. It stretches, or lengthens, the vowel's duration at least twofold (cf. Sievers 1901: 243, 245). Or, as the operation of assimilatory vowel lowering suggests, the pausally accented vowel comes to resemble an underlying long vowel: both consist of at least two parts (see Praetorius 1897: 16–17; cf. Philippi 1898: 1675).

7.3. BH full vowels, then, exhibit two vowel lengths. On the one hand, a full vowel may be short. Short vowels are subject to deletion and are lowered to *pathaḥ* in contiguity to a root-final, verbal pharyngeal or glottal fricative. On the other hand, a full vowel may be long. Long vowels are undeletable and appear as two vowels (V + *pathaḥ*) in assimilatory vowel lowering. Thus BH internally differentiates short from long vowels.

7.4. This distinction between vowel lengths is supported by the conditions governing *nesiga*, an accent shift sensitive to phonosyntax. In one form of the rule, a word-final *_CVC_[47] syllable may lose the accent to the preceding open syllable when the next word, which is phrase-final and closely related to the preceding word, is accent-initial (GKC §§29e–g; Revell 1983, 1987).

*תֹּאכַל לֶחֶם	>	תֹּ֣אכַל לֶ֔חֶם	'you will eat bread' (Gen 3:19)
*וִיפַת תֹּאַר	>	וִ֣יפַת תֹּ֔אַר	'and beautiful' (1 Sam 25:3)
*וְכִחֵשׁ בּוֹ	>	וְכִ֥חֶשׁ בּ֗וֹ[48]	'it denies him' (Job 8:18)

Yet when the accented ultima is *_C_$\bar{V}$_C_, the accent does not shift.

דָּבָ֣ר טוֹב 'goodwill' (1 Kgs 14:13)
לְמֵשִׁ֣יב נֶ֔פֶשׁ 'renew life' (Ruth 4:15)
וְהָעוֹף יִ֥רֶב 'and let the birds multiply' (Gen 1:22)

Thus as these examples show, _nesiga_ operates on a word-final *_CVC_ syllable only if it contains a short (Revell 1987: 108–10; cf. Ezek 23:40; Job 14:13). _Nesiga_, like other aspects of BH phonology, responds to vowel length.

7.5.1. While assimilatory vowel lowering shows that BH long vowels are compound, there is some difficulty with traditional representations of this compound long vowel. According to current systems (for example, Lambdin 1971: §§6, 10; JBL 1988: 582), this compound long vowel is conveyed as [$\bar{\text{V}}$a] in assimilatory vowel lowering. Thus הוֹדִיעַ = [hōdīaᶜ], יַפְרִיחַ = [yaprīaḥ], and תְּבַקֵּעַ = [təbaqqēaᶜ]; the long vowel, then, would remain long in addition to engendering a _pathaḥ_.

7.5.2. Yet this representation is inconsistent with the behavior of the nonlow component in the complex. For as the following examples show, _nesiga_ operates on this vowel (Malone 1978: 135; cf. Revell 1987: 112 with n. 14).

בֹּ֤וקַֽע מַ֨יִם֙ 'who divided the waters' (Isa 63:12)
מֹ֣נֵֽעַ בָּ֭ר 'he who withholds grain' (Prov 11:26)
בֹּ֣צֵֽעַ בָּ֑צַע 'who pursue unjust gain' (Prov 1:19)
וְ֝שֹׁ֗לֵֽחַ מַ֗יִם 'and who sends water' (Job 5:10)

Since _nesiga_ retracts the accent only from a _short_ vowel when the ultima is closed, the _ṣere_ in these examples must be short (cf. Yeivin 1980: 236–37;

47. Retraction also takes place from word-final *-_C_$\bar{V}$, under otherwise identical conditions. See §3.2.1.

48. On so-called "virtual gemination," see GKB 1 §28a.

and, differently, Revell 1987: 80). And that the *ṣere* must have been accented to prompt *nesiga* suggests that the former of the two-part long vowel receives the accent. Thus, a BH long vowel is equivalent to two short vowels (see Jones 1967: 116; cf. Lehiste 1970: 33–34, 43–49); in representation, [V̄] = [VV], and [V̄́] = [V́V] (Malone 1978: 131–35, 156 n. 26; cf. Ben-David 1957–58: 10).

8.1. Hebrew long vowels develop from three sources. One set of long vowels corresponds to reconstructed, proto long vowels. For the most part,[49] these proto vowels are qualitatively unaltered in their Hebrew outcome. For example, **qīl* nouns show *ḥireq*.

גִּיד ‘sinew’
קִיר ‘wall’
רִיר ‘spittle’

**qūl* nouns do not change in Hebrew representation either.

חוּט ‘thread’
טוּב ‘goodness’
שׁוּר ‘wall’

**ā*, however, is different; under certain positional and accentual conditions, **ā* > [ō],[50] obscuring the original vowel altogether.

**qātil*:	אוֹכֵל	‘eating’
	כֹּהֵן	‘priest’
**qātal*:	עוֹלָם	‘eternity’
**qatāl*:	לָשׁוֹן	‘tongue’
	שָׁלוֹם	‘peace’
	שָׁלוֹשׁ	‘three’

And since the quality of the vowel changes, the rules governing **ā* differ from those governing **ī* and **ū*. Except for the maverick **ā*, proto long vowels do not change color in their Tiberian reflex (see Joüon 1923: §6i).

49. Exceptions include **CV̄CC* sequences (GKB 1 §23a) and unaccented, word-final **CV̄C* syllables (see §3.1.2).

50. The change is unconditional in word-internal position (Goetze 1939: 450 n. 62); word-finally, **ā* > [ō] only under the accent (BL §14j, for the accent).

8.2.1. A second set of Hebrew long vowels arises through monophthongization (see Lehiste 1970: 44). Under specific conditions,[51] the heterogeneous diphthongs contract: **ay* is replaced by [ē],[52] and **aw* changes into [ō]. **ay*, like **aw*, is composed of a low, back vowel + high semivowel. And in both cases, monophthongization results in a mid-high phone: when the semivocalic component is labial and back, the resultant mid-high vowel is also labial and back; when the semivowel is nonlabial and nonback, so too the new mid-high vowel. Monophthongization, then, is an assimilatory process (Brockelmann 1966: §71): high and low phones mutually assimilate and merge at an intermediate point (see Hoenigswald 1960: 74).

8.2.2. With the homogeneous diphthongs **iy* and **uw*, assimilation also takes place.[53] Yet because homogeneous diphthongs contain pairs of phones whose height, labiality, and backness are identical, the resulting monophthong perpetuates these same features. Vowel quality does not change.[54] The process, however, is the same as that of heterogeneous diphthong contraction: the vocalic and semivocalic halves mutually assimilate and merge into a long vowel.

8.3.0. The third type of Hebrew long vowel originates in a short vowel that, under certain syllabic-accentual conditions, is lengthened (see GKC §§27e–h). As in pause, the short vowel is reduplicated and is pronounced, durationally, as a doubled short vowel (see Joüon 1923: §6f; Malone 1972: 445). Schematically, $*\hat{V} >$ [VV], which subsequently merges into [$\bar{\text{V}}$].

8.3.1. This representation, however, conceals the qualitative change that takes place in vowel lengthening. When, for example, **i* is lengthened, its Hebrew outcome is [ē]; in its development, the high phone is lowered to mid-high *ṣere*. Similarly, **u* is lengthened to [ō]; the high labial vowel becomes a mid-high labial *ḥolem*. Like the contraction of heterogeneous diphthongs (see Olshausen 1861: §57a), the reduplication and merger of short vowels exhibit a qualitative change.

8.4. Whereas **î* and **û* are lowered, **â* is not. On the contrary, this proto low vowel is *raised* when lengthened. For example, in syllable-closing

51. For details, see GKB 1 §§17g–h, l and BL §§17r, v–y (on **ay*); and GKB 1 §17g and BL §§17c′–j′ (on **aw*). Contraction, though, is generally stalled when the semivowel is geminate (GKB 1 §17g; see also n. 19). Secondarily formed diphthongs, too, are exempt: for example, וַיְהִי 'it was' < **wayyəhī* and רַוְחָתִי 'my respite' (Lam 3:56) < **rawaḥatī* (?). Cf. [-ō] 'him, his' < **-ahū*.

52. In word-final position, however, the reflex is [ε̄], except in constructs, imperatives, infinitives absolute, and miscellaneous lexical items.

53. In the sequence **iyC* and **uwC*, and when **iya* and **uwa* are morpheme-internal (see GKB 1 §17d and BL §§14s, 17e–g; see also Brockelmann 1966: §§40g, 43kα).

54. Except in word-final position, where **iy* > [ē] in the construct, imperative, and infinitive absolute, and [ε̄] in absolute nouns and other verbal forms.

position *aleph* is lost to the preceding vowel, which, in turn, is lengthened (GKB 1 §§15b–d, including exceptions). In the sequence **Ciʾ*, the outcome is [Cē].

**śaniʾ* > שָׂנֵא 'he hates, hated' (Deut 12:31, 16:22; 2 Sam 13:22; Mal 2:16; Prov 6:16)
**māṣiʾt* > מֹצֵאת 'finding, who finds' (2 Sam 18:22 [pausal]; Cant 8:10); see especially
**maliʾtī* > מָלֵתִי 'I am full' (Job 32:18)

Similarly, **Cuʾ* > [Cō].

**quruʾ*[55] > (לִ)קְרֹא
**buʾr* > בֹּאר 'cistern, pit'; see also
בּוֹר 'cistern, pit'

8.5.1. Yet when **Caʾ* contracts, **a* is generally[56] lengthened and raised to *qameṣ*.

**maṣaʾ* > מָצָא 'he found'
**maṣaʾtī* > מָצָאתִי 'I found'; see also
מָצָתִי 'I found' (Num 11:11)
**yaṣaʾtī* > יָצָתִי 'I left' (Job 1:21)

Or, when *yodh* syncopates between two low vowels, the resulting contiguous **a* vowels contract; the outcome, again, is mid *qameṣ* (BL §25n′).

**banaya* > *banaa* > בָּנָה 'he built'
**qanaya* > *qanaa* > קָנָה 'he acquired' (Gen 25:10, 47:22, 49:30, 50:13; Josh 24:32; 2 Sam 12:3); see also
*(*wa*)*ʿaśayat* > (*wa*)*ʿaśaat* > וְעָשָׂת 'it will produce' (Lev 25:21)

Unlike **î* and **û*, which are neither raised nor rounded, **â* changes in both these respects (see Olshausen 1861: §5c; Joüon 1923: §6i). The outcome of **â*, then, is doubly idiosyncratic: the low, back, nonlabial vowel raises and rounds to [ɔ̄].

8.5.2. Although the outcome of **â* is unique among the lengthened vowels, the lengthening of **a* > [ɔ̄] is not unique within Hebrew phonology.

55. On the form, see Joüon 1923: §49a.
56. For exceptions, see GKB 1 §§15b, d.

The raising and rounding of *â is reminiscent of an earlier sound change, the Canaanite vowel shift. In an old stage of Hebrew, *ā was largely replaced by [ō]; phonetically, the back, nonlabial, low long vowel became back, labial, and mid-high. This shift was isolated among the long proto vowels: the Hebrew reflexes of *ī and *ū did not change in height or labiality; *ā, however, was both raised and rounded. So the Canaanite vowel shift, in turn, provided a model for the newly lengthened *a (Harris 1939: 61; cf. Meyer 1966–72: §11.1c): like the raising and rounding of *ā, so too *â was raised and rounded. The replacement of *â by *qameṣ*—a mid, labial, back vowel—therefore conforms to demonstrated, language-internal, phonological patterns (cf. Brockelmann 1966: §51gη).

9.0. It is now possible to return to those forms that gave rise to this discussion of the BH vowel system and its internal relationships. From those forms it appeared that *í was regularly replaced by *ṣere* and *ú by *ḥolem*. *á, however, showed a differential behavior—זָכַר vs. זָכָר, and נַחַל vs. שָׁחוּ.

9.1. In the former pair, the different reflexes of *a are governed by a morphophonological rule. Verbs, specifically finite verbs, participate in accent-conditioned vowel lowering whereby high vowels become mid-high—*í > [é] and *ú > [ó]—and low vowels remain low—*á > [ɑ́]. Further, the uniform representation of *á by Hebrew *pathaḥ* (except in pause), as well as the uniform replacement of tonic vowels by [ɑ] in assimilatory vowel lowering (except in pause), suggest that *all* verbal accented vowels are, by inference, short (Philippi 1897: 40; GKB 1 §10d). In finite verbs, then, short accented vowels participate in a rule of vowel lowering. The change is qualitative, not quantitative.

9.2.1. In nouns, *í is likewise represented by *ṣere*, and *ú by *ḥolem*. Yet in contradistinction to verbs, *á > *qameṣ*. This behavior, however, is identical to the lengthening that occurs when a syllable-closing *aleph* is lost to a preceding short vowel. In both cases, not only are *i(ʾ) and *u(ʾ) lowered to *ṣere* and *ḥolem*, respectively, but *a(ʾ) is raised and rounded to *qameṣ*. Originally short, tonic vowels in nouns behave like compensatorily lengthened vowels (see Harris 1941: 144).

9.2.2. Tonic vowels in nouns behave like lengthened vowels in another respect too. When the ultima of a noun contains an underlying short high vowel followed by a root-final pharyngeal or glottal fricative, the resultant form shows a mid-high vowel + *pathaḥ*.

**maqtil*:	מַפְתֵּחַ	'key'
	מַרְזֵחַ	'orgy'; see also
	מִזְבֵּחַ	'altar'

As in pause (see Brockelmann 1966: §43pλ), the single tonic vowel splits into two. Nouns, then, participate in vowel lengthening.

9.3. Nouns are not the only forms that participate in vowel lengthening. As already noted (§1.1), adjectives also exhibit this feature. For example, [ḥɔ̄zɔ̄q] 'strong', [yɔ̄šɔ̄r] 'upright', and [šɔ̄pɔ̄l] 'low' pattern like [zɔ̄kɔ̄r] rather than [zɔ̄kɑr]. Even when the adjective functions as predicate—for example, in 1 Kgs 18:2, 2 Sam 19:7, and Lev 13:20, respectively—it exhibits tonic vowel lengthening.

9.4.1. In open syllables, however, a wider distribution of forms exhibit tonic vowel lengthening. Adverbs are one example. For as the form [kɔ̄́kɔ̄] 'thus' < **ká+kă̄* (see BDB 462a) shows, open-syllabic **á* is lengthened. Similarly, verbs + objective suffix show this feature. For example, [məṣɔ̄ʾɔ̄́tɑm] 'it had befallen them' (Exod 18:8) < **maṣaʾátam* exhibits tonic lengthening of open-syllabic **á*.

9.4.2. There is evidence that interrogatives participate in open-syllabic, tonic vowel lengthening as well. The term 'why' usually appears as לָמָּה, accented on the penult and carrying a diacritical point in the *mem*. When, however, לָמָּה is closely bound to a following guttural-initial word, its form and accent changes: לָ֫מָּה > לָמָ֫ה, an oxytone word lacking diacritical point (Mirsky 1940–41; Malamat 1942–43). This accent shift, moreover, is not restricted to למה but occurs in other forms; in all but one (Ps 90:8) example, the shift takes place when a paroxytone term ending in two open syllables is closely united to a following guttural-initial word (GKB 1 §28q; see also the comparisons in Mirsky 1940–41: 299). And since למה participates in this shift, its accented penult must therefore be open too.[57] In which case, לָ֫מָה < **lá+mă̄* by tonic lengthening.

9.5. The rules governing tonic vowel lengthening are twofold. In open syllables, Hebrew participates in a phonological rule of accent-conditioned vowel lengthening. In closed syllables, Hebrew participates in a morphophonological rule whereby tonic vowels are lengthened only in nouns and adjectives.[58] That is, nouns participate in tonic vowel lengthening; nonnouns do not, but they participate in tonic vowel lowering.

9.6. Yet vowel lowering and vowel lengthening are not mutually exclusive. Rather, they largely effect the same qualitative result. High vowels become mid-high, and low vowels remain low (except, again, **â*).

57. For the function of the diacritical point, see Olshausen 1861: §§83b, 91f; Stade 1879: §§39b, 138*b*; GKC §20i; Meyer 1966–72: §14.2b; and especially GKC §20k; GKB 1 §10y; and Lambert 1972: §74.3.

58. From a diachronic perspective, these two rules reflect a single phonological operation (see Brockelmann 1940: 335–36, 364–65; and Blau 1976: §§9.1.3–9.1.4. Cf. GKB 1 §21k; and Kuryłowicz 1959).

Their sole difference, in fact, lies in the feature of length itself (and its concomitant changes). Vowel length, then, would appear to be an added feature.

The qualitative change posited in vowel lengthening reinforces the priority of lowering over lengthening. *ī becomes a long, mid-high *ṣere*; *û is lowered to a long *ḥolem*. If lengthening had preceded lowering, *i would split into *ii*, and *u into *uu*. Whereas the attested outcome would require that these reduplicated vowels lower to mid-high phones, the parallel contraction of homogeneous diphthongs does not change in color (except in the cases listed in n. 54). The contraction of homogeneous diphthongs suggests that quality does not change when like phones contract. To uphold this regular sound change, vowel lowering should be ordered before vowel lengthening: *í is lowered to *é*, lengthened by reduplication to *ée*, and contracted to [ḗ]; and *ú > *ó* > *óo* > [ṓ]. These sound changes therefore require the precedence of vowel lowering over vowel lengthening. Or in terms of morphophonology, all forms jointly participate in vowel lowering. Later, vowel lengthening was mapped onto nouns (see Malone 1974: 399).

9.7.0. The morphophonological distinction between nouns and nonnouns does not solve the difficulty presented by the pair נַחַל vs. שָׂחוּ. *á becomes *pathaḥ* in one *qatl form, and *á > *qameṣ* in the other. Other final weak (*waw*) monosyllabs do not help the investigation, for the *ṣere* in שֵׂכוּ and the *ḥolem* in בֹּהוּ are quantitatively ambiguous. Even the *qameṣ* itself in שָׂחוּ admits multiple explanations. The vowel may be long, despite the formal identity between שָׂחוּ and נַחַל. Or the *qameṣ* may be short but rounded in the environment of final *ū; just as *mawt > [mɔwɛt], so too *śaḥū > [śɔḥū] in near-adjacency to the labial phone.

9.7.1. If, however, Hebrew had a rule of near-adjacency rounding, all *a vowels would be expected to round in this environment. Yet in וַיִּשְׁתַּחוּ 'he bowed', *a becomes *pathaḥ* despite the final labial [ū], and also despite formal similarity to שָׂחוּ (*-aḥū#* < *-*aḥw#*). A rule of near-adjacency rounding therefore fails (cf. Malone 1984: 77).

That *a becomes *qameṣ* in שָׂחוּ but *pathaḥ* in וַיִּשְׁתַּחוּ is significant. For this distribution conforms to an established morphophonological distinction between nouns and nonnouns: the former participate in accent-conditioned vowel lengthening; the latter do not. Like [zɔ̄kar], the accented vowel in וַיִּשְׁתַּחוּ is short, and, like [zɔ̄kɔ̄r], so too the vowel in שָׂחוּ is long.

9.7.2. Nevertheless, there is a discrepancy between the outcome of *á in שָׂחוּ vs. that in נַחַל. Yet despite identical morphologies, the two nouns differ phonologically. [naḥal] developed like other segholate nouns, by anaptyxis; *naḥl gained a vowel between the second and third consonants, which then assimilated to the preceding *ḥeth* (BL §§201, o). The outcome is [naḥal]. שָׂחוּ, however, developed differently. The proto form, *śaḥw, ended with a vowelless semivowel. According to regular sound change, such a semivowel, bound on one side by a word boundary and on the other by a consonant, is replaced by its vocalic counterpart (Joüon 1923: §26d).[59] For example, **pary* > *parī* > פְּרִי, and **laḥy* > *laḥī* > לֶחִי. Or in initial position, **wərəʾūbēn* > וּרְאוּבֵן 'and Reuben' (Josh 18:7), and **wəšəmūʾēl* > וּשְׁמוּאֵל 'and Samuel' (Brockelmann 1966: §36h; see also §69gβ, on Aramaic). שָׂחוּ too participated in this change: **śaḥw* > *śaḥū*. נַחַל, then, developed by anaptyxis; שָׂחוּ by semivowel vocalization (Malone 1978: 127–28).

9.7.3. The different processes affecting נַחַל and שָׂחוּ account for their different outcomes. Those forms that participate in anaptyxis do not show vowel lengthening. Nouns whose final, semivocalic radical is replaced by a homoorganic long vowel exhibit vowel lengthening. שָׂחוּ, then, is to be transcribed as [sɔ̄ḥū], and נַחַל as [naḥal].

10. The BH vowel system is primarily quality-sensitive, arranged in a four-tier structure of vowel height. The upper three tiers contain pairs of vowels, internally differentiated by backness and labiality. On the lowest tier lies the nonlabial, back [ɑ].[60]

i	u
e	o
ɛ	ɔ
	ɑ

Each vowel sign represents a unique vowel quality.

This system also accommodates vowel length. Yet since length is not intrinsic to any one vowel, this feature must be uncovered by grammatical investigation. Whereas vowel quality is overt in BH, vowel quantity is covert (GKB 1 §10d).

59. Cf. analogical בֶּכֶה 'weeping' ~ בְּכִי 'weeping', and Joüon 1923: §96Aq.

60. For the graphic arrangement, see Ladefoged 1982: 75.

Bibliography

Aartun, Kjell

1967 Althebräische Nomina mit konserviertem kurzem Vokal in der Hauptdrucksilbe. *Zeitschrift der Deutschen Morgenländischen Gesellschaft* 117: 247–65.

Abercrombie, David

1967 *Elements of General Phonetics*. Chicago: Aldine.

Baer, Seligman

1885 The Dāghēsh in Initial Letters. *Hebraica* 1: 145–52.

Barth, Jacob

1894 Zur vergleichenden semitischen Grammatik. *Zeitschrift der Deutschen Morgenländischen Gesellschaft* 48: 1–21.

1913 *Die Pronominalbildung in den semitischen Sprachen*. Leipzig: J. C. Hinrichs.

Bauer, Hans, and Pontus Leander

1927 *Grammatik des Biblisch-Aramäischen*. Halle a.S.: Max Niemeyer.

BDB Francis Brown, S. R. Driver, and Charles A. Briggs (eds.), *A Hebrew and English Lexicon of the Old Testament*. Oxford: Clarendon, 1907 (repr. 1953 with corrections).

Ben-David, Abba

1957–58 The Source of the Division of Vowels into Long and Short? *Leshonenu* 22: 7–35, 110–36 [Hebrew].

BHS K. Elliger and W. Rudolph (eds.), *Biblia Hebraica Stuttgartensia*. Stuttgart: Deutsche Bibelgesellschaft, 1967/1977, 1983.

BL Hans Bauer and Pontus Leander, *Historische Grammatik der hebräischen Sprache des Alten Testamentes*. Hildesheim: Georg Olms, 1965 reprint.

Blake, Frank R.

1953 Studies in Semitic Grammar V. *Journal of the American Oriental Society* 73: 7–16.

Blau, Joshua

1968 Bibelhebräische Nomina, die auf *pataḥ–ᶜayin* enden. *Zeitschrift der Deutschen Morgenländischen Gesellschaft* 118: 257–58.

1976 *A Grammar of Biblical Hebrew*. Porta Linguarum Orientalium, Neue Serie 12. Wiesbaden: Otto Harrassowitz.

Bloomfield, Leonard

1933 *Language*. New York: Henry Holt.

Boyarin, Daniel

1978 On the History of the Babylonian Jewish Aramaic Reading Traditions: The Reflexes of *a and *ā. *Journal of Near Eastern Studies* 37: 141–60.

Brockelmann, Carl

1940 Neuere Theorien zur Geschichte des Akzents und des Vokalismus im Hebräischen und Aramäischen. *Zeitschrift der Deutschen Morgenländlischen Gesellschaft* 94: 332–71.

1966 *Grundriss der vergleichenden Grammatik der semitischen Sprachen* 1. 1908. Hildesheim: Georg Olms.

Chomsky, Noam, and Morris Halle

1968 *The Sound Pattern of English*. New York: Harper & Row.

Chomsky, William

1952 *David Ḳimḥi's Hebrew Grammar (Mikhlol)*. New York: Bloch.

1971 Problems of Pronunciation in Hebrew. Pp. 21–27 in *Gratz College Anniversary Volume*, ed. Isidore David Passow and Samuel Tobias Lachs. Philadelphia: Gratz College.

Dalman, Gustaf

1978 *Grammatik des jüdisch-palästinischen Aramäisch*. 2d ed. 1905. Darmstadt: Wissenschaftliche Buchgesellschaft.

Dolgopolsky, Aharon B.
1977 Emphatic Consonants in Semitic. *Israel Oriental Studies* 7: 1–13.

Ewald, Heinrich
1870 *Ausführliches Lehrbuch der hebräischen Sprache des Alten Bundes.* 8th ed. Göttingen: Dieterichsche Buchhandlung.

Geiger, Abraham
1856 Schreiben des Herrn Dr. Geiger in Breslau an Herrn Ignaz Blumenfeld in Wien. *Ozar Nehmad* 1: 96–119 [Hebrew].

GKB Gotthelf Bergsträsser, *Hebräische Grammatik.* 2 vols. Hildesheim: Georg Olms, 1962 reprint.

GKC E. Kautzsch and A. E. Cowley (eds.), *Gesenius' Hebrew Grammar.* 2d English ed. Oxford: Clarendon, 1910.

Gleason, H. A.
1965 *An Introduction to Descriptive Linguistics.* New York: Holt, Rinehart and Winston.

Goetze, Albrecht
1939 Accent and Vocalism in Hebrew. *Journal of the American Oriental Society* 59: 431–59.

Grimme, Hubert
1896 *Grundzüge der hebraeischen Akzent- und Vokallehre.* Collectanea Friburgensia 5. Freiburg: Commissionsverlag der Universitaetsbuchhandlung.

Hallo, William W.
1958 Isaiah 28:9–13 and the Ugaritic Abecedaries. *Journal of Biblical Literature* 77: 324–38.

Harris, Zellig S.
1939 *Development of the Canaanite Dialects.* American Oriental Series 16. New Haven: American Oriental Society.
1941 Linguistic Structure of Hebrew. *Journal of the American Oriental Society* 61: 143–67.

Heffner, R-M. S.
1937 Notes on the Length of Vowels. *American Speech* 12: 128–34.

Hoenigswald, Henry M.
1960 *Linguistic Change and Linguistic Reconstruction.* Chicago: University of Chicago.

Hyman, Larry M.
1975 *Phonology: Theory and Analysis.* New York: Holt, Rinehart and Winston.

IPA
1949 *The Principles of the International Phonetic Association.* London: IPA.

Jastrow, Morris
1885 Abu Zakarijjâ Jaḥjâ ben Dawûd Ḥajjûǧ und seine zwei grammatischen Schriften über die Verben mit schwachen Buchstaben und die Verben mit Doppelbuchstaben. *Zeitschrift für die alttestamentliche Wissenschaft* 5: 193–221.

JBL
1988 Instructions for Contributors. *Journal of Biblical Literature* 107: 579–596.

Jones, Daniel
1967 *The Phoneme: Its Nature and Use.* 3d ed. Cambridge: W. Heffer.

Joüon, Paul
1923 *Grammaire de l'hébreu biblique*. Rome: Pontifical Biblical Institute.
Kahle, Paul
1966 *Masoreten des Ostens*. 1913. Hildesheim: Georg Olms.
KB Ludwig Koehler and Walter Baumgartner, *Lexicon in Veteris Testamenti Libros*. Leiden: E. J. Brill, 1958.
Kimchi, Joseph
1888 *Sepher Sikkaron. Grammatik der hebräischen Sprache*, ed. A. Berliner. Berlin: H. Engel [Hebrew].
Kuryłowicz, Jerzy
1959 The Accentuation of the Verb in Indo-European and in Hebrew. *Word* 15: 123–29.
Ladefoged, Peter
1975 *A Course in Phonetics*. New York: Harcourt Brace Jovanovich.
1982 *A Course in Phonetics*. 2d ed. New York: Harcourt Brace Jovanovich.
Lambdin, Thomas O.
1953 Egyptian Loan Words in the Old Testament. *Journal of the American Oriental Society* 73: 145–55.
1971 *Introduction to Biblical Hebrew*. New York: Charles Scribner's Sons.
Lambert, Mayer
1893 Les points-voyelles en hébreu. *Révue des Études Juives* 26: 274–77.
1911 De la prononciation en *a* et en *o* chez les juifs et les syriens. *Journal Asiatique* 10/17: 394–98.
1972 *Traité de grammaire hébraïque*. 1946. Hildesheim: H. A. Gerstenberg.
Lehiste, Ilse
1970 *Suprasegmentals*. Cambridge: M.I.T.
Malamat, Abraham
1942–43 The Accent of "למה" Before Guttural Letters. *Tarbiz* 14: 143–44 [Hebrew].
Malmberg, Bertil
1963 *Phonetics*. New York: Dover.
Malone, Joseph L.
1972 A Hebrew Flip-Flop Rule and Its Historical Origins. *Lingua* 30: 422–48.
1974 The Isolation of "Schematisierung": A Service of Linguistics to Philology. *Journal of the American Oriental Society* 94: 395–400.
1976 Messrs Sampson, Chomsky and Halle, and Hebrew Phonology. *Foundations of Language* 14: 251–56.
1978 'Heavy Segments' vs. the Paradoxes of Segment Length: The Evidence of Tiberian Hebrew. *Linguistics*, special issue: 119–58.
1984 Tiberian Hebrew Phonology. MS, Barnard College Linguistics Department.
n.d. Messrs McCarthy and Prince, and the Problem of Hebrew Vowel Color.
Meyer, Rudolf
1966–72 *Hebräische Grammatik*. 4 vols. Berlin: Walter de Gruyter.

Mirsky, Aaron
1940–41 The Accent of "למה" Before Guttural Letters. *Tarbiz* 12: 297–99 [Hebrew].

Olshausen, Justus
1861 *Lehrbuch der hebräischen Sprache*. Braunschweig: Friedrich Vieweg und Sohn.

Philippi, F. W. M.
1897 Review of *Hebräische Grammatik*, by W. Gesenius. *Theologische Literaturzeitung* 22: 38–41.
1898 Review of *Über den rückweichenden Accent im Hebräischen*, by F. Praetorius. *Deutsche Litteraturzeitung* 19: 1673–79.

Praetorius, Franz
1897 *Über den rückweichenden Accent im Hebräischen*. Halle a.S.: Waisenhaus.

Revell, E. J.
1981 Syntactic/Semantic Structure and the Reflexes of Original Short *a* in Tiberian Pointing. *Hebrew Annual Review* 5: 75–100.
1983 *Nesiga* and the History of the Masorah. Pp. 37–48 in *Estudios Masoreticos . . . Dedicados a Harry M. Orlinsky*, ed. Emilia Fernández Tejero. Madrid: Instituto "Arias Montano."
1985 The Voweling of '*i* Type' Segolates in Tiberian Hebrew. *Journal of Near Eastern Studies* 44: 319–38.
1987 *Nesiga (Retraction of Word Stress) in Tiberian Hebrew*. Textos y Estudios "Cardenal Cisneros." Madrid: Instituto de Filología, Departamento de Filología Bíblica y de Oriente Antiguo.

SBL
1980 Society of Biblical Literature Member's Handbook. N.p.: Scholars Press.

Schramm, Gene M.
1964 *The Graphemes of Tiberian Hebrew*. University of California Publications, Near Eastern Studies 2. Berkeley: University of California.

Schreiner, Martin
1886 Zur Geschichte der Aussprache des Hebräischen. *Zeitschrift für die alttestamentliche Wissenschaft* 6: 213–59.

Sievers, Eduard
1901 *Metrische Studien* 1/1. Abhandlungen der philologisch-historischen Classe der Königlichen Sächsischen Gesellschaft der Wissenschaften 21/1. Leipzig: B. G. Teubner.

Sperber, Alexander
1941 Hebrew Phonology. *Hebrew Union College Annual* 16: 415–82.
1959 *A Grammar of Masoretic Hebrew*. Corpus Codicum Hebraicorum Medii Aevi 2. Copenhagen: Ejnar Munksgaard.

Stade, Bernhard
1879 *Lehrbuch der hebräischen Grammatik*. Leipzig: F. C. W. Vogel.

Steiner, Richard C.
1977 *The Case for Fricative-Laterals in Proto-Semitic*. American Oriental Series 59. New Haven: American Oriental Society.

Wang, William S-Y.
1968 Vowel Features, Paired Variables, and the English Vowel Shift. *Language* 44: 695–708.

Weinberg, Werner
1968 The *qamāṣ qāṭān* Structures. *Journal of Biblical Literature* 87: 151–65.

Yalon, Henoch
1965 The Pronunciation of Vowels. *Tarbiz* 34: 129–35 [Hebrew].

Yeivin, Israel
1980 *Introduction to the Tiberian Masorah*. Trans. and ed. E. J. Revell. Masoretic Studies 5. Missoula: Scholars Press.

A Historiographic Commentary on Ezra 1–6: Achronological Narrative and Dual Chronology in Israelite Historiography

Baruch Halpern
York University

> O God! that one might read the book of fate,
> And see the revolution of the times. . . .
>
> —*Henry IV, Part 2*

Because of the nature of the historical agenda of eighteenth-century Europe, critical theological scholarship has always had a great genius for questions of authorship. The issue of multiple narrative strands in the Pentateuch was, of course, freighted with implications, not all of them threatening to the Church (so Astruc 1753: I). But as, in the course of the late eighteenth-century, there emerged a scholarly community among which the literal claims of the Pentateuch, and of Genesis in particular, were no longer accorded an undiluted allegiance, the quest for the Bible's "sources" assumed a different cast: the presence, partisanship, and date of a source could warrant—as ecclesiastical tradition and Mosaic authority, now discredited, could not—the essential accuracy of biblical reports. One could construe Israel's history, examine Israelite religion historically, only through the procedures of literary criticism.

This study was accomplished with the support of the Alexander von Humboldt-Stiftung, and a Faculty of Arts Research Leave at York University. An early draft was delivered before the Consultation on Chronicles at the Society of Biblical Literature Annual Meeting at Atlanta in 1986. It has shamelessly harvested the produce of close readings by W. H. Propp, D. N. Freedman, and F. M. Cross, and suggestions by R. G. Boling, E. F. Campbell, and D. R. Hillers, who bear no responsibility whatever for my errors, but to whom I am sincerely grateful.

That this conviction led scholarship into a solipsistic quagmire of mutual discord is a perception widely held, and widely published, in this century. The enterprise was bold, and insufficiently controlled, and spawned therefore a vast and varied literature. How does one persuade a scholarly community that a hypothecated source, no longer intact, can be defined to the part of the verse? Despite the difficulties, a centrist consensus emerged, rough or fine, firm or fragile, on the Pentateuch, based on the work of Hupfeld (1853), on the Former Prophets, based on that of de Wette (1807), and, of course, on Chronicles-Ezra-Nehemiah, at least since the time of Abravanel.

Challenges are regularly mounted against all the centrist positions. That which affirms the common authorship of Chronicles, Ezra, and Nehemiah, has been called into the most effective dispute. In recent years, a small group of scholars have assembled a well-constructed and essentially sound case for the separate authorship of these works (esp. Japhet 1968). The case rests most heavily on differences in usage, culture, and party interests. It deals in the issues to which, hitherto, the exponents of common authorship appealed.

Independent of this reassessment of common authorship, the scholarship of the last four decades has had a tendency, if not to vindicate the Chronicler, at least to mitigate the charge of unbridled confection levelled against him by nineteenth-century critics. Chr, more benevolently regarded, takes on the hue of an ancient "exegete." It is a by-product of this rehabilitation that scholars today entertain the possibility that Chr enjoyed access to preexilic sources unavailable to us (already Noth 1943: 133). At least in connection with Hezekiah's and Josiah's reforms, Amaziah's treatment of the Edomites' gods, and Manasseh's deportation (e.g., Cogan 1974: 116–17, 67 n. 15; cf. Avigad 1983: 35–60) scholars evince an increasing willingness to rely on Chr's testimony, in the conviction that he had such sources and used them ably.

In fact, the trends toward increasing reliance on Chr and toward detaching Chr from Ezra and Nehemiah are not discrete. Those revisionists who deny the unity of Chr-Ezra-Neh base themselves heavily on ideological differences in the corpus (so Freedman 1961: 441). They presume, then, that each element of the text harmoniously expresses the historians' ideologies. This argument has force, but in inverse proportion to the reliance the historian placed on sources. Even Wellhausen agreed that, in recapitulating Samuel, Chr altered his source material less than he abridged and supplemented it, according to principles Wellhausen took to be improper, but which are susceptible to alternative assessments.

If Chr had an interest in history, his selection, reconstructions, and representations of events will have expressed antiquarian, not just ideological, concerns. And antiquarian interests may then have induced Chr to introduce or preserve sources whose themes and views were out of step with his own commitments. I have elsewhere argued the importance of antiquarianism in the formation of Israelite historiography (1983), and the availability to Chr of at least one preexilic source no longer extant (1981b; so also Naʾaman 1986, 1987). Regardless of how those arguments are received, the specters they raise have ramifications for Chr, and for the common authorship of Ezra and Chr. After all, inconsistencies in a unified Chronicles-Ezra-Nehemiah could as easily derive from differences between sources, or from different perspectives on different periods, as from a difference in authorship.

A key to sophisticating the case for or against the common authorship of Chronicles and Ezra—and a key to consolidating our purchase on Israel's historiography and history—lies in investigating the ways in which ancient authors worked with their sources. It is not my brief to direct a counter-thrust against the revisionist programs concerning Chr—against those who defend Chr's reliability or dispute its common authorship with Ezra and Nehemiah. However, until Chr's historiographic (not historiosophic) practices are exposed, the mechanics of assembly and composition, which they conditioned, will remain veiled, only half-known, and the subject of ceaseless controversy and conjecture.

This is the handicap that fettered nineteenth-century critics: they assumed that the "redactors" selected and arranged their sources freely. The assumption freed them to imagine all redactors much as they imagined Chr: as blackguards and fools. If redactors were dishonest or irrational, then no logical standard could be applied to competing literary analyses. In Genesis, parallel narrative strands afforded some control. This phenomenon did not characterize Chr and the Former Prophets.

In consequence, the consensus concerning the authorship of Dtr, at least, has always been fragile. Noth's *Überlieferungsgeschichtliche Studien* (1943), a work whose magisterial tone sometimes obscures its logic, owes its longevity precisely to its postulate that Israelite historians worked in good faith: the assumption weathered four full decades without difficulty. Until we have plumbed the redactors' historical methods, I suspect Noth will remain the last, though not the undisputed, word on the subject.

I. The Problem of Chronicles

To investigate comprehensively Chr's use of sources would involve three tasks, each of which has occasionally been undertaken (esp. Willi 1972; Wellhausen 1883; Noth 1943; see Japhet 1985 for the literature, to which add Micheel 1983): (1) defining and, to the extent possible, reconstituting the sources themselves—all of them, including those contemporary practices retrojected by Chr into antiquity; (2) describing Chr's methods in compiling, reordering, rewriting, abridging, and interpreting the sources, and in free composition with and without evidence from them; and (3) establishing the several motivations, thematic and institutional, underlying Chr's reconstructions and presentation, and the interplay between them.

Execution of any part of this agenda is sure to evoke controversy. The first, upon which the others depend, already entails speculation. Noth (1943: 133ff.) made the argument that accurate material preserved in Chronicles but not in Kings implied the use of sources (also Albright 1950). Just what texts fall into this category has remained in issue (as North 1974), though legitimate candidates are numerous (as 2 Chr 11:6–10, 18–21; 12:3–4; 13:4, 19, 21 [cf. Klein 1983]; 14:8–14; 17:7–9, 11; 19:5–10; 20:1, 20ff.; 21:2, 4, 16–19; 24:20–21, 25; 25:5–10, 13, 14; 26:6–11, 15, 16–20; 27:3, 5; 28:7, 9, 12, 18; 29:20–36; 30:1–11, 23; 31:11–20; 33:11–13 [despite North 1974], 14–17).

Nor is source analysis geared to the work's internal structure apt to produce general agreement. Discontinuity in themes or usage can be traced either to the content of the history or to the thematic interests of the compiler. For example, from Rehoboam through Hezekiah, Chr exhibits a fascination for royal expansion in the countryside (2 Chr 11:5–12; 13:19[?]; 14:5–6 + 15:8; 17:2 + 21:3; 26:6, 9–10, 15; 27:3–4; 32:28–29), where losses are sustained by kings judged negatively (21:17, 22:9, 24:23, 25:23, 28:17–18). A notice about Manasseh's expansion (33:14) is the only positive one restricted to Jerusalem, and, thereafter, the historian evinces no related interest. Although numerous other themes and patterns, developed from the reign of Solomon forward, break down in connection with Hezekiah (for some, see Halpern 1981b), one may link this change in focus to Judah's territorial restriction in the era after 701. Conversely, Chr gives the first hint of Judah's coming destruction at the end of his account of Hezekiah's reign (32:26, refracting Kings). Doom, hurtling down like a hawk on a lamb, perhaps extinguished the interests ignited by tales of happier times.

In the circumstances, we must recur to the sources we are able to isolate confidently in Chronicles, Ezra, and Nehemiah. The case of Chronicles itself is, however, too intricate to furnish a starting point: The view that Chr has no sources other than Samuel–Kings validates itself in Wellhausen's or Willi's perspective that Chr is a liar or midrashist. The inverse view, that Chr departs from Samuel–Kings only based on other data, endorses a conservative view of his methods. But to start without either view leaves one up in the air as to how far Chr is rewriting and correcting Kings, and how far copying or paraphrasing from another document. Because scholarly sentiment lies today between the alternatives, and because Chronicles represents such a complex composition, it may be best to approach it obliquely, only after general agreement has been won on historiographic issues generally.

A limited corpus offering fertile ground, and hopes of an early consensus, is found in Ezra 1–6. In this area, Hugh Williamson (1983) has laid an important groundwork. Ezra 1–6 stands apart from the narrative about Ezra and from Chronicles. How it handles sources may cast light on the relationship between Ezra and Chr, and, ultimately, on the use of sources in each. Finally, if Japhet and Williamson, among others, are right, attention to this text offers the possibility of locating the limits of Chr's work.

The following pages concern themselves with identifying the sources of this clever bit of history-writing. The treatment, which breaks the narrative into convenient sections not meant to correspond to full stops in the continuous text, considers the source problem at length. It focuses ultimately on the chronography of Ezra 1–6 and Chronicles. The chronography, it will be seen, is of a type with that of royal temple-building inscriptions, including exemplars in a scribal tradition to which Babylonian Jews were exposed. It reflects the sorts of sources apparently employed in the construction of the text—the segment was originally a variation on a Mesopotamian temple dedication. The sources once isolated, then, it will be clear that these chronographic connections have implications for the idea of history (or genre of history) embodied in Ezra 1–6. Such findings can be brought into comparison with corresponding practice in Chr, where the chronography is markedly different. This result will want extensive discussion. It does not alone suffice to settle the riddles posed above.

II. Sources in Ezra 1–6

Ezra 1

Three biblical texts make undisguised reference to Cyrus's proclamation of Judah's Restoration: 2 Chr 36:22 summarizes it, Deutero-Isaiah (44:26–28; 45:1–7, 13) alludes to it, and the edict figures in three forms in Ezra 1–6. Ezra 1:1–4 cites it directly. The Judaeans then supply an epitome to Tattenai, who relays their precis to the court at 5:13–15. And, in a letter written to Tattenai, Darius quotes a "memorandum" of the decree (6:3–5) found in Ecbatana.

These citations have occasioned disharmony. Arguments against the authenticity of the memorandum have been met (de Vaux 1972: 89–93; Tadmor 1983: 15). This means that 6:3–5 cannot depend on 1:2–4 or 5:13–15. Still, the relationship between 1:2–4, 5:13–15, and the memorandum remains controverted. Bickermann has made a case that 1:2–4 stems from an oral proclamation, as opposed to the memorandum (1946: 249ff.). The elements of the texts are:

Ezra 1:2–4	*Ezra 5:13–15*	*Ezra 6:3–5*	*Isaiah 44–45*
Yhwh appointed Cyrus			Yhwh appointed Cyrus
return ordered	(15): implied return in Sheshbazzar's taking vessels home		return ordered
Diaspora to contribute		court to pay costs	
1:6–11			aliens pay tribute
neighbors lend support			
	(see 5:8)	dimensions and materials specified	
temple vessels returned from Babylonian temple via Sheshbazzar	temple vessels returned from Babylonian temple via Sheshbazzar	temple vessels returned from Babylon	
vessels listed			
temple to be rebuilt	temple to be rebuilt	temple to be rebuilt	temple, town to be rebuilt

Scholars lay widely differing stress on the differences among the accounts in Ezra. Williamson, for example, arguing the independence of 1:2–4, notes that 6:3–5 does not mention the return from exile or Yhwh's electing Cyrus; further, the return of the temple vessels is related outside of the decree in 1:2–4, not within it as in 6:3–5 (1985: 7). We may add that 6:3–5 has the court furnishing the funds for the temple's reconstruction, where 1:2–4 implies that the Diaspora underwrote the project. Williamson also holds that the narrative following 1:2–4 speaks of donations from non-Jews (1:6; 1985: 16). He takes this as an indication that the historian was attempting to draw parallels to the Exodus, but was constrained by the wording of his source from introducing the motif into 1:4. This would suggest that 1:2–4 was cited verbatim from a record of Cyrus's proclamation.

If all this comprises a credible analysis, it does involve multiplying sources. In a sense, that makes for a simple solution. But the issue is not so simply resolved.

Ezra 1 and 5:13–15 both mention that Nebuchadnezzar housed the Jerusalem temple vessels in "the temple of his god." In addition, both texts identify Sheshbazzar as the official (1:8 *nāśîʾ*, 5:14 *peḥâ*) responsible for the vessels' return; 6:3–5 mentions no Judaean official. Finally, 6:5 makes the return of the temple vessels a part of the edict itself, but 5:14–15, like 1:2–11, distinguishes the edict (5:13) from Cyrus's transferring the vessels to Sheshbazzar; the latter is narrated, not included in the edict. In detail, 5:13–15 conforms more to chap. 1 than to 6:3–5.

Nevertheless, there are several correlations between 5:13–15 and 6:3–5. At points, the language is identical:

5:13	brm bšnt ḥdh lkwrš mlkʾ dy bbl kwrš mlkʾ śm ṭʿm
6:3	bšnt ḥdh lkwrš mlkʾ kwrš mlkʾ śm ṭʿm
5:13	byt ʾlhʾ dnh lbnʾ
6:3	byt ʾlhʾ byrwšlm bytʾ ytbnʾ
5:14	wʾp mʾnyʾ dy byt ʾlhʾ dy dhbh wkspʾ dy nbwkdnṣr hnpq mn
6:5	wʾp mʾny byt ʾlhʾ dy dhbh wkspʾ dy nbwkdnṣr hnpq mn
5:14	hyklʾ dy byrwšlm whybl hmw lhyklʾ dy bbl
6:5	hyklʾ dy byrwšlm whybl lbbl
6:5	[a]wyhk [b]lhyklʾ dy byrwšlm [c]lʾtrh [d]wtḥt [e]bbyt ʾlhʾ
5:15	[a]ʾzl [d]ʾḥt hmw [b]bhyklʾ dy byrwšlm [e]wbyt ʾlhʾ ytbnʾ [c]ʿl ʾtrh.

Where the texts coincide in substance, the language coincides; elsewhere, the variation may be traced to the texts' different functions. Ezra 5:13–15 contains the Judaeans' representations to Tattenai. It cites what is germane to the argument: that Cyrus licensed the building; that the restored temple vessels are evidence of this. The return and the building subsidies are not mentioned. The former is an accomplished fact, not relevant to the further question of whether the returnees are to be permitted to continue building. The latter is also immaterial to the question of permission to build, and, with the building underway and therefore temporarily funded (perhaps through local crown revenues), is of secondary concern. Moreover, the Judaeans do not want to bring down on themselves blame for the noncompletion of the project (below), such as an interruption in the building (but not the revenues?) would perhaps imply.

The Judaeans in chap. 5 are intent only on securing the speedy restoration of the temple. It may have been the intent of 1:4 and 6:4 that the subsidy be applied from Judaean tax monies; alternatively, it is possible that the narrator has the Judaeans refrain from requesting a renewal of Cyrus's subsidy in order to avoid an excess of demands. This is the reading the text overtly demands (further below, pp. 89–91). Simultaneously, the text evades the issue of why Cyrus's edict was never completed; by omitting mention of the return(s), it covers up questions about the chronological relationship of Sheshbazzar to Zerubbabel (see below, on Ezra 4:1–5, and section III).

It is noteworthy that 5:15 provides that the temple be built "on its [old] site." The memorandum (6:5) agrees, as does Darius's renewal of Cyrus's order in 6:7. This element reflects an authentic concern for the correct restoration of sanctuaries, which is attested in connection with the Elephantine shrine in *AP* 32:8, precisely an aide-mémoire (*lmbnyh bʾtrh*). There is no semantic or substantive equivalent in chap. 1. However, the list in chap. 2 (v 68) and the narrative in 3:3 do mention former loci.

It is the correlation of 5:13–15 to 6:3–5 that the narrative demands. The edict found in 6:3–5 functions as documentary confirmation of the claims the Judaeans make in 5:13–15. To the degree that it echoes their words, the confirmation rings. Further, both texts fall within the so-called "Aramaic source," a corpus fairly homogeneous in its compositional techniques, especially its extensive quotation of correspondence as evidence.

Still, 1:1ff. provide the reader with the background for reading 5:13–15, and some correspondence is therefore expected. Disagreement between 5:13–15 and 1:2–4 is the surprise. Some of the differences arise from the change in language; others, notably the fact that 1:1 calls Cyrus "king of Persia," not "king of Babylon" (5:13, 6:3), are not so easily disposed of. Even 1:7, which speaks of the vessels Nebuchadnezzar took, differs in several particulars (no "of gold and silver"; no "temple in" Jerusalem; no "to Babylon") from the nearly identical formulations of 5:15 and 6:5. This is not to mention the different audiences the Hebrew and Aramaic texts address.

Does 1:2–4 stem, then, from an independent source? From the materials at hand, the historian was quite capable of reconstructing it, as an epitome of the original edict to which 5:13–15 refers, and which is recorded in an aide-mémoire in 6:3–5. The following points merit notice:

1. Ezra 1:1–4 heralds the Restoration, and alerts the reader to the purpose of the returnees from Babylon.

a. After 1:2–3, there is no narrative statement that the exiles decided to rebuild the temple: Ezra 1:5 speaks of exiles *who* were moved to do so—these are the returnees of 538. Only in 2:68 is a decision to rebuild narrated. But this is already in the time of Zerubbabel, probably around 521, and is followed swiftly by the account of the actual building.

b. Similarly, Sheshbazzar's return in 538 is referred to (1:11, 5:16) but never directly reported. The first report of a return describes Zerubbabel's migration (2:1, 70). In the case of Sheshbazzar, only the incipient action is recorded (1:5, "The lineage heads, etc., arose . . ."). The action is not explicitly described, but assumed (1:11). Again, the narrative strategy is confusing to modern sensibilities; its most obvious purpose is to avoid portraying Sheshbazzar's expedition as abortive.

The principal implications of this strategy remain to be explored (see below to on Ezra 3:7–13 and 4:1–5); it has even propelled readers to the extremity of identifying Sheshbazzar with Zerubbabel (Mandelkern 1959: 1529). In any case, the historian's selection from the edict was in large measure determined by the functions of his summary.

2. The edict in 1:1–4 is a directive to the exiles. It also doubled for a detailed narrative of Sheshbazzar's return, to create an impression of continuity between his activity and that of Zerubbabel, a continuity reflected in the Judaeans' plea in 5:13ff. (see below; Japhet 1982: 66–98; Japhet 1983: 218–29). Ezra 1 thus functions as a sort of prologue, furnishing the information to substantiate the claims of 5:13–15. This is why the two texts agree. It also meant that some elements were not germane to the narrative purpose and premises of the text:

a. limitations on the size and location of the building (as 6:3–5)
b. specifications of the materials for construction (but note that 3:7 links the acquisition of timber and stone "to the license of Cyrus, king of Persia"; the reference is to 6:4)
c. a command to Persian officials to return the temple vessels looted from Jerusalem by Nebuchadnezzar
d. a command to Persian officials to remit money for the project

What *was* material was an enjoinder to other exiles to subsidize the returnees (1:4). Scholars generally assume (but contrast Tadmor 1983: 15) that the royal subsidy was to come from local taxes—as a local affair, it is not mentioned in the brief to Tattenai (5:13–15). If so, 1:4 no more than recasts as an exhortation to the Judaeans what 6:4 in effect enjoins on the Persian authorities.

Another particular also suggests that 1:2–4 is derivative. Ezra 1 relates the return of the temple vessels in direct historical narrative: (*a*) because it was inappropriate to include it in Cyrus's edict to the exiles, who were powerless to effect it, and (*b*) in order to create narrative movement and linkage to the list of vv 8–11. The memorandum (6:3–5), however, suggests that the vessels' return was provided for in the original decree, something that Cyrus would have mentioned, in testimony to his piety and generosity, in any public pronouncement. Along with other omissions in 1:2–4 (especially of "the old site" of the temple or of the fact that a temple formerly existed on the site), this suggests that the narrator is not providing the full text of a source in 1:2–4, but either epitomizing or reconstructing the proclamation, adapted to the demands of the context.

3. Except for the list of vessels returned (1:8–11), usually imputed to an invoice much like the one Ezra preserves (8:25–27, 34), the information in chap. 1 is such that the author could have derived it from sources other than a documentary record of Cyrus's proclamation. Ezra 1 furnishes information to sustain the claims in 5:13–15, and nothing more, as a logical prologue to the account as a whole.

a. The notion that Yhwh elected Cyrus was current in the Restoration community, and was enshrined in Isaiah 44–45, a text with contacts with the Cyrus cylinder (Rawlinson 1884: 35; Berger 1975). The cylinder itself indicates that Cyrus applied just such language to Marduk, a fact that would be known to educated Babylonian Judaeans. *UET* 1:307 applies the same language to Sîn (see Tadmor 1983: 14), and the verisimilitude in Ezra 1:3, along with that of Yhwh's epithet in 1:2, can have been based on broad exposure to Persian epigraphs in Mesopotamia.

b. The element of communal support for the project is explicable on the grounds exposed above (#2): local taxes were probably understood to have been diverted to the construction; this deduction can have been based, if nothing else, on 6:4. Further, Cyrus plainly permitted a general return, which entailed the alienation of Judaean property in Mesopotamia. And, the practice of sending tribute to Yhwh in Jerusalem persisted probably throughout the Persian period, and certainly thereafter, as the character of relations between Elephantine and Jerusalem (*AP* 30–32) and texts in the Talmud and Josephus bear witness.

c. Sheshbazzar's return was a known fact (5:15–16) and source of disappointment (Haggai).

d. Ezra 1:6, if it claims that non-Jews subvened the venture, answers not only to the similar motif in Exodus (11:2–3, 12:35–36), but also to a motif, that of universal tribute, common in texts about temple-building and in hymnody (for example, *ANET* 574:72, 81–83, 89–92; Falkenstein and von Soden 1953: 147, 152; Langdon 1912: 122.26ff., 124.26ff., 146.12ff.; and Ps 68:32–33, 76:12, 96:8; Isa 18:7). This is the source of the motif in Exodus (see 15:18): the temple is the cosmos, and both are built after a triumph eliciting tribute the world over. Similar concepts attach to Zerubbabel's temple in Haggai (2:7), Zechariah (8:20–23), and Trito-Isaiah (60:5–18), and, significantly, in the immediate aftermath of Deutero-Isaiah's Cyrus hymn (Isa 45:14–17, the language parallel to that of 60:5ff.). Finally, Ezra 1:4 ("all who remain") may in fact have the subjects of 1:6 ("all those around them") in view; or, 1:6 may represent a deliberate heightening of 1:4. In any other case, the dissonance between 1:6 and 1:4 is strong evidence for Bickermann's view (Williamson 1985: 16).

e. The restoration of the temple vessels to Sheshbazzar was known from two sources: the edict in 6:5 (and reference in 5:14–15), and the inventory preserved in 1:9–11, presumably with the name of Mithridates (v 8; Galling 1964: 80–81). Some dedicatory record probably was established in Jerusalem. The inclusion of the list in 1:9–11 now helps to establish ties with 2:68–69, again linking Sheshbazzar and Zerubbabel (see below on Ezra 2, 3:7–13, 4:1–5 [subpoints #3–4, and the conclusion on pp. 115–16], 4:6–5:2 [subpoint #2], 5:3–6:12, and IIIA).

f. That the temple vessels had been deposited in a temple in Babylon was noted in 5:14, and could probably have been deduced from the fact that their number remained virtually intact.

This does not mean that no record of Cyrus's proclamation existed (cf. Galling 1964: 61–76). The coincidence of ideas between 1:1–4 and Isaiah 44–45 suggests that both are echoing the language of the edict. Still, in 5:13–16 the returnees cannot demonstrate that the proclamation was made (where was the list of 1:9–11?). Only the retrieval of records from Ecbatana (Tadmor 1983: 15) documents their claim (5:17, 6:1–2). We need not take this seriously—the real issue may have been that Darius needed to reconfirm the edict. It does suggest that Judaean and other repatriations were implemented in isolation from the policy of restoring ruined temples. The Cyrus cylinder (lines 30–34) claims that Cyrus restored a number of peoples and gods to their lands, including settling gods of various towns in temples that had long been in ruins (there is a question whether the line implies this or that they had long since been founded; cf. Gadd 1958). This juxtaposition notwithstanding, the presence of Zerubbabel and Jeshua does not itself suffice, in Ezra 5:13–15 and the discussion with Tattenai, to show that an order to rebuild the temple had been issued. Thus, repatriation could occur without permission being granted to rebuild temples or fortifications. In turn, this implies that 6:3–5 may quote a complete document, without reference to the Judaeans' repatriation.

More telling is the reference to Cyrus as king of Persia in 1:1, 2, 8; 3:7; and 4:3. This precludes the notion that the historian was quoting from a contemporary document: "king of Persia" was not a title otherwise published by Cyrus (see Graf 1984: 18–19). Contrariwise, the Aramaic source (5:13; cf. 6:3) calls Cyrus king of Babylon.

That the Hebrew in 1:8 calls Sheshbazzar Judah's *nāśîʾ* where the Aramaic source calls him *peḥâ* might be thought evidence of an independent source (on the terms, see below). It has latterly been the fashion to deny Sheshbazzar's identity with the Shenazzar of 1 Chr 3:18 (Berger 1971: 98–100; Dion 1983: 111–12) and thus his claim to Davidic antecedents. This is not altogether clear-cut. The argument runs, *ššbṣr* < Šamaš-ab-uṣur, which could not generate *šnʾṣr* in 1 Chr 3:18. But the Greek for Sheshbazzar is

Sanabassar, presupposing a Hebrew like *šnbṣr* or, more fully, *šnᵓbᵓṣr*. Here, original *šmšᵓb* > *šnb*. Further, the name, Šamaš-šuma-ukin produces Aramaic *srmg* (demotic srmnḳy: Steiner and Nims 1985: 70 XVII 10–11). The source is Assyrian, which is why *š* > *s* and *k* > *g* (see Millard 1976). Were the source Babylonian, *šmšš* would presumably have produced *šr*. The irregular reduction of *šmš* before bilabials in these instances means that the identification of Sheshbazzar with Shenazzar remains tenable, if impossible to prove (further, Japhet 1982: 94–98).

On the positive side, then, the titulature *nāśîᵓ* in Ezra 1:8 is the remaining argument that Sheshbazzar was a scion of Jesse. Williamson (1985: 17–18) cites cases where a *nāśîᵓ*, is not royal; he argues that Sheshbazzar in 1:8 is *nāśîᵓ*, of Judah, and not of all Israel, so that it is illegitimate to equate him with Ezekiel's Davidic *nāśîᵓ*. But Ezekiel's Israelite leader is a Davidic ruler of a restored community, focused in Jerusalem; and, like the Chronicler, the author of Ezra 1–6 sees in the Restoration community the only legitimate political expression of Israelite nationhood—thus the *nāśîᵓ* of Judah is *de jure* ruler of all Israel (so, for example, 1:3; 3:11; 4:1, 3; 6:14, 21). The argument against Sheshbazzar's Davidic affiliation thus consists solely of his putative omission from the Chronicler's tables. In any event, the historian in Ezra 1–6 may have thought him a Davidide.

It remains to observe why 1:8 adopts a titulature different from that of 5:14. The *nāśîᵓ* was an officer of a lineage group, probably one accorded formal recognition by the state, who mediated the interests of a kin-group to the (segmentary) authority at the next level up (clan to "tribe," tribe to state: Halpern 1981a: 206–15). The expression refers primarily, however, to the status of the officer in his own kin-group, as in Ezekiel and, for example, 1 Kgs 11:34 (read MT). Contrariwise, *peḥâ* denotes an officer appointed and supported through the power of the Persian empire, whose bailiwick is not necessarily organized on kinship lines: he is an officer of the crown. This term describes the position to which Cyrus appointed Sheshbazzar, as 5:14 claims.

In other words, 1:8 employs the title appropriate before Sheshbazzar's appointment as governor in Jerusalem, which is incidentally described in that verse. Sheshbazzar, the historian claims, was a leading figure among the Jews in Babylon. But the avoidance of royal titulature in the restoration community (the closest one comes is Hag 2:21–23 with Jer 22:24; and Zech 3:8, 6:11–13) combined with the orientation of chap. 1 toward the returnees to dictate the use of *nāśîᵓ*. There is no implication of a separate source; the linkage between the temple vessels and the edict remains quite close, so that the correlation of 1:1ff. and 5:13–15 is complete; and, it is at best unlikely that Cyrus would have preferred the term in question to *peḥâ*, which would, again, have alluded to his own role in the Restoration.

A last consideration is that, in comparison with the list of 1:8–11, where loanwords from Persian and Aramaic abound, the Hebrew of 1:2–4 is quite ordinary. The Cyrus cylinder, of course, was written by a Babylonian scribe in Akkadian (further, cf. *UET* 1:307; Weissbach 1911: 3.XI, 8–9.Ib; *UVB* 1.31; and Teixidor 1978; the Aramaic documents from Asshur, etc.); so conceivably, the original edict was composed in Hebrew. But Babylon was a major center, with the temple of Marduk already standing inside it. Jerusalem's was a different case. Further, 1:2–4 contains late phraseology, including the term king of Persia (above) and the Aramaic calque, *pqd* ^{c}*l*, for 'commissioned' (Tadmor 1983: 14–15). At the same time, the existence of an original edict is to be inferred from the fact of the first return. The difficulty is, the same inference was open to the historian composing Ezra 1–6, so that the attempt to reconstruct it would have been a legitimate historical endeavor.

The foregoing indicates that the historian may have reconstructed the edict based on documentary sources (the Tattenai correspondence), on contemporary models (such as the Cyrus cylinder), on Isaiah 44–45, and on transmitted recollections. The argument with potency for Bickermann's view is Williamson's claim (1985: 16) that 1:4 and 1:6 refer to different groups of donors. This is not altogether certain; and there is much evidence to balance it that favors the contradictory position. With relative assurance, however, we can conclude that in either event the text in 1:1–4 is a paraphrase, not a direct quotation, and reflects only a part of the proclamation at best. The remainder of chap. 1 is cobbled together on the basis of materials in Aramaic and of the invoice in 1:8–11.

Ezra 2

Distinctive source problems make it expedient to treat Ezra 2 separately from 3:1–6. At issue, with important implications for source-use and, ultimately, chronography, is the relationship of the register here to that in Nehemiah 7. Williamson (1983: 2–8; 1985: 29–30) adduces four arguments for the dependence of Ezra 2 on Nehemiah 7:

1. The seventh month (3:1) is germane in Neh 8:2, but out of place in Ezra 3. This is not strictly accurate. In effect, 3:1 links to 2:70 by invoking an assembly in the seventh month. Then 3:2–3 mentions the preceding preparation (the construction of the altar, placed, if one dates the foundation in Darius's second year, from the twenty-fourth day of the sixth month, with Hag 1:13–15; for other *yaqtul* pluperfects see Judg 2:6ff. after 1:1; 2 Chr 12:4–8; 30:2–3). Ezra 3:4–5 leaps forward to Sukkot, and v 6 reverts to the first of the month, capping vv 1–3 and closing the whole segment with a date for the inception of the

restoration cult. In sequence, the verses run: 2–3, 6, 1, 4, 5. Ezra 3:1, where it is, intimates the participation of the entire community not just in the festivals of the seventh month, but also in the rebuilding of the altar (3:2–3). If the effect is conscious (see below, section III), Williamson's argument is indeterminate.

2. Ezra 2:68–69 rounds up the figures furnished in Neh 7:69–70 (where Williamson emends the number of priestly garments), which suggests dependence on Nehemiah. Ezra does not break down the categories of donors, as does Neh 7:69–70, with *tirshatah*, lineage heads, others. This, despite Polybius's warning (3:33) about historians who concoct specific numbers to give the impression of having special knowledge, seems to preclude Nehemiah's dependence on Ezra.
3. Ezra 2:68, "when they came to the house of Yhwh, which is in Jerusalem, [donated] to the house of the god to erect it on its base," is a plus, within Ezra 2:68–69, to the parallel in Neh 7:70. Ezra 2:68 links the lineage heads to the building, and Nehemiah would have had no reason to delete it. But in Nehemiah, where Ezra's reading the law, now set in Nehemiah's time, follows, the line would divert attention from Nehemiah's current project. Probably correct, the argument is not decisive.
4. Neh 7:72a (the people are in their towns) belongs to the Nehemiah Memoir, as a fragment linking 7:1–5 (in a depopulated Jerusalem) with its original, direct continuation in 11:1–4 (they sent representatives to Jerusalem). A piece of this text appears, in slightly expanded form, in Ezra 2:70. So Ezra depends directly on Nehemiah.

This last is a central argument. Neh 11:3–4 $<$ 7:72a = Ezra 2:70. The odd form of Ezra 2:70 ("some of the people" and "all Israel" are awkwardly juxtaposed) evokes the following versions:

Ezra 2:70: The priests and Levites and some of the people and the singers and gatekeepers and Nethinim dwelt in their towns, and all Israel in their towns. The first "in their towns" is expansive, to relieve the redundancy inherent in "some of the people" and "all Israel" (Williamson 1985: 273).

Neh 7:72a: The priests and the Levites and the gatekeepers and the singers and some of the people and the Nethinim dwelt [in Jerusalem?], and all Israel in their towns. Not, with Williamson (1985) "even all Israel in their towns," referring to the inhabitants of the countryside and of Jerusalem, because "some of the people" jars in that context, despite Gunneweg's harmony (1981: 157). Neh 11:4 uses the same expression to distinguish laity settled in Jerusalem. Williamson, reading the text as a fragment of which Neh 11:1 is the continuation, nevertheless fails to resolve the grammatical tension.

1 Esdr 5:45: The priests and the Levites and some of the people dwelt in Jerusalem and its environs, and the singers and gatekeepers and all Israel in their towns. If this expansion on the Nehemiah version is correct in gross, it differs from the situation reflected elsewhere in Nehemiah (as 11:20). It presupposes the Ezra 2:70 order of enumeration.

This text fits the list of returnees regardless of the continuation in Nehemiah, and effectively expands on information found at the outset of the list (Ezra 2:1, Neh 7:6). The exiles returned in order to populate both Jerusalem and its hinterland. The linkage of Neh 7:72a to Neh 11:1–4 reflects Nehemiah's concern to repopulate the capital; this he accomplished by the covenant ceremony in Nehemiah 9–10 (and 11–12). Most commentators remove Nehemiah 8–10 as displaced text. In the present recension, however, they are integral to the narrative. Thus, 7:72b–8:1, locating the reading of the law in the seventh month, follows from 6:15, placing the end of Jerusalem's fortification at the end of the sixth. The reading of the law and the ensuing covenant are set between the completion of the wall and its consecration. We cannot deny the possibility, therefore, that 7:72a formed part of the source consulted by Nehemiah (7:5). Nor is the time element between 7:1–5 and 8:1 such as to demand mediation from 7:72a, taken as narrative.

The sequence in Nehemiah 6:15–11:1 deliberately yokes the work of Ezra and Nehemiah (*contra* Torrey 1910: 252–84), rightly or not. This means the narrative resumes no later than Neh 7:72b and 8:1, when chronological data places us in the seventh month, after the completion of the wall in the sixth month (Neh 6:15). The implication is that 7:72b resumes Nehemiah's narrative flow: it was not found in his source (7:5), the use of which is the strongest argument, otherwise, for a common original. Yet Ezra 3:1 = Neh 7:72b–8:1a, introducing an assembly in Jerusalem in the seventh month. It is another argument against a common original that this introduction must have had a continuation: either Ezra or Nehemiah presumably contains the original continuation. That conceded, it follows that Ezra 2, which cannot be the source for Nehemiah (see #2, above), can only have come from Nehemiah. Here, Williamson's position finds vindication.

This view has one unfortunate ramification. There were a minimum of three stages in the compilation of Ezra–Nehemiah: the memoirs of each principal, the assembly of Ezra 7–Nehemiah 13, and the construction of Ezra 1–6. In other words, the author who situated Nehemiah 8–10 could not also have introduced Ezra 1–6. The epicycle could be avoided by hypothesizing that a single hand drew Neh 7:1–72a from the memoir and used the same continuation in Neh 7:72b and in Ezra 3:1. But while possible, this seems awkward. Further, were there no parallel text, it would be an issue where

Nehemiah's "book of the register" leaves off, and narrative recommences. One might think that the source ended at Neh 7:60, and that 7:69 refers to Nehemiah (the only other character to whom the title, *tirshatah*, is applied). Were the later author concerned to avoid this confusion, the alterations made in Ezra 2 would adequately serve. Ezra 2 in effect guides our reading of Nehemiah 7: it interprets a text received in the form it takes in Nehemiah.

In an argument to date the list to 538–520, Williamson (1985) claims that it is composite (so 2:3–20 vs. 21–29 vs. 30–35). This is not a concern here, since it all antedates Neh 7:5. However, this claim holds only if the shift from personal to place names is significant: it may simply differentiate Jerusalemites from non-Jerusalemites per 2:1, "Jerusalem and Judah." The shift from "men of GN" to "sons of GN" is not beyond a scribe collecting an original list.

Regardless, the list denominates either returnees with Zerubbabel (2:2), or a combination of Zerubbabel's and Sheshbazzar's personnel in Jerusalem, comprising therefore a list of those endowed with tax privileges (*kidinnūtu*) for the temple work (cf. 7:24 and above on Ezra 1). Jeshua appears as a returnee in Ezra 2 (v 2): his subsequent installation as high priest is dated by Zechariah 3 to the autumn of 520 (second year of Darius), which Williamson rightly makes his *terminus ad quem*. Meanwhile, the inclusion of Jeshua and possibly Tobiah the Nathin (2:60; Neh 7:62; Zech 6:10, 14; but Neh 13:4, 7, 8) and Yedayah (2:36; Neh 7:39; Zech 6:10, 14; but Neh 11:10; 12:7, 19, 21; esp. 1 Chr 9:10, 24:7) in the list precludes a date before Zerubbabel's return—this, as we shall see, must be dated to 521. The suggestion is very strong, then, that the list is in fact not composite, but enumerates subordinates of Zerubbabel: it must have been compiled after 522 and before the end of 520.

In all, Nehemiah 7 must be the source of Ezra 2. In the integration of this text into the narrative, four features are to be observed:

1. Chronological derangement as a result of retaining 3:1 from the source in Neh 7:72b–8:1a (see on Ezra 3:1–6 below).
2. The echoing of 5:15 and 6:5, 7 in 2:68, "to erect it on its site": this is a significant plus against Nehemiah 7.
3. The lack of any explicit passage of time between 1:11 and 2:1, suggesting the identity of the two episodes.
4. The mirroring of 1:9–11 in 2:68–69 (with round figures for priestly garments and precious metals in the former): again, an identity of Zerubbabel's with Sheshbazzar's return is implied.

For the chronography of Ezra 1–6, each of these features will prove important.

Ezra 3:1–6

For chronographic purposes, Ezra 3:1–6 is to be severed from 3:7–13, as we shall see. The structure of 3:1–6 has been examined under Ezra 2, above. Verses 2–3 break the time sequence from v 1, which is itself taken over, probably deliberately, from a source (Neh 7:72b–8:1a). Verse 6 then closes the segment by breaking the sequence again, taking us back to the time before 3:4, but after 3:3. So:

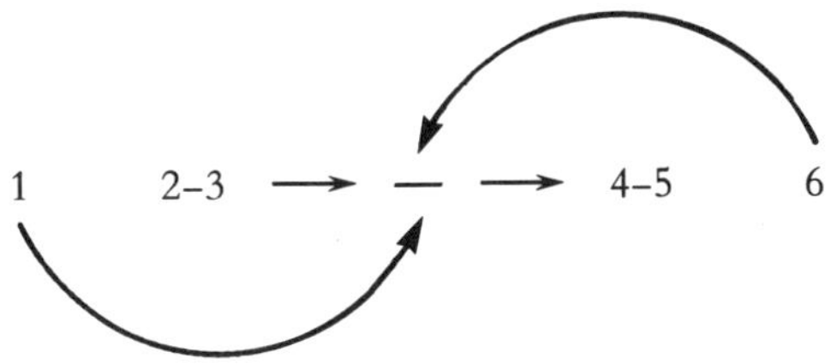

As noted above, the effect is to flatten the shifts in time and to coordinate all the aspects of the altar building.

As sources of this text, and of 3:7–13, Williamson cites Haggai, Zechariah (1983: 23–26), Nehemiah 7–8 (for 3:1), the Aramaic texts in 4:6ff., and Num 29:1–38 (for 3:4–6). The dependence on Haggai is marked. Thus Hag 1:14–15 dates the first work on the temple to Elul 24, from which 3:1–3, 6 (on Tishri 1) follows, and, thereafter, the onset of Sukkot (Tishri 15 in 3:4–5; cf. the fertility language of Hag 1:10–11). Later still, Hag 2:3–9, dated to Tishri 21, provides parallels to Ezra 3:12–13 (Hag 2:3) and 3:7 (Hag 1:8, 2:7–8). This last text also correlates in its details about importing materials to Ezra 6:4, to reality, and to reports of Solomon's temple-building with which the chapter has other contacts (Braun 1979: 52–64). It should, however, be noted that the notices concerning Solomon's materials mention Israelite workmen (1 Chr 22:2–3), metalwork (1 Chr 22:2–3, 2 Chr 2:6), and a variety of trees (2 Chr 2:7, but not 1 Chr 22:4) and agricultural commodities (1 Kgs 5:24–32, 7:13ff.). Ezra 3:7, in contrast, is rather vague. Similarly, the parallel drawn between Solomon's seven-year-long project (1 Kgs 6:38; see Levenson 1984: 288–89) and the seven years between Zerubbabel's arrival and the completion of his temple (3:8 + 6:15) is a bit forced: the historian, had he thought the comparison worth pressing, could have been considerably more clear both in 3:8 (which on this reading is construed to imply inactivity for two years) and overall (further on this below, on Ezra 4:1–5); and, as opposed to the supposed seven years of Ezra 3, those of Solomon do not include the time taken for preparations. Essentially, elements such as the procurement of timber from Lebanon fall into the category of historical coincidence conditioned by practical considerations, or by the desire of the returnees to recapitulate the Solomonic program.

Williamson's only hesitation arises over the identification of Jeshua and Zerubbabel as the builders of the altar in vv 2–3. They are listed in this order only here, and the claim that they built the altar before laying the foundations entails tension with 5:16, where Sheshbazzar is said to have laid the foundations presumably before their arrival (but see below on 3:7–13). Both points suggest the possibility of another source.

Actually, Jeshua appears in conjunction with Zerubbabel, but before him, in Zechariah's night vision. In 3:1–7, Jeshua is installed (cf. esp. Num 8:1–4, 5–22; 19:1ff.; Lev 8:1ff., 33–36). Zech 4:6b–10a probably belongs after 3:8; regardless, 3:8, a proclamation to Jeshua, announces the Davidide and 4:6b–10a soon thereafter names him (Halpern 1978: 169–70). The oracle about Jeshua's installation precedes that, to Jeshua, about Zerubbabel's (3:7, first occurrence of *gam* perhaps refers to Jeshua's ancestor, or to the gods, or to the still uninstalled Zerubbabel). Again, in 6:11–13, Jeshua is crowned; only then is Zerubbabel crowned (4:7, 9–10) and introduced in an oracle to Jeshua. Zechariah thus suggests that in a certain cultic environment, the governor was presented to the (installed) high priest.

Under the circumstances, it is piquing that in Zech 2:1–4, on the heels of an announcement of restoration (1:8–17), the action revolves around "four horns." These symbolize the horns of Judah's old oppressors (Asshur and Babel?). Nevertheless, the image being played upon is that of a four-horned altar (hence the need for stonemasons, against Good 1982: 56–59). In sum, like Ezra 3, and unlike standard Near Eastern accounts of temple-building, Zechariah links the first activity in Zerubbabel's temple-building (and in the Restoration) to the altar, probably figuring the purification of its old site prefatory to its rebuilding; and, like Ezra 3, Zechariah presents Jeshua and Zerubbabel, in connection with the reconstruction of the temple, in that order. Nowhere else is the same order preserved.

This correspondence, which confirms Williamson's position that Zechariah 1–6 furnished a source for Ezra 3, might be thought both to sustain and draw strength from the argument that the night vision comprises a prophetic reverie rendering the ritual of the temple's foundation theologically accessible, by a flight on the wings of symbol (Halpern 1978). D. L. Petersen, however, has subjected this position to a stinging attack (1984: 195–206).

Against an association of the night vision with the temple foundation, Petersen ranges four arguments: (1) "most" references to the temple in the text occur in oracular materials, not in visions, and the two forms cannot be joined (the oracles being secondary); (2) not all visions contain cult imagery (5:1–4, the "covenant curse," is the example); (3) not all the cultic imagery (the altar is the example) relates to the temple-building; and (4) my earlier argument that the text reflects a widespread myth for temple-building rituals is vitiated because the mythic texts from which the pattern is drawn portray the Divine Warrior in active combat, where Zechariah 1–6 do not. Petersen also demurs against the presumption of "pervasive mythic patterns" in the ancient Near East: "These visions focus even less on cultic matters than does Jeremiah's vision of the almond rod focus on ancient Near Eastern horticulture." The arguments are answered in turn.

To the first argument, it would suffice to plead that the historian in Ezra 1–6 had a full text of Zechariah before him, and construed it as on my model. But Petersen's urge to sequester oracular from visionary material stems ultimately from a form-critical broadjump made by J. W. Rothstein (1910). A. Petitjean (1969: 53–88) observes that the two corpora have different orientations and data. Of course they do! Oracular material often serves to render visionary material penetrable—as in passages such as 1 Kgs 22:19–23 and Jer 1:11–19 (Petersen's parallel); it is by nature a sort of prosaizing denaturing of visionary metaphor.

What is the justification for sundering a vision from its interpretation? A decent reflection would divulge that the night vision, if deprived of its explanatory apparatus, would communicate, if at all, only to accomplished mentalists. Consider Petersen's reading: things are " 'in between,' " "on the move," "cosmic"; Zechariah is " 'doing' theology." What did this mean to the hearer? The temple was under construction. The world was being set to rights—theologically, to be sure, and cultically. That there are contacts in the visionary material to the temple at all indicates the integration of visionary with oracular pronouncements: the altar, Jeshua's shriving, the menorah, and the flying scroll all constitute such contacts; and the "first stone" of 3:9–10 and 4:7 relates directly to the seven eyes of 4:10. Finally, the oracular segments contain authentic recollections of the temple building (as 4:6b–10, 3:9–10, 6:9ff.: Petitjean 1969: 179–85; Halpern 1978: 168ff.; and Petersen 1974: 368–71). Even if Zechariah's bizarre visions were transmitted alone, in what context and why were contemporary oracular snippets preserved? What process led the redactor who inserted them to read the night vision as I have done? Did he, too, suffer from the delusion that Zechariah could " 'do' theology" and talk sense both at the same time?

Second, not every vision in the reverie need relate to the temple. Yet, Petersen's example, the covenant curse (Zech 5:1–4), *is* closely tied to the temple: the dimensions of the curse (5:2) are those of the tabernacle, and of the porch (*ʾwlm*, played on by *ʾlh*) of Solomon's temple. Psalms 15 and 24 apply similar sanctions against just the sorts of transgression to which this covenant curse is oriented; the latter is transparently the liturgy of a temple processional. And, in the context of the Restoration (and Ezra 7–Nehemiah 13), no other locus for a covenant curse than the temple is even plausible.

Again, overt links to the temple in several visions (see above) are grounds to take the oracular material seriously, and to seek links between the temple and the remaining visions.

Third, some of the imagery in Zechariah 1–6 has no direct link to the reconstruction of the temple. But in light of Ezra 3, the altar building must be vouchsafed a place in that process. And 4:1–6a, 10b–14 surely figures the ceremony of the temple's foundation (Halpern 1978: 176–77). The installation of the high priest (3:1–7) and the invocation of the covenant curse (5:1–4) are also best related to that occasion: the night vision dates to Shebat 24 of Darius's second year; we are entitled to expect that listeners would take these elements as comment on the cosmogonic program on which they had embarked.

Concerning Petersen's last argument, it is disingenuous to compare mythic with human temple construction. Mesopotamian texts on building and building rituals are purely mundane; their language and sequence link the rituals they describe to the pattern (enshrined in cosmogonic myth) that Zechariah seems to impose on Zerubbabel's temple building. Similarly, Zechariah 1–6 seems to be based on a ritual of temple building (see Halpern 1978: 167ff.), which it reads, allowing for the peculiarities of a monadic cult, as a process of exorcising enemies—those of Israel and the Divine Warrior. It should be added, in defense of the "pervasive mythic pattern" (for which Petersen allows [1984: 198 and n. 11]), that Zechariah's contacts with Mesopotamian building ritual and myth may arise from exposure to Babylonian practice, in a period in which the reconstruction of ruined sanctuaries reached vertiginous heights—indeed, other evidence of influence from Nabonidus's temple-building activities will be adduced below (esp. under the discussion on 4:1–5). Still, preexilic Israelite texts evince the same mythology: sanctuaries were built on the backs of Yhwh's and Israel's enemies (Halpern 1981a: 19–31); if demolished, they were abandoned by the god to chaos, and had to be won back from foes mundane or demonic. This is not to say that the myth (cosmogony) always travelled with the ritual of temple-building: it was a perspective on temple-building available for theologians to draw on. As Enuma Elish illustrates, the myth was linked to the ritual of construction, as a commentary on the divine corollary of it; the ritual was probably adapted to the myth (see Eliade 1943, with comparative evidence; Levenson 1984; and esp. Hurowitz 1983).

All the foregoing tells against Petersen's view, as, too, do the citation of Zechariah's role in Ezra 5:1 and 6:14, Haggai's concern with the temple in the same period, the date of Zech 1:8ff., and the focus of Zechariah 1–6 on chaps. 3–4 (in which the links to the construction are strongest). Zechariah 1–6 culminates in an oracle related to the building in 6:11ff. The relationship between Zechariah 2 and Ezra 3, logically, confirms this line of reasoning. In the relationship it is logical to see further evidence for Williamson's analysis.

Ezra 3:7–13

Concerning the derivation of vv 7 and 12–13, with v 13 a reinterpretation of Hag 2:3, 9, see above on Ezra 3:1–6. Ezra 3:8–11 was presumably derived from ideas of how the sacerdotal orders would have executed the dedication, based in the historian's experience (cf. 1 Chronicles 15; 2 Chronicles 15, 24, 29–30, 34–35), and in the example of Solomon (Braun 1976). (On the chronology, see below on 4:1–5 and section III; for the names of 3:9, see Williamson 1985.) Two features merit remark.

1. Ezra 3:10 mentions singers only of the Asaph guild. The list of returnees with Zerubbabel mentions only Asaphite "singers" (Ezr 2:41 [128], Neh 7:44 [148], 1 Esdr 5:27 [128]). Gese (1974: 147–58) assigns this to an early milieu, before the guild differentiated into three groups, Heman, Asaph and Jeduthun.

Ezra 3:10 has the Asaphites, with priests "dressed" in trumpets (closest is 2 Chr 5:12), singing a refrain (common in Psalms, and 1 Chr 15:34, 16:42; 2 Chr 5:12–13, 20:21, 29:30) identified with Asaph in 1 Chr 15:34, and with Asaph and David here and in 2 Chr 29:30. This refrain is the close of Asaph's song at the ark's placement in David's tent (1 Chr 16:8–34). However, Heman and Jeduthun perform the same song (1 Chr 16:41–42). In these other passages, three guilds of singers are generally active, as throughout Chronicles.

So 1 Chr 6:16–32 traces the lineage of Asaph (Gershom), Heman (Qehath), and Ethan (Merari), who in 1 Chr 15:16–24 and 16:5–6 squire the ark's move. 1 Chr 16:41–42 introduces Heman and Jeduthun (cf. 2 Chr 7:6), and sons of Jeduthun, like Obed Edom (16:38). Thus, Chr includes both Ethan and Jeduthun. In subsequent texts, the singers stem from Asaph, Heman, and Jeduthun (1 Chr 25:1–4, 9–31; 2 Chr 5:12–13; 29:13–15; 35:15; in 2 Chr 20:19–21 Asaph, Qehath [= Heman?], and Qorah [= Qehath!]). 1 Chr 9:15–16 (= Neh 11:17) is an exception, with Asaph and Jeduthun.

None of this signals a shift from an Asaph-Heman-Ethan to an Asaph-Heman-Jeduthun triad. The list of 1 Chr 15:21 and 16:5 includes Obed Edom, son of Jeduthun. Ethan occurs as an individual (1 Chr 6:16–17, 28–32), based on Chr's reconstruction from 1 Kgs 5:11. The picture, then, is of a trio, with omissions in 1 Chr 9:15–16 (Heman), 15:20–21 (Jeduthun), and 2 Chr 20:19, 21 (?Jeduthun). Chr's picture is consistent, and late (Gese 1974).

In linking Asaphites alone to the foundation ceremony, the author of Ezra 3:10 thus follows the list in Ezra 2 rather than the evidence of the later cult. This is not a conclusion to which he was driven: he was entitled to reconstruct two returns—one under Sheshbazzar (1:8, 11; 4:5, 24–5:2; 5:14–16) in 538 and one, under Zerubbabel, before Darius's second year (2:2, 4:24–5:2, 6:15). So, were he reconstructing a foundation under Zerubbabel, and keeping Sheshbazzar's return separate, he might have presumed that all three orders had returned in 538, while Zerubbabel brought only Asaphites. In the absence of an explicit identification of Sheshbazzar with Zerubbabel, and in light of 3:3 and 4:4–5, the text contributes to the impression that Zerubbabel's return, along with all building activity, occurred under Cyrus and Sheshbazzar (5:14–16; see below, section III; cf. above on Ezra 2, Ezra 1 [subpoint 3e], and just below). This will take on considerable significance.

2. The date for the foundation, in the second month of the second year after Zerubbabel's arrival (Ezra 3:8), is peculiar (see below on 4:1–5 for chronology). If set in Darius's second year, it conflicts with later dates in Haggai (1:1–12, 14–15; 2:18), which the historian in Ezra is known to have used (see above on 3:1–6). Williamson suggests the historian is making typological comparison to Solomon by choosing the second month (1985: 47; but cf. Streck 1916: 2.2:11ff.).

Consistent with Williamson's observation is the fact that, against the practice elsewhere in Ezra, no day in the second month is specified—none is given for the start of Solomon's building (1 Kgs 6:1, 2 Chr 3:2 with Naples manuscript, and 𝔊𝔖𝔙𝔄). The "second month," based on Haggai (Darius's second year, ninth month, twenty-fourth day), Zechariah (sometime around Darius's second year, eleventh month, twenty-fourth day), and 4:24 + 3:6, must be that of Darius's third year.

It may seem that a desire to avoid taking the foundation down to Darius's third year (against Hag 2:18) motivated the historian to switch from dating by regnal years in chap. 1 to dating by years of the return in chap. 3. Ezra 3:8 dates the foundation with reference to "the second year of their coming to the house of the god, to Jerusalem" (see below on 4:1–5). This minimized tensions with dates elsewhere. The whole frame of reference was changed: when was "their coming"—under Sheshbazzar/Cyrus, Sheshbazzar/Zerubbabel/Cyrus, or Zerubbabel/Darius?; and, the idea of "the second year" remained. Again, the chronological implications of the text are misleading, either vaguely or deliberately. But further factors are involved (see below on 4:1–5).

Another difficulty is the fact that the Judaeans in 5:16 claim that Sheshbazzar laid the foundation of the temple at the time of the first return. Yet, here, Zerubbabel and Jeshua do the same job, and there is no mention of an earlier attempt. Again, any break between Sheshbazzar and Zerubbabel is being obscured (see #1 in this section). This, it will develop, is also the reason for the switch from regnal- to return-year dating.

The conflicting dates for the foundation defy sure solution. What foundation meant is not clear. It could mean the inauguration of continuous building (cf. 2 Chr 24:27), by Sheshbazzar (per 5:16) and then Zerubbabel, or on-site preparation for building: hence the use of the term to mean the official start of a journey (Ezra 7:9). A ceremony in the second month of Darius's third year is not precluded, even in imitation of Solomon, with the intention of dissolving the builders' temporal status and securing to them the blessings and emoluments lavished on that king (further, Braun 1976, 1979).

Zech 4:8 sees the foundation as the replacement of the first stone (date in 1:8?). Esarhaddon separates the two (Assur A V 3–12, before the first brick in V 17–26). Other Mesopotamian inscriptions confirm what we must in any event have supposed, that the brickwork was laid after the foundation. To the earlier stage belonged extensive ceremony (as Gadd 1953: 124:26–29; Langdon 1912: 256:40). Hag 2:18 may pertain to the first stage (2:15), Zech 4:6b–10a, with the replacement of the first stone, to the later stage.

In any case, if Sheshbazzar did lay a foundation around 538, years of exposure to the elements and vegetation would have necessitated clearing, reorientation by the builders with regard to directional bearings, extensive repair, and a ceremony invoking the god's aid in the completion of the project, cursed by a previous failure. Nabopolassar describes none of this when celebrating the completion of an unfinished temple (Langdon 1912: 66–69; but compare Langdon 1912: 236.1.40–240.3.3, 242.1.43–244.2.10, 246.2.29–250.3.46, 254.16–256.40; and Wetzel and Weissbach 1938:47:39–40, to focus on Neo-Babylonian parallels).

Ezra 4:1–5

Ezra 4:1–5 is the linchpin of Ezra's chronology. Its implications reach back past chap. 3 and forward to chap. 5. Ezra 4:1–3, the rebuff of the "enemies" come to help build, links to 3:8–13. In the absence of other references to Esarhaddon's deportation (4:2), and given a citation of a resettlement by Ashurbanipal (Millard 1976: 1–15; Cogan 1974: 101 n. 23) in 4:10, Williamson suggests that 4:1–3 was culled from one of the letters in 4:6–17 (1983: 26). These letters date, however, from the reigns of Xerxes and Artaxerxes. To judge from the one quoted at length (4:8–16), they argued that the Judaeans, who had long since completed the temple, should be enjoined from compassing the city of Jerusalem as a whole with a defensive fortification.

Williamson's suggestion means that the authors of one of the letters denouncing the fortification, thirty-five years after the event, and implacable in their opposition to Jerusalem, dredged up an episode connected with the temple's construction; the account shows that they, too, had sought *kidinnūtu*, and, worse, that they acknowledged the legitimacy of the temple. This is possible, if their letter argued that, allowed to wall Jerusalem, the Judaeans would exclude outsiders from the temple. Ezra 4:8–16, urging Jerusalem's illegitimacy, contradicts this line. True, 4:8–16 comes from a group other than those in 4:1–5 or 4:6 (on 4:7, see Garbini 1985). But were the opponents in 4:1 identical with those of 4:6, the details of the latter would have enabled the narrator to name the (anonymous) antagonists in 4:1.

The difference between 4:10 (resettlement by Ashurbanipal) and 4:2 (Esarhaddon) is best construed to imply that the historian in 4:2 has some particular group in mind (the memory of deportation being preserved as in 4:10, and in the cases of Israel and Judah); or, that the historian consciously meant to dissociate the figures of 4:1–3 from those of 4:6ff. Whether the approach of the gentile neighbors in 4:1–3 has a literary source in the petition of "Bethel-Sarezzer" and his cohorts (Zech 7:1–7) is a question. As noted below, the text conforms to the standard presentation of temple construction (and Zech 8:20–22, commenting on 7:2). At any rate, references to the terms of Cyrus's edict, and to Cyrus as king of Persia, establish links with chap. 1. Only the content of v 2 could come from a substantive, as distinct from paradigmatic, source.

In fact, there is a strong case against a substantive source. Ezra 4:1–3 has a clear-cut purpose. It explains the delays in building that prevent the completion of the temple until the sixth year of Darius. The starting-point of the delay will be isolated below; but the whole structure together will suggest that 4:1–3 represents an invention, or literary device, based on a retrojection of the incidents of 4:6, 8–23. After all, Zechariah and Haggai never intimate that the "enemies of Judah"—the neighbors transplanted by the Assyrians—impeded the building of the temple. On the contrary, the Judaeans alone are responsible for the delay (Hag 1:2–11), or Yhwh and Mesopotamian powers restrained them (Zech 1:12–15). The neighbors, by contrast, are cooperative, indeed, fellow travelers to the returnees (Zech 7:2–3, 8:18–22, Hag 2:7). And the neighbors' comportment in 4:1–3 fits the impression Haggai and Zechariah create.

Even more tangled is the chronology of 4:4–5, the claim that the gentile neighbors obstructed the builders. Williamson takes these verses as a reprise of 3:3—the altar-builders were fearful of "the peoples of the lands." So, 3:1–6 describes activity in the reign of Cyrus, while 3:7–4:3 introduces the activity of Zerubbabel and Jeshua in Darius's time (Williamson 1985: 44; cf. Talmon 1976: 322). Williamson adds, "It did not serve the purpose of the author's narrative to emphasize the time gap between the two parts of his description at this point" (1985: 47); that is, the author's focus was on positive aspects of the building, not on the issue of communal negligence that looms so large in Haggai (1:1–4, 9). Thus, 4:4–5 takes us from 3:1–6 to 3:7–4:3. This tactic allows Williamson to place the erection of the altar (3:1–6) in a period before Darius. Then 4:4–5, which describes harassment from the time of Cyrus to that of Darius, refers to the pre-Darius contretemps of 3:3—it was because of this contretemps that Zerubbabel, in Darius's time, rejected the gentiles' offer to help (4:3).

This reading represents a decided advance on previous interpretations. Particularly well-founded is the argument that any confusion over the sequence of Achaemenid kings is illusory, a function of an assumption that the text is a chronologically sequential narrative. Jettisoning this assumption, Williamson correctly concludes (following Talmon 1976) that Ezra 4:6–22, which concerns itself with the later city fortification instead of the temple construction, presents parenthetical documentation for the historian's reconstruction of opposition from the people of the land in 3:3 and 4:4–5. The temporal sequence, thus, resumes only in 4:24, in Darius's reign. For all its advantages, the reading does entail problems.

1. Ezra 3:1–6 dates the dedication of the altar to Tishri in the first year of Zerubbabel's return (after 2:68). Ezra 3:7 then describes preparations for building. And 3:8 dates the foundation to Iyyar of the second year of Jeshua's and Zerubbabel's "coming to the [site of the] house of god, to Jerusalem." Williamson must find a chronological seam between 3:1–6, the building of the altar in the time before Darius, and 3:8, the foundation of the temple (set by Haggai and Zechariah in Darius's time). This means placing 3:8 two years after Zerubbabel and Jeshua began collecting materials: Williamson must take "the second year of their coming to the house of god" to mean the second year after they began to devote themselves to reconstructing the building (v 7).

Is so elliptical a reading of 3:8 condign? Nowhere else does "coming to" mean "turning one's attention to (the job of [re]building)." Further, the continuum from 3:1, 4, 6 (seventh month of Zerubbabel's and Jeshua's return) to 3:8 (second month, second year of their return) is strong. Look at the sequence: 2:68, at the outset of Zerubbabel's return, says that "on their coming to the house of Yhwh which is in Jerusalem" the lineage heads made donations; their coming to the temple demanded mention because the lineage heads were, in the terms of 2:1, 70, settled across the countryside. The contrast is to Sheshbazzar (1:11), who came only to Jerusalem (cf. Williamson 1983: 24). Next, 3:1, 6, from the same source as 2:68, speaks of action in the seventh month of the same year; and 3:8 begins, "In the second year of their coming to the house of God, to Jerusalem, in the second month"—the second year after 2:68, at the time of Zerubbabel's return. Whatever the chronological reality, the narrator must have expected that the reader would take this to mean the second year after the return—that is, the time seven months, not two years, after 3:1–6. Otherwise, he would have provided an absolute date, the omission of which is momentous. The altar, therefore, is built in the seventh month of the year of the return, and 3:8 locates the foundation in the second month of the next year.

Had the author meant to assign two years to procuring building materials, he could have said so. He might have said that preparations took a year in 3:7, or written in 3:8 not of "the second year of their coming to the house of the god, to Jerusalem," but "the second year of their preparations." The formulation of 3:8, "their coming to the temple of the god, to Jerusalem," speaks against Williamson's proposal. The least forced reading of 3:8 (and 2:68) identifies "their coming to the temple . . ." with that stage in repatriation when the returnees first arrived, before they dispersed to their lands. We thus have no warrant to read into the passage a temporal break between the altar dedication and the foundation ceremony.

2. Why does Ezra 3:8 fail to date the foundation to the second year of Darius, to which Zerubbabel's foundation of the temple was fixed by Haggai (1:1–2, 2:18), Zechariah (1:8 + 4:9; also 8:9), and references in Ezra 4:5 and 4:24–6:22? If 3:1–6 described events in Cyrus's time, and if there were a temporal break between 2:68–3:6 when Zerubbabel arrived and 3:7 when, after an indeterminate delay, he began to worry about construction, this option could have been exercised. The urge to mortise Ezra 3:8 into the prophetic texts expressed itself in two manuscripts (Myers 1974: 63) that identify the second year in question as that of Darius.

3. If the historian is reconstructing an altar dedication under Cyrus (cf. Japhet 1982: 94), why does he not link it to Sheshbazzar, as 5:16 suggests he should? At no point does he give signs of identifying Zerubbabel with Sheshbazzar, so appeal to such a theory is contraindicated. To the contrary, Sheshbazzar is consistently tied to the time of the Cyrus edict (1:8, 11; 5:14–16), while no such dating of Zerubbabel *need* be implied by any data in Ezra (see below). We may suspect that a source (see below on 6:13–22) associated the foundation with Zerubbabel, not Sheshbazzar, and that, in line with his program to dispel any impression of discontinuity in the construction except that occasioned by local obstructionism, the historian avoided attributing an abortive first foundation to 538. But the same considerations do not apply to the construction of the altar.

4. What led the author of 1 Esdr 3:1–5:1 to deduce that Zerubbabel returned at the start of Darius's reign? His reading of Ezra required him to remove Ezra 4:7–24, under Artaxerxes, to a position before Ezra 2 (1 Esdr 2:15–25). Since he places a reign of Artaxerxes between Cyrus and Darius, he could have avoided this cumbersome expedient by situating Ezra 3:1–6 in Cyrus's reign.

1 Esdras places Zerubbabel's activity in Darius's reign—including the altar dedication (1 Esdr 5:46–52)—presumably because of the traditions in Haggai, Zechariah, and Ezra cited above. This merits remark. 1 Esdras must wrestle with a problematic sequence: Ezra 3:8 sets the foundation of the temple in the second year of Zerubbabel's return; in Ezra 4:1 the enemies of Judah hear and volunteer to help. After their rebuff, 4:4–5 summarizes: "The people of the land discouraged the people of Judah, and impeded their building, and hired advisors against them to frustrate their counsel, all the days of Cyrus king of Persia until the reign of Darius king of Persia." Next come letters to Xerxes and Artaxerxes (4:6–23); and Artaxerxes orders work on the *fortifications* halted. Then 4:24 reads, "Then the work *of the house of the god* that is in Jerusalem halted, and remained at a standstill until the second year of the reign of Darius king of Persia." From this juncture, the narrative proceeds consecutively in the reign of Darius.

From the jumping around (Ezra 3:8, second year of the return; 4:4–5, from Cyrus to Darius; 4:6, Xerxes; 4:7–23, Artaxerxes; 4:24, Darius), 1 Esdras concludes that Ezra 4:6–23 preceded Ezra 3:1–4:3. It further takes Ezra 4:4–5 as a historical reason for Zerubbabel's rejection of the help of the people of the land (1 Esdr 5:69–71), sandwiched between 1 Esdr 5:68 and 6:1ff. (with the error "for two years until," for MT's "until the second year of"). This reading placed the events of Ezra 4:6–24 before Zerubbabel's activity, as the background to his rebuff to the neighbors.

The revision of the sequence in 1 Esdras turns on two considerations: (*a*) Zerubbabel founded the temple with Jeshua in Darius's second year, and therefore Ezra 4:4–5, which starts from the time of Cyrus, was retrospective; (*b*) the Ezra narrative resumes in Darius's second year after 4:24, so that 4:6–24 was to be placed sequentially before Zerubbabel, containing the specifics of the retrospective introduced in 4:4–5, as background to the rationale laid out in 4:4–5. In turn this implied that "the second year of [Zerubbabel's and Jeshua's] coming to the house of the god" (Ezra 3:8) was also Darius's second year, and that Zerubbabel first arrived in Jerusalem a few months after Darius's accession (or after the first New Year after his accession).

The reading in 1 Esdras is thus a nuanced one, not too dissimilar in approach from what Williamson proposes. It recognizes rhetorical resumption, or epanalepsis, as a technique for inserting narrative out of sequence. What comes between Ezra 4:5, the statement that the people of the land impeded building until Darius's reign, and 4:24, a notice that work ceased until Darius's reign, is such an insertion. But 1 Esdras takes it as a retrospective insertion. Josephus is even more explicit: he places a first foundation by Zerubbabel in 538, much along the lines Ezra 1–6 means to suggest (see below) and identifies Artaxerxes in Ezra 4:7–23 as Cambyses (*Antiquities*

11:1:3–2:2). Williamson has shown this is not necessary. He concurs with the author of 1 Esdras that 4:4–5 is a retrospective remark. The materials of 4:6–23 then constitute the temporal digression Williamson has already identified, the thread of the narrative resuming in 5:1, after 4:24 recapitulates 4:5. Ezra 5:1 in fact refers to prophecies by Haggai and Zechariah dated to Darius's second year.

Ezra 4:6–23 is proleptic, not retrospective. It leaps forward to the time of Xerxes and Artaxerxes, Darius's successors, not his predecessors. Hence, the exchange with Artaxerxes concerns the fortification of the town, an issue different from and later than the construction of the temple. Williamson scores the thesis that the historian of Ezra 1–6 misdated Artaxerxes: 6:14 lists the Persian kings in the correct order, not the incorrect, and in any case nothing in 4:6–23 warrants the inclusion of Artaxerxes in such a list (1985: 58, 83–84). Were the narrative sequential, and Artaxerxes Cambyses, 4:6–23 would have been inserted before 2:1, 3:1, or 3:8.

Allowing that 4:4–5 (and 4:6–23) refers to the whole period from 538 on (5:16 corroborates the inference; note Japhet 1982: 69–71, 90–91, 94, where the treatment is similar) resolves the seeming contradictions. There is no chronological break between 3:1–6 and 3:7–4:3. The break occurs rather at 2:1, at the transition from Sheshbazzar in 1:8–11 to Zerubbabel in 2:1–2: the historian requires (for purposes explored below, and in section III) that his readers recognize that the two leaders (termed *pḥh* in 5:14 and in Hag 1:1, 14; 2:2, 21) were active in different periods. This in turn places the altar dedication in Darius's reign, with no links to Sheshbazzar. The foundation in 3:8–13 would then pertain to the second month either of Darius's second year, or, more likely, of his third, the second year after Zerubbabel's return to Jerusalem.

But why does the historian pursue relations with the neighbors down to Artaxerxes in 4:6–23, when the issue is obstruction in Darius's time? The text suggests that Zerubbabel's rebuff provoked the neighbors' enmity: the rebuff (4:1–3) leads to the articulation of their antagonism from the time of Cyrus to that of Darius (4:4–5); then comes 4:6–23, a history of subsequent conflict. The sequence sets the rebuff, and with it the temple foundation, at the start of the trouble with the neighbors. In other words, *ostensibly*, it sets the rebuff and the temple foundation in *Cyrus's reign*.

Now the reason for the switch from regnal-year to return-year dating becomes clear. This obscured the obvious break between Sheshbazzar and Zerubbabel. This is why chaps. 2–3 provide no absolute date for the altar-building, or for anything else. This is why the neighbors must be blamed for obstructing the temple-building. This is why there is no return under Sheshbazzar, but only one under Zerubbabel—there is no explicit temporal shift between 1:11 when Sheshbazzar's return is at the ready, and 2:1 when

Zerubbabel's begins. Zerubbabel's return *was* the return under Sheshbazzar, and it seems likely that the historian expected the reader to identify the *tirshatah* in 2:63 as Sheshbazzar. The same thinking led the historian to identify Sheshbazzar twice as the leader of the Restoration—only he is called *peḥâ*—but to leave the governor unnamed in 6:7, where Zerubbabel must be in point. Scholars have made much of the fact that Zerubbabel disappears when this history leaves off. Even more striking is the fact that Sheshbazzar vanishes in the midst of it.

The historian insinuates that all the action through 4:4 belongs in the period from 538–537—that Zerubbabel returned, built the altar, and founded the temple under Sheshbazzar. So all the delay from 538 to 520 in the building of the temple is blamed on the interference of the neighbors. The transition to Darius is mentioned only at 4:5, 24. Likewise, the renewal of Cyrus's license to build the temple is not an issue until 5:3. Like 1:1, 7, Ezra 3:7 and 4:3, 5 speak of Cyrus as though he were still on the throne. Ezra 5:13, 14, 17 and 6:3, 14 are clear on the fact that he is dead. This is also why the foundation ceremony in 3:10 involves only Asaphite singers: the historian is implying that only the one return took place—that of chap. 2, under both Sheshbazzar and Zerubbabel. For this reason, too, the narrator put in the exiles' mouth in 5:16 the peculiar assertion that Sheshbazzar founded the temple: the exiles are not lying; yet there is no narrative correlative (Josephus supplies one—*Antiquities* 11:2:1). Zerubbabel's foundation is being placed, by implication, under Sheshbazzar. If the reader does not recognize that Zerubbabel's activity all dated to Darius's reign, the chronological seam between 1:11 and 2:1 (and on Williamson's reading between 3:6 and 3:8) is invisible.

Another factor contributes to the general effect. Ezra 3:3 states that the exiles constructed the altar while "in fear from the peoples of the lands." This links to the claim in 4:4–5 that under kings from Cyrus to Darius, the people of the land hectored the exiles. Williamson (1985; cf. Talmon 1976: 322) concludes that 4:4–5 refers to 3:3 to explain why Zerubbabel rebuffs the neighbors. Since the conflict antedates Darius's reign, he reasons, 3:3 must be set before that time. Now, the temple is founded in 3:8, and this occurred in Darius's second year. Here, then, is the reason Williamson must insert two years between 3:6 and 3:8—to remove 3:3 (and the altar) back out of Darius's reign. The expedient, as we have seen, is contraindicated.

Ezra 4:4–5 does not start just before Darius's accession, as Williamson suggests. It covers "all the days of Cyrus . . . and until the reign of Darius" (4:5)—this is the formulation that governs the reconstructions of both 1 Esdras and Josephus. The problem is not Williamson's link to 3:3, though, which is sound. Rather, Williamson—and most other commentators—are misled by the Euclidean axiom that the foundation of the temple is set in

Darius's second year. The author of 1 Esdras does not entirely share this premise. He is a chronological Lobachevskian.

At no point does our sly historian violate the real chronology, in which building begins (Hag 1:2) on Zerubbabel's arrival under Darius. Sheshbazzar plays no active role after chap. 1, and readers who distinguish Sheshbazzar's term as governor from Zerubbabel's (so 1 Esdras) will infer a shift after chap. 1. But the changeover from regnal-year to return-year dating after chap. 1 (and back again in chap. 4) suggests that the ambiguity is deliberate. And the digression to Artaxerxes clouds the shift to Darius in a general chronological upheaval that confounds readers even today: 4:4–23 furnishes background to Zerubbabel's rebuff of the neighbors. Yet it is placed after the foundation in Darius's second year, again concealing the fact that Darius was already on the throne. This must be conscious camouflage.

The historian labors hard to imply that Zerubbabel founded the temple under Cyrus. Thus, in 4:24, the epanalepsis of 4:4-5 starts with *bēʾdayin* 'then': then work stopped until the reign of Darius, as though Darius came *after* Artaxerxes. The text thus *invites* the readings of 1 Esdras and Josephus: Ezra 4:1–5 is followed by obstruction in 4:6–23, and this, in turn, by the resumption under Darius in 4:24ff. But the invitation is ambiguous. 'Then', *bēʾdayin*, can be nonsequential, 'at that time'. In 4:24, it refers not to the time of Artaxerxes, but to that of 4:4–5 in Darius's day (see Williamson 1985: 65). This is probably true of the same term in 5:2, where the coordination of Haggai's and Zechariah's prophecy with the beginning of the building is underscored (5:1, 2b). The ambiguity of the term, however, is so pronounced as probably to be deliberate (see also section III).

Until chap. 4, there is no break in the chronological sequence. The return is ordered, a return occurs; the altar is built, the temple founded; the neighbors hear and are rebuffed. And then 4:4–5 states that they obstructed the building "all the days of Cyrus" through to "the reign of Darius." This is the first indication of a transition from Cyrus to Darius. So, until 4:4, the narrator leaves us around 538, with Cyrus the only relevant font of authority (4:3, 3:7). This vindicates Williamson's link from 3:3 to 4:5: Ezra 3:3 is the first notice of the neighbors' meddling, but, as 4:5 implies, it belongs at the start of Cyrus's reign.

This is also the reason that Haggai and Zechariah are introduced only in chap. 5. Their own books tie them to the foundation of chap. 3, in Darius's second year. But they cannot be brought up in this connection in Ezra, because the historian is implying that the original foundation occurred in 537, under Cyrus. Chap. 3, then, describes Sheshbazzar's foundation, chap. 5 the resumption under Zerubbabel.

In sum, uncritical reading produces the following chronology: (1) the exiles return with Zerubbabel when Cyrus appoints Sheshbazzar governor,

(2) the exiles found the temple, (3) the neighbors turn up and inaugurate a vendetta, and (4) work ceases until the second year of Darius, when Haggai and Zechariah instigate renewed action. Only this reading squares with all the indications reviewed above. Josephus shares it: he departs from 1 Esdras to date the foundation to Cyrus and Sheshbazzar (*Antiquities* 11:2:1).

Overall, Ezra 1–6 presents a dual sequence. In the real chronology, Zerubbabel founds the temple in 520. In the ostensible one, he does so around 537. Only 5:16, the claim that Sheshbazzar laid the foundation (= 3:8–13), may violate the pure duality of the text. The object of this legerdemain is to suggest that work on the temple started early and continued. The "people of the land" obstructed it (see also table 1):

Hebrew	*Aramaic*	*Ostensible Date*	*Real Date*
1. first Return (1)		538	538
2. second Return, founding (2–3)		538–537	521–520
3. neighbors' rebuff (4:1–3)		537	520
4. history of tension (4:4–5)		537–520	—
5.	history of tension later		
	(4:6–23)	?537–460	480–460
	= 4:4–5 (4:24)	?–520	?–520
6.	building starts (5:1–2)	520	520
7.	Tattenai inquiry (5:3–17)	520	520
8.	Darius edict (6:1–12)	520	520
9.	completion (6:13–15)	515	515
10.	dedication (6:16–18)	515	515
11. Passover (6:19–22)		515	515

Some further points must be noted:

1. The first segments record the start without reference to the opposition to it that the historian hypothesizes.
2. The next segments concern themselves with the animosity of the neighbors and the problems this engendered with the Persian authorities, with the exception of 5:1–2, which recapitulates in Aramaic the gist of chap. 3 in the Hebrew: this is necessary to resituate the reader before the introduction of the Tattenai episode in 5:3–6:13.
3. The final segments (nos. 9, 10, 11, and, arguably, 8) deal only with the successful completion of the temple and its celebration.

In short, the chapters are organized by subject matter, not chronology. This is a familiar pattern in Mesopotamian royal inscriptions (as Wiseman 1951: 23; Wiseman 1956: 117ff.; Wiseman 1964: 119–21; Tadmor 1973: 141 [Shea 1979 creates difficulties for dating Joash, and presumes that Adad-Nirari's stelae are all pre-796, not "summary inscriptions"]; Tadmor 1958: 30–32, 35–36 [a geographically ordered original underlying the Nimrud

Prism and Khorsabad annals], 92; Levine 1981:63–64 [Shalmaneser III and Sennacherib]; Cogan and Tadmor 1977: 65–85; and esp. Tadmor 1965). It permits the historian to relocate 4:6–23 from its proper place after chap. 6.

Other than camouflaging the chronology, what are the effects of this strategy? First, after the break in the narrative of temple-building (4:1–3), it became necessary to insert a text, such as 5:1–2, to resume the thread of 3:7–10a (with Williamson 1983, 5:1–2 comes from the historian). The insertion of 4:6–23 softens the repetition. Second, the insertion of 4:6–23 blurs the distinction between the temple-building and fortification, cloaking the latter in the shining raiment of sacred duty that distinguished the former. This is also the impact of Artaxerxes' mention in 6:14, for, regardless of that king's support for the temple (7:15–24), the structure had long since been completed in his day. The fortification becomes the extension, or even the culmination of the temple-building.

The third effect of inserting 4:6–23 at this juncture is to give the impression so vivid in 1 Esdras: that a local opposition instigated the royal decree halting work on the temple in the era from Cyrus to Darius. Without these verses, the inquiry of Tattenai reflects official interest, not a history of opposition: the continuation of the work during the inquiry (5:5) reflects a benevolent disposition. Ezra 4:4–5, at best vaguely consonant with Haggai, did not sufficiently explain the delay in construction. The insertion of 4:6–23, however, effectively absolves the returnees of blame. This is the reason for the tight join between 4:23 and 4:24, including the use of *bʾdyn* in the latter. The historian, who (with Williamson) composed both verses, deliberately dissolved the distinction, chronologically and substantively, between the Artaxerxes correspondence and earlier local opposition, if any. This antedating of the tension with the Assyrian transplants also prepared the reader for Ezra's measures against miscegenation: Zerubbabel's rebuff (4:5) is overtly motivated only by xenophobia.

For the narrative's structure, some comparative evidence is germane. The temple construction scheme in Ezra 1–6 recapitulates predictable Near Eastern topoi (for which see Hurowitz 1983). The Cyrus edict, for example, cites the king's military achievements as a preface to the divine command to build a temple. There follows the enrolment of a labor force (itself called by the god), and contributions (tribute) from the world over. Also included are the elements of securing timber from the mountains, assembling other materials, a joyous sacrificial consecration, and the (rough) coincidence of the consecration with the coming of the New Year (6:15, 19; cf. Gudea Cylinder B).

There are also texts in which temple building is interrupted—the building of the Tabernacle (Exodus 24–40, Leviticus 8–10) furnishes an instance in which the divine command to construct a sanctuary (Exodus

24–31) is followed by revolt (Exodus 32–34) before being fulfilled (oral observation, V. Hurowitz). Not too far removed is the course of events in Nabonidus's Harran inscription: in a dream, the god Sîn ordered him to rebuild Ehulhul in Harran (Gadd 1958: 56.11–14); but trouble and treachery among the people of Akkad (56.14–58.22) led to a ten-year delay (58.23–27). This is the period of his sojourn in Teima, from the fourth to the thirteenth year of his reign (Tadmor 1965: 356). Finally, Nabonidus pacified his foes, and returned to execute the project entrusted him (58.28–64.22, possibly with a second dream in 62.3.3–4). Here, the sequence resembles that in Ezra, and "neighbors" interrupt the building.

A different recension appears in Nabonidus's Sippar cylinder. There, the order to build is warrantied by a sign—the defeat of the Umman-Manda (cf. the dream requiring explication in Gudea Cylinder A; note Thureau-Dangin 1925). The fulfilment of this sign indicates that the time has come to act (Langdon 1912: 218–20.1.16–35). Three parallels merit remark: the temple, like that of Solomon, is in ruins; the Umman-Manda (corresponding to the Babylonians, or, later, to the local opponents) destroyed it and now obstruct its rebuilding (1.23–24); and, it is not Nabonidus himself (like the returnees), but Cyrus (as against Babylon, or like Darius *vis-à-vis* the neighbors) who overcomes them (1.28–32). It is important to note that underlying this elaborate treatment is the disquieting conviction that Nabonidus should have restored the sanctuary at the start of his reign (Tadmor 1981:23). What is more, the inscription deliberately uses imprecise chronological terminology to antedate the work on Ehulhul to Nabonidus's sixth year (when the Medes were defeated) or even his third year: the phrases *rēš šarrūti* 'accession-year' and *ina šalulti šatti* 'in the third year' are used figuratively to denote the "early part of the reign" and "the culmination of the cycle of events" respectively (Tadmor 1965: 352–58). The Babylon stela may be even more radical in this respect, possibly tracing the work in Harran to Nabonidus's accession (Langdon 1912: 285.10.12ff.).

Nabonidus's Sippar cylinder attributes the demolition of the sanctuary to the god's rage against Harran (cf. Gadd 1958: 46.6–9; Langdon 1912: 218.1.1.8–13, 270.8.1.1–274.2.41, 284.10.12–19). This is standard with ruined sanctuaries. Merodach-Baladan deals identically with the Assyrian domination of Babylon (Gadd 1953: 123.8–9). Esarhaddon exploits the motif against this king when relating the rebuilding of Babylon and Esagila (after a devastation that Marduk originally decreed to be seventy years long; Borger 1956: 13.5, 14.8, 15f.10), much as Cyrus deploys it (Cylinder 9–10, 31–35) against Nabonidus. It is used, thus, both by builders who complete interrupted projects and by those who through conquest come into possession of unfinished works (see also Cogan 1974: 9–21). Sargon detaches the motif from temple-building (Marduk summoned him against Merodach-Baladan) in the Khorsabad annals composed in 706, three years after he became king of Babylon (Lie 1929: 42.268–73).

Ezra 5:12 tells the same story, prefacing it to an account of the Cyrus edict (5:13–15), although, addressed to the Persian authorities, it does not introduce the element of the god's forgiveness. The displacement in the paradigm is that it is not the god's, but the authorities' permission that must be sought to build the temple: the Persian state stands to the returnees as Yhwh to the Israelites after Exodus 32, as Marduk to Esarhaddon, or as Marduk and Sîn to Nabonidus. But there is no affront for the Persians to forgive. Ezra 4:6–23 supplies one: the town was "rebellious and wicked" (vv 12, 15, 19); the records show it.

That this is a concern at all has to do with the narrator's strategy of mixing together the issues of temple-building and fortification. The relationship between the Rehum and the Tattenai correspondence is the key. Tattenai's inquiry (5:3–4) might have elicited the simple answer that Cyrus authorized the reconstruction of the temple. Instead, we have a long historical recital, quoted in Tattenai's letter, in 5:11–16. This responds as much to Rehum's and Artaxerxes' concerns as to immediate historical circumstance. It airs those concerns because they are germane to the theology of temple reconstruction in the paradigm the author of Ezra has adopted.

Ezra 5:11–16 characterizes the (temple) construction as follows: (1) The Judaeans are building in their capacity as "servants of the god of heaven and earth" (5:11). They are not intent on revolt, as Rehum claims (4:13). (2) They are rebuilding an old and venerable structure (5:11), evidence that the task on which they are engaged is sacred, not political (against 4:12–13, 15–16). (3) The temple was first built by a great king (5:11), whom they emulate in the sacral realm; the reconquest of the region is not their aim (against 4:20, read to imply that it is). (4) Sin against their god precipitated their ancestors' ruin (5:12), implying that the temple's reconstitution is necessary for placation, and that a history of political rebellion (against 4:12, 15, 19) is not germane. (5) It was Nebuchadnezzar who exiled them (5:12), Cyrus who championed them (5:13ff.), so that their loyalties are to the Achaemenids, proof against hostile agitation. Formal links between the Tattenai correspondence and that of Rehum are also to be noted: Artaxerxes' archive work divulges the truth of Rehum's accusations, Darius's that of the Judaeans' defense (4:15, 19; 5:17; 6:1). Artaxerxes appears alongside Cyrus and Darius in 6:14. And the Rehum exchange is inserted precisely at Darius's second year, the time of the Tattenai inquiry: this was a deliberate decision, as 4:5b need not have appeared until after 4:24.

In sum, the motif of suspended building in 4:6–24 and 5:3–6:12 (despite 5:5, the effect is similar) is adopted as an opportunity to pursue the narrator's strategy of integrating the temple-building with the wall-building, a linkage already intimated in Isaiah 44–45 and Zechariah 1–6. Ezra 4:6–23 furnishes an opportunity to introduce the motif of divine abandonment, in a theologically acceptable form, in 5:11ff. This in turn carries the implication that the issue, in Ezra 5–6 and, too, in 4:6–23, is removed from the realm of politics, and plugged into that of piety. The loyalty of the restoration community is incontestable.

There were other options available for the presentation of the same data. Nabopolassar records that he completed a temple begun by an earlier king, introducing the project and its history only after a prologue in which he mentions the overthrow of his foes by Marduk (Langdon 1912: 69.15–24; closely parallel is Neriglissar 2). But Nabopolassar spotlights his own achievements, not those of the Babylonians as a whole, so that it is unnecessary for him to explain the interruption in construction. A dedication inscription of Zerubbabel might assume very much the same cast. Our historian, however, is concerned not with the glory of Zerubbabel, but with the history of the Restoration community as a whole, so that this model is inappropriate to him.

Another, intermediate option appears in Merodach-Baladan's inscription concerning the restoration of Eanna, the temple of Ishtar in Uruk. This text speaks first of a longstanding need for repair (lines 1–7), the wrath of the god and consequent lordship of the Assyrians, which prevented the temple's restoration, and, finally, the defeat of the Assyrians and reconstruction of Eanna by the king. Here, again, an external enemy (whose regime is the product of earlier divine wrath) has prevented the reconstruction. One might expect some sin, therefore, to be imputed to the royal predecessors. Instead, the epigraph seems to imply that it was the earlier kings' inaction with regard to Eanna that precipitated Marduk's wrath, but that the key problem was "the wicked Assyrians." Both the predecessors' inaction (cf. Haggai) and the neighbors are blamed.

In other words, Ezra 1–6 exploits established modes of conceptualizing and describing the reconstruction of a ruined temple. What historically occasioned the delay in the construction between 538 and 520 we cannot know. But the first opportunity to explain it, without breaking into the narrative with a fabrication, came after 4:3. It is noteworthy that 4:3 enjoys a sort of parallel in Esarhaddon Assur A (Borger 1956: 7.13–15): Esarhaddon introduced gifts from across the world to the newly dedicated sanctuary, but to placate Asshur kept foreigners away from it (also Ezek 44:7).

The use of a similar motif in Ezra services several narrative concerns: to exonerate the returnees from the charge (Haggai) of failing to execute their sacred duty to complete the temple; to underscore the continuity of efforts to rebuild the temple from the time of Cyrus on; to document the indurate enmity between Jerusalem and its "foes" in the countryside; to equate Jerusalem's fortification with the temple-building; and, definitively, to interpret the causes of Judah's earlier destruction, so as to reassure secular authorities of her continuing loyalty, to win their assent to her ongoing development, and, by avoiding Merodach-Baladan's tactic (above), to accomplish the other programmatic aims, apologetic and polemical, listed here.

Overall, however, the narrative's tessellated chronography reflects a sense that, in spirit, all the action of the Restoration could legitimately be homogenized into a "first movement" of the Return—that it all should have been, in fact. This homogenization—including the nonchronological use of *bēʾdayin*—has parallels in Mesopotamian historiography not just in the texts of Nabonidus, but stretching back to Sargon II (Tadmor 1981: 14–25), and in the notion of a king's achieving universal "victory" in a single year (Stuart 1976, to which add Tadmor 1973: 141, 143 and nn. 14–18 with cases from Shamshi-Iluna and the Suppiluliuma-Mattiwaza treaty [BoSt 8: 14.46]). Closely parallel, too, are the texts in which Esarhaddon antedates the reconstruction of Babylon to his *rēš šarrūti* (accession year; see Cogan 1983: 85–87); here, however, the chronological terminology is applied literally—there is no dual chronology, as in Ezra or the texts of Nabonidus. The ancient Near Eastern notion appears to have been that the king ideally acted out, in the first year, his accomplishments for the rest of time: "The which observ'd, a man may prophesy, with a near aim, of the main chance of things as yet not come to life, which in their seeds and weak beginnings lie intreasured. Such things become the hatch and brood of time" (*Henry IV*, Part 2).

Ezra 4:6–5:2

Ezra 4:6–22 is based on letters, two cited extensively (4:8–16, 17–22; on 4:9–10, 17b see Porten 1983; on the rubrics see below on 5:3–6:5; on the terminology see Dion 1981). This material is inserted achronologically (for what follows, see above on 4:1–5). Ezra 4:23 caps the sequential fillip, while 4:24 recurs to 4:5. However, 4:4–5 is also out of sequence, spanning the period from 2:1 forward, or 3:1 (hence already 3:3), ostensibly under Cyrus.

If, with Williamson (1983), we are to avoid hypothesizing a compilation of the Aramaic source before the writing of Ezra 1–6, the historian must have supplied 4:24–5:2. This is consonant with the logic actuating the insertion of 4:6–23, which advances ideological programs already in evidence in the Hebrew (for example, no break between Sheshbazzar and Zerubbabel, exoneration of the returnees, fixing blame on local opponents, etc.). It also dovetails with the coordination of the answer to Tattenai with the concerns raised in the Artaxerxes correspondence (see above on 4:1–5).

Gunneweg (1982) has refurbished the old case for an Aramaic source, noting: (1) the absence of Levites in the Aramaic until 6:18, 20; (2) the use of "elders" in the Aramaic, against "lineage heads" in the Hebrew, the former with external, the latter with domestic authority; (3) the resistance in Aramaic being to the fortification, not the temple-building; (4) the deranged chronology in 4:4ff.; (5) the lack of an interruption of the temple-building, despite the demands of the Hebrew in 4:5; and (6) the naming of opponents in the Aramaic, who obstruct the Judaeans at the court, not locally, as in 4:4–5.

Of these arguments, *(1)* and *(2)* reflect the difference in subject matter (and usage) in the segments covered. (For the elders and external relations, see Halpern 1981b: 198–206; cf. Reviv 1983.) Items *(3)* and *(4)* collapse on the view of 4:6–23 offered above (in the discussion of 4:1–5), and chronological derangement is not limited to this pericope. Item *(5)* in effect conflicts with *(4)*, since it is precisely the report of interruption, in 4:8–23 (albeit of the fortification) that permits the historian to satisfy the demands of the Hebrew. And *(6)* is a function of the historian's reluctance to identify the group of 4:1–3 with that active in Artaxerxes' time: this would have queered his dual chronology.

There are other differences between the Hebrew and Aramaic segments:

1. Ezra 5:11 and 6:5, 7 are explicit that reconstruction, not new construction, is in point. Ezra 1:1–4 does not make the distinction. The variation is puzzling.
2. Ezra 5:16 claims Sheshbazzar founded the temple, while chap. 1 makes no such claim. This expedient denies discontinuity either between Sheshbazzar and Zerubbabel, or in the reconstruction of the temple (see above under 3:1–6, 3:7–13, and 4:1–5, and below on section III). It answers Rehum (and 4:12); it is the only text in which the ostensible (not real) chronology of Ezra 1–6 is unambiguously set forth, and alleges that Cyrus's license to build never lapsed (against 4:24), in which sense its import does not contradict the real chronology (see above, p. 88). Depending how one takes the term "foundations," there may or may not be a contradiction in substance.
3. Ezra 4:10 attributes deportations to Asnappar, 4:2 to Esarhaddon. Different groups are in point (see above), writing different letters (4:6, 8).
4. Ezra 5:14 terms Sheshbazzar a *pḥh*; 1:8 uses *nāśîʾ*. (See above on Ezra 1.)
5. Ezra 5:13 rightly calls Cyrus king of Babylon (6:3 has no title). Ezra 1:1, 2, 8; 3:7; and 4:3 call him king of Persia. The Hebrew references are anachronistic, derived from later titulature, in contexts in which the historian is reconstructing. Ezra 5:13–15 cites the proclamation and 6:3–5. The latter may originally have identified Cyrus as king of

Babylon, but lost the designation by a haplography that was then partially restored. The fact that 6:14, in Aramaic, calls Cyrus (and Darius and Artaxerxes) king of Persia suggests that the correct title in 5:13 comes from a different document.

6. Ezra 4:24 has a construction stoppage until the second year of Darius, 4:5 until the reign of Darius. The reader's tendency is to link 4:24, if not to the order of Artaxerxes in 4:21–22, to the action of the neighbors in 4:4–5. In other words, the passage reads like a *progressive* epanalepsis (as in Gen 15:12, 17; Judg 3:23a, 24a; or Judg 3:26a, 26c), in which the second member of the epanalepsis picks up the action described in the first member at a later stage. It dates the cessation of work to the period before 521. The natural reading identifies the cessation with that period mentioned in 4:5, "all the days of Cyrus and until the reign of Darius." Ezra 4:5 thus advances the subtext of continuity, implying that 3:1–6 takes place under Cyrus and Sheshbazzar (see table 1, and above on 3:7–13 and 4:1–5). In reality, however, 4:24 is an epanalepsis recapitulating 4:4–5, not following from it. The historian has hooked suspension in the temple building until Darius in 4:24 onto the later order of Artaxerxes to suspend the fortification. So, in the real chronology, 4:24 restates 4:4–5: from Cyrus's *and Sheshbazzar's* day in chap. 1 to Zerubbabel's in chap. 2, the gentiles had blocked the building; hence, when Zerubbabel resumed construction (3:2, 8), he rebuffed the neighbors (4:1–3). In the ostensible chronology, 4:24 implies that the temple building ceased from Cyrus's and *Zerubbabel's* time, in 3:8–13, to Darius's (and Zerubbabel's) time in 5:1–2.
7. Ezra 5:1–2 and 6:14 (Aramaic) mention the role of Haggai and Zechariah in the construction of the temple; chap. 3 does not. The object is to dissociate the ministry of the prophets from action the historian's ostensible (not real) chronology places in the period before Darius. While Zerubbabel could be antedated into Cyrus's or Cambyses' time, after all, Haggai and Zechariah could not. The historian elected to link the prophets' efforts to the renewed building he reconstructed in Darius's second year.

Overall, there is no cause to hypothesize a compilation of the Aramaic material prior to the writing of Ezra 1–6. The chronological irregularities in 4:24–5:2 line up with others in the Hebrew, sustaining Williamson's point. Thus, 4:24 picks up the thread of a segment (4:4–5) that was already out of its chronological environment. Ezra 4:24 takes us back before 2:1 (or 4:4). Then, 5:1–2 brings us up to Darius's second year on the ostensible chronology, contemporary with 3:1 on the real chronology.

The time sequence through 5:2 may be represented as follows:

$$1 \rightarrow 2 \rightarrow 3 \rightarrow 4{:}1\text{-}3 \parallel 4{:}4\text{-}5 \parallel 4{:}6\text{-}23 \parallel 4{:}24 \rightarrow 5{:}1\text{-}2$$

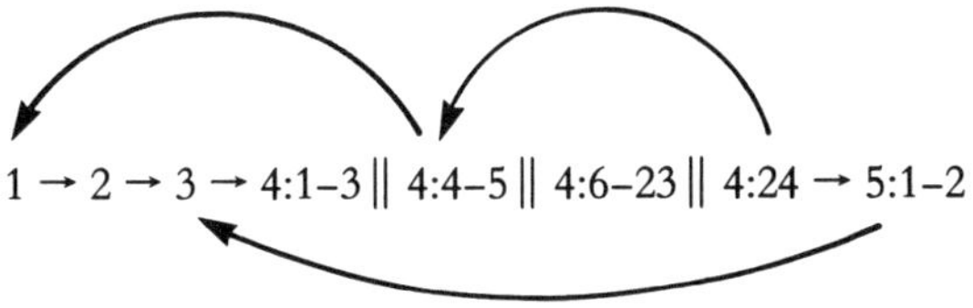

From this juncture, the chronological sequence is unbroken.

Ezra 5:3–6:12

Ezra 5:3–6:12 is source-based: letters are cited in 5:6–17 and 6:1–12. Ezra 5:3–5, framing the first letter, derives from it. Verse 3b comes from v 9b, without the opening. Verse 4a takes its opening from v 9, while v 4b recasts v 10a in direct address, modeled on v 9. The first-person usage of v 4, derivative from v 9, suggests the use of an original. Tattenai's name and rank certainly came from some source, probably this letter (*VAS* 4:152:25; Olmstead 1944). There is additional verisimilitude in Tattenai's request for an archive search in Babylon (5:17), where Cyrus issued the edict, ending in a find at Ecbatana (6:2; see Tadmor 1983: 15). Tattenai's inquiry after the names of the leaders also elicits no real answer; this implies that his letter is excerpted. At the least, an annex with the names has been suppressed. Darius's response mentions the "governor" (6:7), where in Tattenai's report only Sheshbazzar, long in the past, is so called (5:14); here we have another blurring of the lines between Zerubbabel and Sheshbazzar—only the latter is identified as governor. Last, the claim of 5:5 that work on the temple continued presumably reflects consultation with a source, given the tendency observed above to identify later interruptions of the fortification with delays in the temple building. It derives from Tattenai's submission, or from a close reading of 5:8, along the lines Williamson suggests (1985: 77). The historian will not have foregone the opportunity to lay a cessation of the building at the doorstep of the community's opponents.

The correspondence between the Judaeans' defense in 5:11–16 and the Rehum correspondence (see above on 4:1–5) indicates that the historian worked the letters over. Ezra 5:11–17 also relates closely to Darius's answer in 6:1ff. (see above on Ezra 1). The correlation between 5:8 and 6:14 on the progress of the work is explicable by the supposition that 6:14 stitches together 5:1–2 (the prophets' role) and 5:8, so that no revision in 5:8 need be postulated. On the other hand, 5:8 does name the building materials, linking both to 6:4 and to 3:7. The thematic dovetail between the letter and its context is hardly aleatory.

Note that the rubrics of the letters in 4:8–10 and 5:6–7 are similar.

4:8–10	*5:6–7*
senders	copy of letter sent
sent letter	senders
topic	—
addressee	addressee
then senders	—
"and now"	—
copy of letter sent him	letter sent him
—	written thus
To Artaxerxes	To Darius, greeting
senders	—
"and now"	—
Let it be known . . .	Let it be known . . .

In each case (the other full rubric to the king is in 4:7), there is notice that a copy is being provided; and, while 5:7 does not repeat the names of the senders, there is duplication between the rubric and the salutation. This is not the case with the royal responses. In 5:17, no information is repeated. One might suggest that the introduction of Rehum's communication eliminated the need to signal the reader that a source is being quoted. In 6:3–6, however, Darius's letter is without a rubric; it flows from direct narration. Haplography is possible, by homoioteleuton from a narrative account of the finding of Cyrus's decree, which duplicated the opening of Darius's letter. However, the technique here resembles that of 1:2–4, although 6:6 implies the start of the letter earlier. And the linkage, artificial insofar as it insinuates that Darius had no personal role in the decision at stake, between 5:17 and 6:1 resembles that between 4:23 and 4:24. A merging of types of discourse (and times) is in point. At a minimum, the use of the letters gives evidence for the historian's editing even of sources he quotes openly.

One other factor also suggests that the historian interprets and recasts his sources rather than rendering them verbatim. Although the concern with sacrifices in Ezra 6:8–10 squares with 6:3–4, the Cyrus cylinder, Ezra 7:17, 21–22, 23 and, for example, Streck 1916: 222–23, the curse in 6:11–12 is without parallel in Darius's inscriptions. These elsewhere refer to his successors, where 6:11–12 is directed ("any king or people") toward foreigners. Modification to redirect the curse to the local opponents may be in evidence.

Ezra 6:13–22

Ezra 6:13–15 follows from the preceding materials, except for the mention of Artaxerxes in 6:14 (explored above). However, the record of the temple's completion must reflect a concern to consecrate it at the New Year (between 6:15 and 6:19; see Morgenstern 1955: 62 n. 3). On the basis of Mesopotamian parallels and the information contained in the account of Solomon's temple-building (see Hurowitz 1983), we should expect some monumental commemoration by Darius and by the builders mentioning the consecration. It is not necessary to hypothesize such a text (see below, and section IIIA). But reliance on one would harden the choice not to describe a foundation by Sheshbazzar, an element mentioned (5:16) only to establish that Cyrus's edict had not lapsed. This concern is one motive to stress the continuity between Sheshbazzar and Zerubbabel. There would have been no (defensible) monument of Sheshbazzar's.

The failure to switch over from Aramaic at this point is puzzling. D. Snell's suggestion that the Aramaic is used to vouch for the authenticity of the sources (1980: 33–34) runs afoul of this peculiarity. Implied is a close link of the construction to the dedication (6:16–18). This does not concern us here, except as the logical conclusion to the narrative. It was all liable to reconstruction, including the elements of "joy" in 6:16 (cf. 1 Chr 16:27 and Neh 8:10) and sacrifice in 6:17 (with the animals of Darius, 6:9, and the sin offerings, as 8:35 and 2 Chr 29:21). However, the same elements would have appeared in a dedicatory inscription, possibly bilingual (in deference to Darius), use of the Aramaic portions of which would adequately explain the historian's remaining in that language through v 18. This is perhaps the sole strong point in favor of an inscription from 515.

Williamson takes the position (1985: 73–74) that the historian has already provided narrative framework in Aramaic (primarily 4:24–5:2), and that he therefore closed the narrative unit in that language. This makes sense in a bilingual environment; but it is difficult to see why the next "unit," and the switch to Hebrew, begins in 6:19 rather than 7:1. Too, the date in 6:15 is drawn from a source (dedicatory or antiquarian); and, if this was not Aramaic, the decision to render it into Aramaic is a curiosity. There is a further consideration: Ezra 6:13 and 14a,c both draw on the evidence of the Tattenai correspondence. But v 14b does not imply close reading in Haggai and Zechariah (contrast on 3:1–6, above). And, the citation of the Torah in 6:18 does not refer to a particular passage, but to (P's) general instructions concerning the installation of the priesthood (see Japhet 1977: 203ff. for similar usage in Chr). In all, we may speak of a generalized citation of Hebrew sources and a close use of Aramaic. For vv 15–18, use of a dedication may be indicated.

The text makes the claim that the Restoration embraces all Israel (v 17; see above on Ezra 1). This is the further implication of vv 19–22, in Hebrew, about the Passover (esp. v 21), which echoes elements of Hezekiah's celebration (as 6:20, 2 Chr 30:3, and above). Here, again, in contrast to the Chronicler's account of that comparable occasion, the exclusion of the neighboring community (v 21) enters into consideration, in line with concerns expressed in 3:3 and 4:1–5 and in the use of the Aramaic materials. This element links to Ezra 7–Nehemiah 13. It explains the purity of the whole community (6:20), as against the problems encountered by Hezekiah. The Passover thus represents the historian's construct, and the shift into Hebrew reflects the fact.

III. Implications

This survey concurs with Williamson's fundamental conclusions on the assembly of Ezra 1–6 in a single stage (without a prior compilation of the Aramaic source) and on its anteriority to Ezra 7–Nehemiah 13, although I depart from him on particulars. The possibility remains open that conclusions concerning the use of sources in Ezra 1–6 may lead to modifications of the preliminary results achieved above. After such extensive remarks, however, a few key points merit special mention.

A. *The Historiographic Profile of Ezra 1–6*

Some of the historiographic properties of the text have long been obvious: close reliance on sources, such that effectively only the details of cultic service (of interest also to Chr), the early interference of Judah's neighbors, and some wording in the correspondence are supplied entirely from the historian's imagination; frequent reference to Chr's accounts of Solomon and Hezekiah (see Braun 1979), another trait of Chr (Halpern 1981b: 36–52; Braun 1976: 581–90); the generalized reference to the Torah (see above on 6:13–22) and the role of normative concerns in the reconstruction and presentation (again characteristic of Chr). I might add the avoidance of anachronism at 3:10, which restricts itself to Asaph, comparable to cases in Chr (Willi 1972: 183–84), but here dictated by the urge to homogenize the return into a single, early movement. Finally, there is the dissection of the Cyrus edict, so that the return of the temple vessels is rendered in direct narrative, but the edict remains in discourse, in chap. 1. This apparently follows from the reconstruction of an edict directed toward the exiles there, based on common sense and on documentation in 6:3–5. None of these properties should excite special historiographic interest.

The sources themselves were few. Perhaps Jeshua and Zerubbabel left a record at the dedication; possibly, such a record of their activity originally formed the endpoint of Chr (Freedman 1961: 440; but see section IIIB below). The list in 1:8–10 was preserved or reconstructed, and Nehemiah 7 was read carefully to imply that the *tirshatah* and Zerubbabel were not one and the same individual. Its list of donations was treated as though equivalent to those Sheshbazzar brought to Jerusalem. The letters in chaps. 4–6 (Tattenai's with detail added) were used to great effect. And Zechariah and Haggai were scrutinized for details of the foundation, even though this was retrojected, somewhat boldly, to Sheshbazzar in the ostensible chronology of the text (one could make a case that Hag 2:18 entitled the historian to sever the foundation from the day of the oracle). Still, the historian did not attribute the foundation to Sheshbazzar himself, in line with Zechariah's statement that "the hands of Zerubbabel founded this temple" (4:9). Ezra 3:1–6 reflects in part Zech 2:1–4, while 3:7–13 exhibits close contact with Zech 4:6–10 and Haggai.

A feature to which insufficient attention has hitherto been paid is the treatment of royal pronouncements in Ezra 1:1ff., 4:17–23, and 6:1–12. In the first and third cases, the decrees are all but interchangeable with direct narrative, so that the lines between them blur (see above on Ezra 1 and 5:3–6:12). Artaxerxes' salutation in 4:17 is treated in a similar vein. The king's word, then, is so charged as to be virtually indistinguishable from its accomplishment: execution follows inexorably; royal commands enjoy a potency comparable only to that of Yhwh's word (cf. Throntveit 1987 on Chr). The exaggerated deference to authority the text exhibits coincides with the implication of the Aramaic material that the loyalty of the returnees is unmitigated (see above on 4:1–5). In sum, kingship remains a focus of the historiography in Ezra 1–6, the mainspring of which, after all, is Cyrus's edict, summarized three times and cited; but it is the Persian kingship that occupies this place, not the Davidic. In connection with royal decrees, therefore, the historian's thematic concerns lead him to modify his mode of citing sources.

Prominent among thematic concerns in the narrative is the continuum from Yhwh, through Cyrus and Sheshbazzar, to Zerubbabel and Darius. No report of a break, chronologically or in the fulfilment of Cyrus's sacred mission, interrupts the sequence from 1:1–4:1. The careful avoidance of Heman and Jeduthun at 3:10, noted above, has the implication, not coincidental, that there was no return other than Zerubbabel's (chap. 2) in the early period, in which singers other than Asaphites might have come to Judah. Ezra 5:16 reinforces this impression, in a segment that has disgorged evidence of the historian's hand (see above on 4:1–5 and 5:3–6:12), probably reworking a source. The source in 3:1 was retained for substantially the same reasons (see above on Ezra 2). And the list of temple vessels returned by Cyrus through Sheshbazzar appears, in 1:8–11 alone, as a mirror image of the donations Zerubbabel extracted from the Judaeans (2:68–69). The historian's techniques for promoting the impression of continuity and for creating a dual chronology have been examined in some detail above (on 4:1–5).

There is, of course, evidence of discontinuity in 4:4–5, 24, the impact of which is magnified deliberately by the insertion of 4:8–23. Still, this material is carefully placed so as to avoid suggesting a transition between Sheshbazzar and Zerubbabel. Even the system of dating in chaps. 2–3 is altered (from regnal years) to leave the revealing chronology overtly vague (see above on 3:7–13): in light of Haggai and Zechariah, the key sources for this part of the account, the omission of an absolute date in Darius's second or third year is little short of incredible. And the technique of relating Sheshbazzar's return only indirectly, implicitly in the use of the sources of chap. 1, helps obscure the distinction between his and Zerubbabel's returns.

All this throws Zerubbabel's activity in the overt chronology back to the time of Cyrus and Sheshbazzar around 538 (see table 1). The effect was, first, to blame local opposition for the suspension of the building; antedating this opposition, against the evidence of Haggai and Zechariah (and Ezra 4:1–3), to the time of the temple's construction exonerated the returnees of divine blame, and carved out a platform position on the conflict between the returnees and the peoples of the land. Second, the antedating endowed Zerubbabel with the legitimacy of Sheshbazzar in respect of the Persian authorities. This was no doubt a contemporary concern in 520, and it might therefore be argued that 5:16 formed an original part of Tattenai's submission.

The concern with continuity does not, however, stop at Zerubbabel. It also manifests itself in the author's view of the returnees' public works. The insertion of 4:6–23 identifies the fortification of Jerusalem as an extension of the temple building. Here, tight linkage between 4:23 and 4:24 (which has valence also to 4:5) plays an important role. Even more important is the dialogue between 4:12ff. and 5:11–13: the latter, which defends the temple building, rebuts the former, which attacks the fortification of the city. The inclusion of Artaxerxes in 6:14 enhances the effect (see above on 4:1–5).

It is his single-minded pursuit of these and related themes that spurs the historian to his most striking methodological virtuosity. Several traits may be isolated in the corpus with relative confidence. The adaptation of source documents has been subject to examination above (on Ezra 1 [subpoints #1–2 and the conclusion], 4:1–5 [beginning paragraphs], and 5:3–6:12). It represents, relatively, a regular feature of the author's compositional repertoire.

This is not an operation that the historian performed with any foul intent. Editing documents is a normal historiographic procedure. Even the probable recasting of 5:11–13 violates the letter more than the spirit of the

TABLE 1. *The Chronology of Ezra 1–6*

Pericope		Leaders	Chronology: Ostensible Date	Chronology: Real Date
1:1–11	*Return ordered*	*Shesh* : *Cyrus*	538	538
1:9–11	30 gold *ʾgrṭl*, 1,000 silver *ʾgrṭl*, 29 "changes," 30 gold bowls, 410 silver (?)secondary bowls, 1,000 other vessels: all the vessels, silver, and gold, 5,400.			
2:1–70	*Return with Zerubbabel*	*Zerub* :	538	521
2:69	61,000 gold drachmas, 5,000 silver minas, 100 priestly robes.			
2:63	The *tirshatah* told them that they would not eat from the "holy of holies"....			
2:68	Of the lineage heads, at their coming to the house of Yhwh, which is in Jerusalem, some made offerings to the house of the god to erect it on its site.			
3:1–6	*Altar dedication*	*Zerub* :	538	521
3:1	And the seventh month arrived, and the children of Israel were in their towns, and the people assembled as one man to Jerusalem.			
3:3	They erected the altar on its site, for they were in fear from the peoples of the land.			
3:6	From the first day of the seventh month, they began to offer offerings to Yhwh, and the temple of Yhwh had not been founded.			
3:7	*Gathering building materials*	*Zerub* : Cyrus	538	521
3:8–13	*Foundation*	*Zerub* :	537	520
3:8	In the second year of their coming to the house of the god, to Jerusalem, in the second month, Zerubbabel and Jeshua and the rest of their brothers... began			
3:13	...for the people raised a great alarum, and the sound was heard afar.			
4:1–3	*Rebuff of neighbors*	*Zerub* : Cyrus	537	520
4:4–5	*Neighbors' obstruction* ("summary statement," after Williamson's "summary notation")	: *Cyrus-Darius*	537–520	538–520
	The people of the land discouraged the people of Judah and impeded their building, and hired advisors against them to "frustrate their counsel," all the days of Cyrus, king of Persia, and until the reign of Darius, king of Persia.			
4:6	*Neighbors to Xerxes*	: *Xerxes*	ca. 480	ca. 480
4:7	*Bishlam to Artaxerxes*	: *Artaxerxes*	ca. 460	ca. 460

TABLE 1, *continued*

Pericope	Leaders	Chronology: Ostensible Date	Chronology: Real Date
4:8–16 *Rehum to Artaxerxes*	: *Artaxerxes*	ca. 460	ca. 460
4:17–23 *Artaxerxes to Rehum*	: *Artaxerxes*	ca. 460	ca. 460
4:24 *Epanalepsis of 4:5*	: *Darius*	537–520	538–520
Then the work of the house of the god that is in Jerusalem halted, and was halted until the second year of the reign of Darius, king of Persia.			
5:1–2 *Building of temple*	*Zerub* :	520	520
5:3–5 *Tattenai's inquiry*	: *Darius*	520	520
5:6–17 *Tattenai to Darius*	: *Darius* (*Shesh* : *Cyrus*)	520	520
5:16 Then that Sheshbazzar came and laid the foundation of the house of the god that is in Jerusalem, and from then until now it has been under construction but has not been completed.			
6:1–12 *Darius to Tattenai*	: *Darius* (: *Cyrus*)	520	520
6:13–15 *Completion*	: *Darius* (: *Cyrus, Artaxerxes*)	520–515	520–515
6:16–18 *Dedication*	:	515	515
6:19–22 *Passover*	:	515	515

source. Certainly, the same is true of chap. 1, with its reconstituted edict. Still, it may be submitted that this property distinguishes the historian from Chr, whose tendency, when not subverting a source's sense, is to copy more than to paraphrase (esp. Micheel 1983).

Most striking of all, however, in a text that covers all of about twenty-three years and focuses largely on six of them, is the frequent chronological derangement in which the author indulges. There is disturbance in the temporal sequence in 3:2–3, 6, in 4:4–5, in 4:6–23, and in 4:24–5:2. The reasons for these disturbances have been explored above and related to central themes of the book. Particularly, they must be traced to the goal of establishing the continuity of the Restoration, from Cyrus's time onward, and to the hope of satisfying the ideological demand that the Restoration be accomplished in the first movement of the Return. A few further observations, however, are in place.

In itself, the chronological oscillation of 3:1–6 would not stand out. Ezra 3:1 functions as a sort of topic sentence, with 3:2–3 recounting preparations for the occasion it describes, and 3:4–5 moving forward from 3:1. This sort of capricious intermittence often summons forth the form-critical scalpel, but it has biblical and epigraphic parallels, including a close one at 2 Chr 30:1ff. In this last text, v 1 is a topic sentence, vv 2–4 explain the process by which the course of action it details was arrived at, and v 5 begins a detailed account of the action. That Ezra 3:6 adds one further move backward is an extra wrinkle. However, in ordinary Hebrew narrative, one would scarcely lay special stress on its presence. Indeed, it is worth noting that, though the choice was conscious and deliberate, dictated by thematic concerns (see above on Ezra 2), the retention of 3:1 from a source is what occasioned most of the disturbance. This is the same as the case of 2 Chr 12:2–11, where v 2a comes from a source and vv 2b–8 expand on preceding events (sin, Shishak in the countryside, Shishak "come" as far as Jerusalem, repentance) before an epanalepsis in v 9a resumes at the juncture at which the source began (Shishak attacking Jerusalem; on the construction of the account see Na^ʾaman 1987: 271). Nevertheless, after the omission of chronological data between Ezra 1:11 and 2:1, the commission of chronological mayhem in 3:1–6 typifies the document as a whole.

The programmatic disconnection begins in 4:4–5. Again, the mechanics and impact of the formulations here and through 5:2 are treated in the body of the survey. What wants stress is the deceptive artlessness with which the disturbance is perpetrated. Ezra 4:4, for example, reads very much like the continuation of 4:3: the foes were rebuffed, and obstructed the construction. To what could this refer except the building project undertaken by Zerubbabel—the only building project commenced, according to our narrator, in fulfilment of Cyrus's edict—begun in 3:8? The formulation conditions us to read the verse as the consequence, not the cause, of the action in 4:3. Yet 4:5 makes it clear that the obstruction began at the time of Sheshbazzar, in 538–537, well before Zerubbabel arrived on the scene (see below).

The join between 4:23 and 4:24 has much the same effect. The concatenation of "they stopped them [from working] by main strength" and "at that time [or, then] the work on the temple that was in Jerusalem stopped, and remained stopped until the second year of Darius's reign," invites the reader to suppose that the chronological sequence is unbroken. In consequence, 1 Esdras and Josephus both place the episode in 4:8–23 before Darius, and Josephus (*Antiquities* 11:2:2), reading sharply, sees it as the transition from Cyrus (1:1–4:4) to Darius (4:24ff.). The historian in Ezra 1–6 evinces the same disingenuousness in his failure to supply a temporal break between 1:11 and 2:1, and in his studied shift in the dating scheme at 2:68 and 3:1, 8; the reversion to Sheshbazzar in 5:16, without mention of Zerubbabel, is another, more muted instance. A comparable case, without chronological connections, is the sly juxtaposition of "the great acclamation" that "was heard afar" (3:13) with the line, "the enemies of Judah and Benjamin heard . . ." (4:1). The suggestion that the enemies heard the cheering is palpable; simultaneously, it is not there: the enemies had general intelligence, and 4:1 continues, "that the exiles were building a temple" (compare, too, 5:17–6:6, where direct discourse and narrative meld together).

In all these cases, the object is to lead the reader. This the historian tries to do without prevarication. Dates, for example, are not invented, but suggestively omitted, or reported in a coded form. The text conceals a literal chronology in the bowels of a historiographic paradigm for temple building, exemplars of which are known from Mesopotamia in the very same period. It exhibits twin chronological structures. It fudges the chronology in order to blame the delay for the temple construction on the neighbors of Judah—instead of invoking Judaean recalcitrance, *à la* Haggai, or Judaean apostasy, *à la* Exodus 32.

The paradigmatic source for the treatment in Ezra 1–6 (as opposed to the substantive sources enumerated above) is most clearly represented by Nabonidus's Sippar cylinder. Just as this text seems to place the building of Ehulhul in the period of Belshazzar's regency, but does not go so far as to mention his participation, Ezra 3 ostensibly sets the foundation of the temple under Sheshbazzar without mentioning *him*. And, as the Sippar cylinder blames the Umman-Manda for the delay in construction, until Cyrus defeats them, Ezra blames the people of the land, until Darius steps in.

There is another resemblance—the system of dual chronology. The real chronology locates the temple foundation in Darius's third or second year. Thus, Hag 2:18 dates it to the ninth month of the second year. On the same date, Hag 2:23 reverses the rejection of Jehoiachin's line (and thus of Zerubbabel's legitimacy) found in Jer 22:24. Further, Zechariah, in the eleventh month of the same year, refers to the foundation (perhaps in the immediate past) under Zerubbabel (4:9) and describes the removal or replacement of the first stone as a current event (4:7), projecting the temple's completion at Zerubbabel's hands (4:9). Ezra 6:15 dates the completion to Darius's sixth year.

This chronology stands up to other considerations as well. Ezra 3 links the foundation to Jeshua and Zerubbabel, without mentioning Sheshbazzar, just like Haggai and Zechariah. Furthermore, widespread upheaval in the empire was the midwife of Darius's accession—of the upheaval, the reflex in Judah's world may well have been the rise and return of Zerubbabel (whom Darius may have sent without having recommissioned the temple project). Zerubbabel would on any reasonable estimate have been rather too young to found a temple or lead a return in 538. Even were he the eldest son of Shealtiel, the second son of Jehoiachin (1 Chr 3:16), Jehoiachin was at most eighteen years old in 597. With a view to infant mortality, the births of sisters, and some disruptions in domestic life occasioned by the exile, 565 seems the probable upper limit for Zerubbabel's birth. More likely still is the era after 560, when Jehoiachin was enfranchised at the king's table (hence the name, "seed of Babylon"). Zerubbabel would have been about twenty to twenty-five years old in 538, but almost forty in 521, and, as a resident of Persian Babylon for seventeen years, an appropriate candidate to lead the province. In all likelihood, the author of Ezra 1–6 was no more deceived about the real chronology of the events than were the scribes of Nabonidus.

The Nabonidus parallels permit extrapolation. Why did the author of Ezra 1–6 not go the whole hog and impose his ostensible chronology unambiguously? Evidently, he feared that his construct would be assailed on the grounds of the chronological data found in Haggai and Zechariah, and in any digest of Zerubbabel's work. Similarly, at Harran, Nabonidus's inscriptions reflect, at least approximately, the authentic chronology of Ehulhul's reconstruction; it is only on Babylonian soil that the dual chronology becomes more radical and more difficult to piece out. In other words, the Sippar cylinder, like Ezra 1–6, is a secondary composition, a text at a moderate remove from the events and those who knew them. Were the remove greater still, no doubt all signs of the accurate chronology would be obliterated.

The concerns that Ezra 1–6 shares with Nabonidus's texts, and, in particular, the techniques it uses to create a dual chronology, intimate that the historian enjoyed a certain familiarity with Nabonidus's Sippar and Babylon inscriptions about Ehulhul. The parallels do not come from a purely local source in 515: it is inconceivable that, in 515, Zerubbabel could have produced an epigraph demoting himself, as the ostensible chronology of Ezra does, from governor of Judah to a subordinate of Sheshbazzar. Further, the historian, probably in Artaxerxes' time, certainly contributed 4:6–24, and probably 5:1–5 as well. These are so integral to the dual chronological structure that it is difficult to imagine what the text would have looked like without them. Unless we posit an intermediate compilation, under Darius, the historian will have been the one who first imposed a dual chronology on the events. This historian was, like his more illustrious contemporary, an assiduous scribe, versed in the models of an establishment Babylonian education.

B. Chronography and Source-Use in Ezra 1–6 and Chronicles

Where the Chronicler introduces new time elements, or rearranges sequences, direct evidence for assessing his techniques is generally wanting. Thus, M. Cogan (1985: 179–209 [1980: 165–72]) can make the claim that Chr is prone to schematic dating: Chr assigns dates to events because he likes certain numbers, rather than for any other reason. However, the cases by which Cogan hopes to establish that Chr is preoccupied with three-year periods can all be called into question—even aside from the fact that the "three-year" period in Nabonidus's Sippar cylinder is in fact a figurative one (cf. 1 Kgs 2:39 and 2 Kgs 24:1).

For example, Rehoboam's three years of fidelity to Yhwh (2 Chr 11:7) arise from the fact that Shishak raided Judah in Rehoboam's fifth year. To Chr, this implied that Rehoboam had been wicked for a period (schematically equated with his fourth year). Yet earlier, he had been guided by Shemaiah's instructions not to invade Jeroboam's kingdom (2 Chr 11:1–4, 1 Kgs 12:21–24); so Chr must hypothesize a transition, leading to Shishak's campaign.

Again, that 2 Chr 18:2 omits the three years of 1 Kgs 22:1 is no evidence that Chr did not take such figures seriously (so Cogan 1985: 207). 1 Kgs 22:1 affects the chronology only of Ahab's reign, which Chr does not treat (cf. the sequence in the Old Greek version of 1 Kings 20–22). This leaves only Jehoshaphat's reform in his third year (Cogan 1985: 207 n. 38; 2 Chr 17:7), which may reflect nothing more than a desire to allow time for the political and religious consolidation of 2 Chr 17:2, 5–6, and a sense that the reform belonged before the Transjordanian wars (2 Chr 18, 20:1–30), in the course of which Jehoshaphat's virtue is much in evidence. The chronology of Jehoshaphat's reign posed problems for Chr, who must have seen that the synchronisms in Kings (Old Greek) implied Jehoshaphat's death around the time of Ahab's. Yet the Transjordanian wars dated to Jehoram's day at least (2 Kings 3).

Cogan's arguments to a stylized antedating of events in Chr are more reasonable in theory but nevertheless problematic. Hezekiah's reform, Cogan asserts, is placed in his first year on typological (paradigmatic) grounds—the parallel is to Esarhaddon's inscriptions dating his reconstruction of Babylon to his first year (Cogan 1985: 200–203, 207 n. 38). Still, this could equally derive from a sequential reading of Kings. There, the reform sits at the start of the regnal account (2 Kgs 18:4); after it come reports of Hezekiah's revolt against Assyria and conquests in Philistia, and only then an Assyrian campaign in the west dated to Hezekiah's fourth year. All this was ample warrant to date the reform early. More telling, Asa's reform is dated to a midpoint in his reign (2 Chr 13:23 + 15:10), despite a complete lack of chronological information about the reform in Kings. Similarly, Jehoshaphat's judicial reform (2 Chr 19:5–11) is late in the reign and basically undated; and Chr makes no serious effort to antedate Solomon's construction of the temple (see below). The evidence for arbitrary antedating by Chr in Hezekiah's case is unpersuasive.

Cogan cites the Josiah account (2 Chr 34:3–7) as an instance of antedating to an alleged age of majority (age 16; 1985: 203–5). Kings locates Josiah's first movement toward reform in his eighteenth year, Chronicles in his eighth. Most likely, this difference reflects a haplography from year eight to year eighteen in a source or *Vorlage* of Kings. Indeed, the choice of the eighth year, when Josiah was sixteen, as that in which Josiah "began to seek Yhwh" (2 Chr 34:3) is peculiar. The reform of the twelfth year, probably exaggerated in 2 Chr 34:3–7 to create an impression of Josiah's native piety, is virtually a doublet for the major reform. If anything, it suggests that Chr could not countenance a temple rededication without a full reform of the cult first.

Overall, the possibility of chronological fiddling remains open. Perhaps some did occur. But to Cogan's specific bill of indictment, one can only return the Scottish verdict of "not proved." These are, however, not the only texts that afford a purchase on Chr's handling of chronology. Indeed, raising the question of chronography helps to isolate Chr's fingerprint. The Chronicler is at work, for example, in 2 Chr 25:14ff., where the Edomite imbroglio of 2 Kgs 14:7–14 becomes the cause for the sack of Jerusalem. Similarly, the phrase "you are he, the god, in the heavens" is inserted in 2 Chr 20:6 in an account about the period in which such sentiments first appear in Kings (1 Kgs 18:39; but cf. 2 Chr 33:13).

Where Chr reverses a time sequence in his sources, he does not shilly-shally about. If a literary pattern demands it, Chr in effect splices the ark narrative of 2 Sam 6:1–11 into the center of 2 Samuel 5 (1 Chronicles 13–14; Halpern 1981b: 37). Here, Chr takes Samuel as achronological: the three-month-long sojourn of the ark in the house of Obed Edom is construed as simultaneous with other events (in 2 Samuel 5). Modern scholars concur with Chr's interpretation: the Samuel report is out of sequence (Mazar 1963).

Again, Chronicles revises the sequence of events in 1 Kgs 22:45–50: Jehoshaphat accepted, rather than rejected, a partnership with Samaria in the venture before, not after, his fleet at Ezion Geber sank (2 Chr 20:35–37). This reconstruction reflects careful contemplation of 1 Kgs 22:45, which states that Jehoshaphat came to terms with his northern neighbor; it treats "then" in 1 Kgs 22:50 as a term demarcating achronological narrative. Conversely, 2 Chr 25:14ff. reads "then" in 2 Kgs 14:8 to mean "just after, and because of, what preceded." Chronicles resolves, then, the ambiguity it discovers in the source.

Another case is that of 2 Kgs 16:5–9, in the reign of Ahaz. Again, the sequence begins with "then"; again, Chr takes it to be nonsequential. To damn Ahaz's appeal to Tiglath-Pileser III, Chr blames upon it the loss of Eilat (2 Chr 28:16–17): this means reading 2 Kgs 16:5–6a separately from 16:6b, and hypothesizing that the latter belonged after, not before 16:7ff. The loss of Eilat follows as a (divine) sanction from Ahaz's negotiations with Assyria rather than inspiring the negotiations in the first place.

In a vein more similar to Ezra, Chronicles also seems to antedate the conspiracy against Amaziah by fifteen years, to the time of Jehoash's sack of Jerusalem (2 Chr 25:27 with 25:14, 25). Here, though, the chronological terminology is elastic: the conspiracy had its origins "from the time when Amaziah turned from after Yhwh"; obviously, it culminated only at the end of his reign. In any event, the last case of chronological revision is egregious: Asa's "gout" (2 Chr 16:12) suggests a senile infidelity, and would match well with a period of unrest. So Asa's war with Baasha comes in the thirty-sixth year of Asa's reign, when Baasha was, like Joe Hill in the song, "ten years dead" (2 Chr 16:1–10, against 1 Kgs 15:33, 16:8). In this case, too, the revision is unambiguous, despite the problems it creates.

There may be other instances (as 2 Chr 23:1–3). If the list of Rehoboam's forts (2 Chr 11:6–10) derives from a reliable source, then the fact that it includes only one name represented on the list of Shishak's targets, and the archeology of Lachish, suggest it belongs after, not before, the account of Shishak's campaign (12:4; but see Naʾaman 1986; on Lachish, and the date of the end of Level V, see Ussishkin 1980; Yadin 1980; Ussishkin et al. 1983:116; cf. Dever 1986: 32–33 n. 34). One may argue about the Chronicler's motivation in each case. But for him one thing may be said. In contradistinction to the Deuteronomist, who indulges frequently in achronological narration (see above, and 1 Kgs 11:14–25; 2 Kgs 20:1–11, 12–19, on which cf. 2 Chr 32:26, 31), he takes a clear stand on relative chronology, and sticks to it.

The one exception to this rule comes in connection with Solomon's temple building. Chronicles antedates the preparations for this project to David's time, and, in this respect, we might speak of a bookend to Sheshbazzar and Zerubbabel (Freedman 1961: 439). Construction starts, with Kings, in Solomon's fourth year. But Kings details how Solomon spent thirteen years on his palace before dedicating the temple. Chronicles omits the palace building (2 Chr 1:18; 2–7). Still, it retains 1 Kgs 9:10, the remark that Solomon spent twenty years building both palace and temple (8:1). As in Ezra, thus, the time of completion remains the same. Only, by inferring from a careful reading of 1 Kings 6–7 that the temple was being outfitted while the palace was being built—by reading Kings as achronological—Chronicles eliminates a thirteen-year delay in dedicating the temple. Again, the degree of ambiguity in the chronology is in fact reduced. Chronicles presents its conclusions in the instance somewhat tentatively; this may be a solitary case of Chr's dabbling in dual chronology. Still, it leaves no doubt in the reader's mind as to the course of events.

The picture in Ezra 1–6 is entirely different. That the historian here was familiar with the chronology seems beyond reasonable dispute: the contrary supposition solves few, if any, problems. Yet the temporal succession of events is embarrassing to his thematic interests. Instead of adopting Chr's recourse and revising the order of events, instead of identifying Zerubbabel with Sheshbazzar, he allows each of his sources to speak, from its own time, on its own subject. By painstaking attention to syntax, to diction, to every aspect of composition, he chooses to soften the chronological focus with the gauze of thematic development; he blurs, disguises, obscures the passage of time, all to good effect in the service of his program, until the eras intermingle, swirling next to and into each other like eddies in the timeless waters of the Flood. But all this is achieved by the art of suggestion. Technically, formally, literally, the use of sources in Ezra 1–6 is apparently impeccable. It is almost as though the narrator, with the eye of the contemporary reader peering over his shoulder, worked to avoid the criticism that chronological chaos would conjure up, while enjoying his frolic nonetheless.

Like Ezra, Chronicles manipulates time in order to antedate temple building. The paradigms for temple building in the two works are perhaps comparable. But ideology, like usage, is not specific to an individual. In the remote depths of historiographic practice, we have evidence of a difference in authorship. Chronicles treats chronology more or less one-dimensionally. It antedates the temple construction. And it approaches the cult as a timeless entity, dreamily merging David's, Solomon's, and Hezekiah's establishments, and that of the Second Temple. But consider the philosophical difference: Ezra creates a dual chronology. Chronicles interprets its *sources* as achronological and tries to resolve their ambiguity in line with the Chronicler's theology. Chronicles does to Kings what Josephus and 1 Esdras find themselves compelled to do to Ezra. Ezra belongs to a historiographic genre only remotely related to that of Chronicles.

The application that the historian of Ezra 1–6 makes to different sources and different events gives the impression that the narrative is not concerned with chronology. Yet his narrative is more successful than are Assyrian royal inscriptions or annals in pursuing chronological homogenization without outright distortion. Ezra 1–6 is, more precisely, achronological, out of time, much like the work whose completion it celebrates. Its historiographic techniques converge, thus, on the locus of its subject—the source of the living waters, the place of eternity (Levenson 1985: 137ff.). The temple was the locus of a supernal confluence, an eternal analepsis. Around it, sequence dissolved. The literature concerning temple-building partakes of this timeless quality. "Time is broke and no proportion kept!" And the scholar must have "the daintiness of ear to check time broke in a disorder'd string" (*Richard II*).

In these considerations, there are strong grounds to deny that Chr wrote Ezra 1–6. Indeed, the relationship of Ezra to 1 Esdras raises a bulwark on behalf of T. C. Eskenazi's position that Chr used Ezra to compose 1 Esdras (1986; see further Williamson 1987: 12–13): the historiographic principles operating on the chronology and on the sources in Chr and 1 Esdras are identical. Unhappily, many of the ideological arguments ranged by Japhet (esp. 1968) against the common authorship of Chronicles and Ezra also apply to Eskenazi's thesis. Japhet's case is not airtight, but is weighty enough to commend caution. Nevertheless, a few contemplations may be offered.

If a historian responsible for much of the final form of Chronicles also produced 1 Esdras, the history of composition of these works must have been unutterably complex. Eskenazi avoids the worst epicycles of her position by stipulating that 1 Esdras was a separate work. But this recourse is contraindicated. 1 Esdras, thus, while duplicating much of 2 Chronicles 35–36, diverges from it significantly. 1 Esdr 1:26, for example, asserts that Jeremiah, not Necho, mediated Yhwh's final oracle to Josiah. Williamson has shown (1982; 1987: 12–13) that here 1 Esdras seems to rely on 2 Chronicles as a source, and this is certainly true of the other changes 1 Esdras works on 2 Chronicles 35–36 (on which see, for example, Myers 1974: 26–29). As shown above (on Ezra 4:1–5), the same relationship obtains between 1 Esdras and Ezra 1–6: reliance on the combined Ezra–Nehemiah is manifest in 1 Esdras's use of Ezra 2, and in its reinterpretation of the temporal bearings of the Rehum letters; Williamson has established (see above on Ezra 2) that only the assembly of Ezra-Nehemiah could have produced the present version of Ezra 1–6, the source for these and other details. Thus, 1 Esdras even reworks the letters of Ezra 4:6ff. to include references to the construction of the temple (1 Esdr 2:17–18; note also 4:43–46, 51–57, in a heavily redacted section construing Zerubbabel's return on the model of Nehemiah's, and melding it with Sheshbazzar's—4:57).

In light of these circumstances, and of Williamson's demonstration that the Chronicler's account of Josiah's death (in Esdras) reflects reliance on a source other than the present version of Kings, it is likely that the present 2 Chronicles 35–36 and Ezra–Nehemiah are the sources of 1 Esdras. But if 1 Esdras is Chr's work (Eskenazi), must we posit that MT has somehow swapped 1 Esdras with its sources in 2 Chronicles 35–36 and Ezra–Nehemiah?

The best model for reconstructing this process begins from the hypothesis of an early edition of Chronicles (Chr[1]), composed around 515. The existence of such a work was long ago inferred on other grounds by D. N. Freedman (1961); F. M. Cross subsequently added fresh argument to a similar effect (1975). Cross, perhaps troubled by the chronological tesselation in Ezra 4, limited Chr^1 to 1 Chronicles 10–2 Chronicles 34, with the *Vorlage* of 1 Esdr 1:1–5:65 (that is, up to the equivalent of Ezra 3:13). Roughly, this must be correct. But 1 Esdras relies on the combined Ezra–Nehemiah (see above). So, in Chr^1, sometime after 515, a historian wed a "chronistic" Hezekian national history to the Deuteronomistic History (probably inserting parts of 1 Chronicles 1–9; see Halpern 1981b, with Freedman 1961: 440), and appended to it an early version of the present 2 Chronicles (33–34) 35–36, along with the dedicatory source underlying Ezra 1–6. The tenor of the work must have been fairly ecumenical, as Chronicles, Haggai, and Zechariah seem to be: if Ezra 4:1–5 represents a reconstruction from the perspective of Artaxerxes' time (see above), the earliest record of the temple building may have blamed Sheshbazzar (as, effectively, Hag 1:2–11) for, or imputed to Yhwh (Zech 1:7–17), the delay in building from 538 to 521. All this varies only slightly from Cross's stance, and lines up, broadly, with that of Freedman: if R. E. Friedman (1981) was right to speak of the vision of Dtr$_2$ as that of a movement "from Egypt to Egypt," the main thrust of Chr^1 is a movement from temple to temple.

Cross proposes that a Chr^2 was produced shortly after Ezra's mission in 458 (1975: 11–14), and Freedman's position is much the same (1961). Cross's Chr^2 contained the *Vorlage* of 1 Esdras as a whole, from which Chr^3 was to lift the continuation of the list of miscegenates in 1 Esdras 9:37–39 for inclusion in Neh 7:72bff., and, secondarily, Ezra 3:1. Allowing that the present 1 Esdras depends on Ezra–Nehemiah (and that Ezra 3:1 is calqued from 1 Esdras 9:37–39 or Neh 7:72b–8:1), another tack is indicated: assume that the *Vorlage* of 1 Esdras was in fact its source—the Ezra memoire; then, probably with a text of Ezra 7–Nehemiah in hand, Chr^2 retained the history of 515, and produced the present Ezra–Nehemiah.

A final stage was one of bifurcation: Chr^3 produced Chronicles and 1 Esdras, the latter dependent on the Ezra memoire and the parallels in Chr^2, with the profane work of Nehemiah politely red-pencilled. But the fuller treatment in Chr^2 of the Restoration somehow emerged as the preferred text, 2 Chronicles 35–36 included: so MT now weds the version of Chronicles found in Chr^3 to the account of Josiah's death and the return in Chr^2. This expedient may reflect antiquarian concerns—to preserve the Nehemiah memoir, and contextualize Ezra's sacred work in contemporary political history. Or it may express a need for a mythic charter for friction with Samaria. Chr^3 then updated the genealogies of 1 Chronicles 1–9 to include Davidides down to around 400 (similarly Freedman 1961).

In the reconstruction of such a literary process there is nothing to inspire confidence. It holds firm if Chr produced 1 Esdras: this can only be

Cross's Chr[3], if Williamson's post-deuteronomistic source is to be accommodated, or his position on the relationship between Ezra 1–6 and Ezra–Nehemiah as a whole. But the skepticism such a complex editorial and textual history is sure to evoke is justified. The reliable implications of the historiographic analysis are more limited: the author of Chronicles is unlikely to have produced Ezra 1–6. He may have used it as a source; he did not himself construct it.

The evidence adduced to identify authors is usually philological or ideological (for example, Kapelrud 1944; Japhet 1968). The case of Ezra 1–6 suggests that more elliptical approaches can yield fruit—that excursions into the calculus of historiography, into the historian's idea of what history is—can also contribute, not just to our understanding of the text, but to the question of authorship as well. I do not assert that the results garnered above are conclusive or even indisputable evidence for separate authorship in Chronicles and Ezra–Nehemiah. But the marshes of usage and theology have often betrayed our most prosperous hopes of finding a solid compositional footing. Perhaps some reconnoitering from more rarefied altitudes can provide a bead on the lay of the literary land.

Bibliography

Albright, W. F.

1950 The Judicial Reform of Jehoshaphat. Pp. 61–82 in *Alexander Marx Jubilee Volume*. New York: Jewish Publication Society.

ANET *Ancient Near Eastern Texts Relating to the Old Testament*. 3d ed. Princeton: Princeton University, 1969.

AP A. Cowley, *Aramaic Papyri of the Fifth Century* B.C. Oxford: Clarendon, 1923.

Astruc, J.

1753 *Conjectures sur les mémoires originaux dont il paroit que Moyse s'est servi pour composer le livre de la Genese. Avec des remarques, qui appuient ou qui éclaircissent ces conjectures*. Brussels: Fricx.

Avigad, N.

1983 *Discovering Jerusalem*. Jerusalem: Shiqmona and Israel Exploration Society.

Berger, P.-R.

1971 Zu den Namen *ššbṣr* und *šnʾṣr*. *Zeitschrift für die alttestamentliche Wissenschaft* 83: 98–100.

1975 Der Kyros-Zylinder mit dem Zusatzfragment BIN II Nr. 32 und die akkadischen Personennamen im Danielbuch. *Zeitschrift für Assyriologie* 64: 192–234.

Bickerman, E. J.

1946 The Edict of Cyrus in Ezra 1. *Journal of Biblical Literature* 65: 249–75.

Borger, R.
1956 *Die Inschriften Asarhaddons Königs von Assyrien.* Archiv für Orientforschung Beiheft 9. Graz: Weidner.
BoSt Boghazköi-Studien.
Braun, R. L.
1976 Solomon, the Chosen Temple Builder: The Significance of 1 Chronicles 22, 28, and 29 for the Theology of Chronicles. *Journal of Biblical Literature* 95: 581–90.
1979 Chronicles, Ezra, and Nehemiah: Theology and Literary History. Pp. 52–64 in *Studies in the Historical Books of the Old Testament*, ed. J. A. Emerton. Supplements to Vetus Testamentum 30. Leiden: Brill.
Cogan, M.
1974 *Imperialism and Religion: Assyria, Judah and Israel in the Eighth and Seventh Centuries B.C.E.* Society of Biblical Literature Monograph Series 19. Missoula: Scholars Press.
1980 Tendentious Chronology in the Book of Chronicles. *Zion* 45: 165–72.
1983 Omens and Ideology in the Babylon Inscription of Esarhaddon. Pp. 76–87 in *History, Historiography and Interpretation: Studies in Biblical and Cuneiform Literatures*, ed. H. Tadmor and M. Weinfeld. Jerusalem: Magnes.
1985 The Chronicler's Use of Chronology as Illuminated by Neo-Assyrian Royal Inscriptions. Pp. 197–209 in *Empirical Models of Biblical Criticism*, ed. J. H. Tigay. Philadelphia: University of Pennsylvania. [Revised English version of Cogan 1980.]
Cogan, M, and H. Tadmor
1977 Gyges and Ashurbanipal. *Orientalia* 46: 65–85.
Cross, F. M.
1975 A Reconstruction of the Judaean Restoration. *Journal of Biblical Literature* 94: 4–18.
Dever, W. G.
1986 Late Bronze Age and Solomonic Defenses at Gezer: New Evidence. *Bulletin of the American Schools of Oriental Research* 262: 9–34.
Dion, P. E.
1981 Aramaic Words for "Letter." *Semeia* 22: 77–88.
1983 *ššbṣr* and *ssnwry*. *Zeitschrift für die alttestamentliche Wissenschaft* 95: 111–12.
Eliade, M.
1943 *Commentarii la legenda Mesterului Manole.* Bucharest.
Eskenazi, T. C.
1986 The Chronicler and the Composition of 1 Esdras. *Catholic Biblical Quarterly* 48: 39–61.
Falkenstein, A., and W. von Soden
1953 *Sumerische und akkadische Hymnen und Gebeten.* Stuttgart: Artemis.
Freedman, D. N.
1961 The Chronicler's Purpose. *Catholic Biblical Quarterly* 23: 436–42.
Friedman, R. E.
1981 From Egypt to Egypt: Dtr^1 and Dtr^2. Pp. 167–92 in *Traditions in Transformation: Turning-Points in Biblical Faith* (FS F. M. Cross), ed. B. Halpern and J. D. Levenson. Winona Lake: Eisenbrauns.

Gadd, C. J.
1953 Inscribed Barrel Cylinder of Marduk-Apla-Iddina II. *Iraq* 15: 123–34.
1958 The Harran Inscriptions of Nabonidus. *Anatolian Studies* 8: 35–92.

Galling, K.
1964 *Studien zur Geschichte Israels im persischen Zeitalter*. Tübingen: Mohr.

Garbini, G.
1985 La lettera di Ṭabʾel (*Ezra* IV, 7). *Henoch* 7: 161–63.

Gese, H.
1974 *Vom Sinai zum Zion*. Munich: Chr. Kaiser.

Good, R. M.
1982 Zechariah's Second Night Vision (Zech 2,1–4). *Biblica* 63: 56–59.

Graf, D. F.
1984 Medism: The Origin and Significance of the Term. *Journal of Hellenic Studies* 104: 15–30.

Gunneweg, A. H. J.
1981 Zur Interpretation der Bücher Esra-Nehemia—zugleich ein Beitrag zur Methode der Exegese. Pp. 146–61 in *Congress Volume: Vienna 1980*, ed. J. A. Emerton. Supplements to Vetus Testamentum 32. Leiden: Brill.
1982 Die aramäische und die hebräische Erzählung über die nachexilische Restaurations—ein Vergleich. *Zeitschrift für die alttestamentliche Wissenschaft* 94: 299–302.

Halpern, B.
1978 The Ritual Background of Zechariah's Temple Song. *Catholic Biblical Quarterly* 40: 167–90.
1981a *The Constitution of the Monarchy in Israel*. Harvard Semitic Monographs 25. Chico: Scholars Press.
1981b Sacred History and Ideology: Chronicles' Thematic Structure—Intimations of an Earlier Source. Pp. 35–54 in *The Creation of Sacred Literature: Composition and Redaction of the Biblical Text*, ed. R. E. Friedman. Near Eastern Studies 22. Los Angeles: University of California.
1983 Doctrine by Misadventure: Between the Israelite Source and the Biblical Historian. Pp. 41–74 in *The Poet and the Historian*, ed. R. E. Friedman. Harvard Semitic Studies 26. Chico: Scholars Press.

Hupfeld, H.
1853 *Die Quellen der Genesis und die Art ihrer Zusammenhang von neuem untersucht*. Berlin: Wiegandt and Grieben.

Hurowitz, V.
1983 Temple Building in the Bible in Light of Mesopotamian and North-West Semitic Writings. Ph.D. diss., Hebrew University of Jerusalem.

Japhet, S.
1968 The Supposed Common Authorship of Chronicles and Ezra–Nehemiah Investigated Anew. *Vetus Testamentum* 18: 330–71.
1977 *The Ideology of the Book of Chronicles and its Place in Biblical Thought*. Jerusalem: Bialik.

1982 Sheshbazzar and Zerubbabel: Against the Background of the Historical and Religious Tendencies of Ezra–Nehemiah. *Zeitschrift für die alttestamentliche Wissenschaft* 94: 66–98.

1983 Sheshbazzar and Zerubbabel: Against the Background of the Historical and Religious Tendencies of Ezra–Nehemiah. *Zeitschrift für die alttestamentliche Wissenschaft* 95: 218–29.

1985 The Historical Reliability of Chronicles. *Journal for the Study of the Old Testament* 33: 83–107.

Kapelrud, A. S.

1944 *The Question of Authorship in the Ezra-Narrative: A Lexical Investigation.* Oslo: Jacob Dybwad.

Klein, R. W.

1983 Abijah's Campaign against the North (II Chr. 13)—What Were the Chronicler's Sources? *Zeitschrift für die alttestamentliche Wissenschaft* 95: 210–17.

Langdon, S. L.

1912 *Die neubabylonischen Königsinschriften.* Vorderasiatische Bibliothek 4. Leipzig: Hinrichs.

Levenson, J. D.

1984 The Temple and the World. *Journal of Religion* 64: 275–98.

1985 *Sinai and Zion: An Entry into the Jewish Bible.* New Voices in Biblical Studies 1. Minneapolis: Winston.

Levine, L. D.

1981 Manuscripts, Texts, and the Study of the Neo-Assyrian Royal Inscriptions. Pp. 49–70 in *Assyrian Royal Inscriptions: New Horizons in Literary, Ideological, and Historical Analysis*, ed. F. M. Fales. Orientis Antiqui Collectio 17. Rome: Istituto per l'Oriente, Centro per la antichità e la storia dell'arte del vicino oriente.

Lie, A. G.

1929 *The Inscriptions of Sargon II, King of Assyria*, Part 1: *The Annals.* Paris: Geuthner.

Mandelkern, S.

1959 *Veteris Testamenti Concordantiae Hebraicae atque Chaldaicae.* 4th ed. Tel-Aviv: Schocken.

Mazar, B.

1963 David's Reign in Hebron and the Conquest of Jerusalem. Pp. 235–44 in *The Time of Harvest: Essays in Honor of Abba Hillel Silver*, ed. D. J. Silver. New York: MacMillan.

Micheel, R.

1983 *Die Seher- und Prophetenüberlieferungen in der Chronik.* Beiträge zur biblischen Exegese und Theologie 18. Frankfurt: Lang.

Millard, A. R.

1976 Assyrian Royal Names in Biblical Hebrew. *Journal of Semitic Studies* 21: 1–15.

Morgenstern, J.
1955 The Calendar of the Book of Jubilees, Its Origin and Its Character. *Vetus Testamentum* 5: 34–76.

Myers, J. M.
1974 *I & II Esdras*. Anchor Bible 42. Garden City: Doubleday.

Na᾿aman, N.
1986 Hezekiah's Fortified Cities and the LMLK Stamps. *Bulletin of the American Schools of Oriental Research* 261: 5–21.
1987 Nomad-Shepherds on the Southwest Fringe of the Kingdom of Judah in the Era of the Divided Monarchy. *Zion* 52: 261–78.

North, R.
1974 Does Archeology Prove Chronicles Sources? Pp. 375–401 in *A Light Unto My Path: Old Testament Studies in Honor of Jacob M. Myers*, ed. H. N. Bream, R. D. Heim, and C. A. Moore. Gettysburg Theological Studies 4. Philadelphia: Temple University.

Noth, M.
1943 *Überlieferungsgeschichtliche Studien*, vol. 1: *Die sammelnden und bearbeitenden Geschichtswerke im Alten Testament*. Schriften der Königsberger Gelehrten Gesellschaft 18. Geisteswissenschaftliche Klasse 2. Halle: M. Niemayer.

Olmstead, A. T.
1944 Tattenai, Governor of "Across the River." *Journal of Near Eastern Studies* 3: 46.

Peterson, D. L.
1974 Zerubbabel and Jerusalem Temple Reconstruction. *Catholic Biblical Quarterly* 36: 366–72.
1984 Zechariah's Visions: A Theological Perspective. *Vetus Testamentum* 34: 195–206.

Petitjean, A.
1969 *Les Oracles du Proto-Zacharie*. Paris: Gabalda.

Porten, B.
1983 The Address Formulae in Aramaic Letters: A New Collation of Cowley 17. *Revue Biblique* 90: 396–415.

Rawlinson, H. C.
1884 *Cuneiform Inscriptions of Western Asia: A Selection from the Miscellaneous Inscriptions of Assyria*. Vol. 5. London: R. E. Bowler.

Reviv, H.
1983 *The Elders in Ancient Israel*. Jerusalem: Magnes.

Rost, P.
1893 *Die Keilschrifttexte Tiglat-Pilesers III*, vol. 1: *Einleitung, Transscription und Uebersetzung, Wörterverzeichnis mit Commentar*. Leipzig: Eduard Pfeiffer.

Rothstein, J. W.
1910 *Die Nachtgesichte des Sacharja*. Beiträge zur Wissenschaft des Alten und Neuen Testament 8. Leipzig: Hinrichs.

Shea, W. H.
1979 Adad-Nirari III and Jehoash of Israel. *Journal of Cuneiform Studies* 30: 101–13.

Snell, D.
1980 "Why is There Aramaic in the Bible?" *Journal for the Study of the Old Testament* 18: 32–51.

Steiner, R. C., and C. F. Nims
1985 Ashurbanipal and Shamash-Shum-Ukin: A Tale of Two Brothers from the Aramaic Text in Demotic Script. *Revue Biblique* 92: 60–81.

Streck, M.
1916 *Assurbanipal und die letzten assyrischen Könige bis zum Untergang Ninevehs.* Vorderasiatische Bibliothek 7. Leipzig: Hinrichs.

Stuart, C. D.
1976 The Sovereign's Day of Conquest: A Possible Ancient Near Eastern Reflex of the Israelite "Day of Yahweh." Pp. 159–64 in *Essays in Honor of George Ernest Wright*, ed. E. F. Campbell and R. G. Boling. Missoula: Scholars Press. (= *Bulletin of the American Schools of Oriental Research* 220/221.)

Tadmor, H.
1958 The Campaigns of Sargon II of Assur: A Chronological-Historical Study. *Journal of Cuneiform Studies* 12: 22–40, 77–100.
1965 The Inscriptions of Nabunaid: Historical Arrangement. Pp. 351–63 in *Studies in Honor of Benno Landsberger on His Seventy-Fifth Birthday*, ed. H. G. Güterbock and T. Jacobsen. Assyriological Studies 16. Chicago: University of Chicago.
1973 The Historical Inscriptions of Adad-Nirari III. *Iraq* 35: 141–50.
1981 History and Ideology in the Assyrian Royal Inscriptions. Pp. 13–33 in *Assyrian Royal Inscriptions: New Horizons in Literary, Ideological, and Historical Analysis*, ed. F. M. Fales. Orientis Antiqui Collectio 17. Rome: Istituto per l'Oriente, Centro per la antichità e la storia dell'arte del vicino oriente.
1983 The Rise of Cyrus and the Historical Background to His Proclamation. Pp. 5–16, 253–55 in *The History of the People Israel: The Return to Zion—the Persian Era*, ed. B. Sasson. Jerusalem: Alexander Peli.

Talmon, S.
1976 Ezra and Nehemiah. Pp. 317–28 in *Interpreter's Dictionary of the Bible Supplementary Volume*, ed. G. A. Buttrick. Nashville: Abingdon.

Teixidor, J.
1978 The Aramaic Text in the Trilingual Stele from Xanthus. *Journal of Near Eastern Studies* 37: 181–85.

Throntveit, M. A.
1987 *When Kings Speak: Royal Speech and Royal Prayer in Chronicles.* Society of Biblical Literature Dissertation Series 93. Decatur: Scholars Press.

Thureau-Dangin, F.
1925 La fin de l'empire assyrien. *Revue d'assyriologie* 22: 27–29.

Torrey, C. C.
1910 *Ezra Studies.* Chicago: University of Chicago.

UET C. J. Gadd and L. Legrain. *Ur Excavation Texts*, vol. 1: *Royal Inscriptions.* London: Oxford University, 1928.

Ussishkin, D.

1980 Was the "Solomonic" City Gate at Megiddo Built by King Solomon? *Bulletin of the American Schools of Oriental Research* 239: 1–18.

Ussishkin, D. et al.

1983 *Excavations at Tel Lachish 1978–1983: Second Preliminary Report.* Tel Aviv: Institute of Archaeology, Tel Aviv University (repr.).

UVB J. Jordan. *Vorläufiger Bericht über die von der Notgemeinschaft der deutschen Wissenschaft in Uruk-Warka unternommenen Ausgrabungen.* Abhandlungen der Preussischen Akademie der Wissenschaften, 1929. Philologisch-historische Klasse 7. Berlin: Akademie der Wissenschaften, 1930.

VAS Vorderasiatische Schriftdenkmäler der Königlichen Museen zu Berlin.

de Vaux, R.

1972 *The Bible and the Ancient Near East.* London: Darton, Longman, and Todd.

Weissbach, F. H.

1911 *Die Keilinschriften der Achämeniden.* Vorderasiatische Bibliothek 3. Leipzig: Hinrichs.

Wellhausen, J.

1883 *Prolegomena zur Geschichte des Volkes Israels.* Berlin: Reimer.

de Wette, W. M. L.

1807 *Beiträge zur Einleitung in das Alte Testament, 2: Kritik der israelitischen Geschichte.* Halle: Schimmelpfennig.

Wetzel, F., and F. H. Weissbach

1938 *Das Hauptheiligtum des Marduk in Babylon, Esagila und Etemenanki.* Wissenschaftliche Veröffentlichungen der deutschen Orient-Gesellschaft 59. Leipzig: Hinrichs.

Willi, T.

1972 *Die Chronik als Auslegung: Untersuchungen zur literarischen Gestaltung der historischen Überlieferung Israels.* Forschungen zur Religion und Literatur des Alten und Neuen Testaments 106. Göttingen: Vandenhoeck and Ruprecht.

Williamson, H. G. M.

1982 The Death of Josiah and the Continuing Development of the Deuteronomic History. *Vetus Testamentum* 32: 242–48.

1983 The Composition of Ezra i–vi. *Journal of Theological Studies* 34: 1–30.

1985 *Ezra, Nehemiah.* Word Biblical Commentary 16. Waco: Word Books.

1987 Reliving the Death of Josiah: A Reply to C. T. Begg. *Vetus Testamentum* 37: 9–15.

Wiseman, D. J.

1951 Two Historical Inscriptions from Nimrud. *Iraq* 13: 21–26.

1956 A Fragmentary Inscription of Tiglath-Pileser III from Nimrud. *Iraq* 18: 116–29.

1964 Fragments of Historical Texts from Nimrud. *Iraq* 26: 118–24.

Yadin, Y.

1980 A Rejoinder. *Bulletin of the American Schools of Oriental Research* 239: 19–23.

The Bible in the University

James L. Kugel
Harvard University

The Origins of Biblical Criticism

My purpose in the following is to examine briefly an aspect of the origins of the discipline known as modern biblical scholarship. I hope that I will be forgiven what amounts to a sustained look at biblical exegesis as it existed some centuries ago—territory that is normally considered somewhat outside the scope of biblical scholarship per se—but this swerve itself is ultimately part of the point I wish to make. For it has always struck me as somewhat ironic that contemporary biblicists rarely stop to consider the intellectual and social foundations of their discipline: after all, for many of us, trying to understand the writings of ancient Israel itself by means of reconstructing its mental and social world is a daily concern. Yet the same sort of sensitivity to historical context does not generally extend to trying to understand the undertaking in which we ourselves are thus engaged—indeed, unlike students of European literatures, or of the history of art or political or intellectual history, biblical scholars often show a surprising lack of interest in, or knowledge of, their own discipline's earlier years. I am not certain that the brief remarks that follow can do much more than to suggest that this state of affairs is lamentable; but in seeking so to do, I would like to begin by evoking one or two specific, and somewhat neglected, points.

The first concerns the time of origin of the intellectual movement we call modern biblical scholarship. And here I should like to say that, contrary to the impression one might gain by reading many standard introductions, modern biblical scholarship did not begin in the nineteenth century, nor yet in the eighteenth, but in the sixteenth, that is, toward the end of the Renaissance and the massive shift in sensibilities and scholarly methods that it had ushered in, first in Italy, then elsewhere on the Continent and in England. This is not to say, of course, that subsequent centuries did not witness further dramatic changes in our understanding of the Bible, changes that may in some respect dwarf the relatively modest achievements of

Renaissance Bible scholars. But it is to say, simply, that the starting point of all such advances is to be located in the sixteenth century, whose innovations in scholarly tools and assumptions caused a whole new field of study to be born—the same field in which biblical critics are engaged today.

The innovations of Renaissance biblical scholarship are usually attributed to changes in the objective conditions under which it was carried out. And it is true that, for example, the incomparably greater knowledge of Hebrew found among Renaissance scholars was itself dependent in some measure on the invention of the printing press and the subsequent rapid diffusion of Hebrew texts of the Bible, Hebrew grammars written in Latin, and dictionaries, lexicons, and even rabbinic texts and commentaries published either in the original or in Latin translation. It is in fact striking in how relatively short a span of time there emerged an almost entirely new class of scholars, collectively known nowadays as the "Christian Hebraists." Trained in Hebrew (as ever) by Jewish teachers,[1] directly or *par personne interposée*, with the aid of Johannes Reuchlin's pioneering Hebrew grammar (1506) or some other early manual,[2] these men sought to master every aspect of the Hebrew Bible: not only did they wish to read and understand the text in its original tongue, but they undertook to translate it anew, no longer confiding in the judgments of Jerome's Vulgate and other received wisdom.[3] Renaissance scholars composed, or referred to, guides to Hebrew style, sometimes identifying in Hebrew various tropes and figures familiar from schoolboy exercises in Latin rhetoric, but also, more significantly, other features without parallel in classical tongues, proper only to the language of the

1. The history of interaction between Jewish teachers and Christian biblical scholars goes back to the very beginnings of Christianity, and is significant not only in late antiquity but again afresh in the Carolingian Renaissance. In the twelfth century, with the founding of the Abbey of St. Victor in Paris (whence: "Victorine scholarship") and such events as the compilation of the Cistercian Bible by Stephen Harding (on the basis of the orally transcribed comments of a "renowned Jewish scholar," probably a member of Rashi's circle) Christian familiarity with Hebrew and the Jewish exegetical tradition reached a new peak. (Smalley 1964 contains a detailed account of the Victorine masters; on Nicholas de Lyra and Jewish scholarship, see Hailperin 1963.) However, all these instances pale before that of the Christian Hebraists of the Renaissance, when for the first time one can speak of thorough-going Jewish learning and a solid grasp of philological issues in Christian circles.

2. Reuchlin's was almost the first work of its kind; it had been immediately preceded by Conrad Pellican's *De modo legendi et intelligendi Hebraeum* (1504). An undated Hebrew grammar, ca. 1500, was prepared by Aldo Manuzio; other, far sketchier works date from the end of the fifteenth century (see Weil 1963: 249–52; and Roth 1959: 142).

3. Here there are of course antecedents; in fact it was in the twelfth century that Christian scholars first began seriously to challenge the authority of Jerome's translation, even turning his phrase *Hebraica veritas* into their rallying-cry; see Grabois 1975, who points to the use of this term by Stephen Harding (*Patrologia latina* 166: 1375). Note that *Hebraica veritas* continued to be the slogan of sixteenth-century translators and commentators.

Bible. They gloried in the *Hebraismus* and all that constituted the *proprietas* of the language. Most strikingly, they were drawn to the entire corpus of postbiblical Jewish writings about the Bible, rabbinic and medieval commentators, the whole body of Jewish law and aggadah, the writings of medieval Jewish grammarians, philologians, and lexicographers, Hebrew liturgical and secular poetry, Jewish philosophy, and, with perhaps the greatest enthusiasm of all, at least in some quarters, the Kabbalah. For Christian Hebraists generally assumed as axiomatic the continuity (just as some modern scholars have assumed the discontinuity) between biblical and postbiblical Jewish civilization: the first place to look for the elucidation of a difficult word or theologically troubling passage was among the "learned Rabbins," and Jewish tradition was, at least initially, consulted as a kind of "native informant" for all matters touching on the Bible.

Typical of this spirit is Sebastian Münster's preface to his popular edition of the Hebrew Bible, מקדש ה׳ *vel Hebraica Biblia* (1534–55), which contains a section entitled "The Commentaries of the Jews are Not to be Condemned." In it he defends the use of the whole corpus of Jewish writings (adducing Jerome as his model and precedent)—targum, Talmud, and, besides the well-known commentary of Rabbi Solomon (Rashi), other works of medieval Jewish exegesis, written by "the many outstanding Rabbis whom the Jews had in Spain, Africa, and other regions." To be sure, Jewish writings contained potential pitfalls, and had to be approached with caution; still, they were an invaluable, and un-ignorable, source of information: "Let neither the reading nor the interpretation of the Rabbis go counter to you, O Christian reader, if you have learned Christ purely; for He will come forth, whether they agree with us or disagree." And as any student of Christian Hebraists knows, Münster's is both an outstanding Christian compendium of Jewish learning and yet hardly unique in its views.[4]

The names of many of the Hebraists of the sixteenth century, Catholic and Protestant—Münster, and his teacher C. Pellican; Egidio Viterbo and Xanctes Pagninus; François Vatable, Jean Le Mercier, G. G. Postel, G. Genebrardus, J. J. Scaliger, F. Junius, Andreas Masius, B. Arias Montano, M. Flacius Illyricus, V. Schindler, and dozens more—are nowadays largely forgotten, but no modern biblical scholar perusing their writings would, I

4. Writing on this subject recently, M. Goshen-Gottstein (1975) has correctly stressed that, despite their enthusiasm for Hebrew language study and for rabbinic and later Jewish learning, Christian scholars never allowed Jews as such to participate in the revolution in biblical studies except as (often paid) tutors, and that that revolution was hardly the result of Christian-Jewish "dialogue": it was, as he notes, a "purely internal Christian affair." Seeing the inherent contradiction in Christian reliance on Jewish exegetes, Luther and his contemporaries specifically limited Jewish "help" to the realm of philology.

think, have difficulty identifying their activity with his own. For what exited already in the sixteenth century was a set of schools and centers, each familiar with the work emanating from elsewhere and collectively embarked upon a thorough reexamination of Scripture. Their interests ranged from the minutely philogical (where they often had recourse to linguistic comparisons, to cognates in "Chaldaic" and occasionally Arabic) to broader issues: the reliability of the Masoretic text, the system of Hebrew poetry, authorship and unity of various books, the nature of prophecy and divine inspiration. At times they pointed out errors or impossibilities in the text; at times they proposed emendations. They referred to each other by name, and relatively frequently; references to more distant predecessors are far less common. None of this is particularly remarkable until it is juxtaposed to the Christian biblical scholarship of just a century or two earlier, whose laconic, crabbed style and flat assertions (usually presented as if already known to the reader, or else bolstered by invocations of the hoariest authorities—even, indeed especially, when seeking slightly to modify or reinterpret the received wisdom) and whose (at times deceptively) static quality and utter submission to text and tradition all seem light-years away from current notions of scholarly inquiry.

It was said that the printing press is often credited with having influenced dramatically the course of biblical scholarship; other "objective" changes are also cited. Thus, the rise of classical scholarship and the rebirth of interest in ancient Greece and Rome certainly presented students of the Bible with a methodological model. They copied the classical scholars' concern for correct texts and manuscript comparisons, and, still more significantly, they took to heart the Renaissance writers' new appreciation of the gap between "us" and "the Ancients," "our" Latin and "theirs." Israel too was an ancient people, indeed, the most ancient, so that even after all translations had been scrutinized and corrected in accordance with the most advanced information, if there nevertheless remained expressions, sentiments, or ideas that seemed foreign or even repugnant, Renaissance scholars were less likely to attribute the difficulties to the domain of divine caprice. They no longer automatically believed, with Augustine, that anything that contradicts doctrine or even simply does not concern right conduct or questions of faith must be interpreted figuratively (*De Doctrina Christiana* 3:10:14). A new respect for the *sensus litteralis* had slowly been built up. (This happened gradually; for its beginnings see Smalley 1964: 281; and Froehlich 1977:34). Now they were more likely to explain a problem in the text with reference to some feature native to the language or culture of Israel: "This is how the Hebrews express strong disapproval"; "Hebrew has no superlative as in Latin, and so must employ a singular substantive followed by the same substantive in the plural, so as to designate the foremost in its class." Commentators were fond of cataloguing Hebrew idioms: *manus lavere* means to dissociate oneself from, *filius* designates membership in a class or affiliation, *ecce ego* indicates both presence and obedience. And they rejoiced in pointing out the absurdities of too literal a translation: "Placuit verbum in oculis meis," "Abrahamus plenus dierum mortuus est," "locutus est deus per manum prophetae," "duxit eam in uxorem" (see Münster 1534–35: 14).

Certainly the Protestant Reformation itself became the greatest "outside" impulse to the new approach—though it is important to stress that the rise of the new movement in biblical studies had itself been a significant factor leading up to that Reformation. Once underway, however, the Reformed denominations were to become a driving force behind the new biblicism. For Reformers were anxious in all things to start afresh, and the notion that the new biblical science might demonstrate the falsity of old Popish interpretations was obviously congenial. This position was highlighted in the well-known motto, *Sola Scriptura.* For if Scripture's *words alone* were to be authoritative, then all previous interpretations of what those words meant were now open to new arbitration. Of course this slogan, or complex of slogans, was not the invention of the Reformers (see Ebeling 1964; and Pfürtner 1977), nor ought the authority vested in Scripture by them be thought of as a wholly new departure. What was significant was the use to which their act of Scriptural obeisance was put—how it was intended, and perceived, as the ideological justification for a new stance toward tradition and traditional authority. In this sense, Scripture's presence was nothing less than electric, the ever renewed dynamo in the Reformers' midst. There is no clearer statement of the power of the Scriptural stance than Luther's famous words before Emperor Charles V at the Diet of Worms in 1521, when he was asked to recant his views:

> Unless I be convinced by evidence of Scripture or by plain reason—for I do not accept the authority of the Pope or the councils alone, since it is demonstrated that they have often erred and contradicted themselves—I am bound by the Scriptures I have cited, and my conscience is captive to the Word of God. I cannot and will not recant anything, for it is neither safe nor right to go against conscience. God help me. Amen.

Here much is made apparent in a few words: the enthronement of Scripture (along with "plain reason") as supreme authority; the pointed opposition of this authority to that of the Pope; and, finally, the suggestion that the latter's errors and contradictions in, among other things, scriptural interpretation have ultimately invalidated the Church's very authority. Almost from the start, the central issue was what Luther elsewhere called the Pope's "right of interpreting Sacred Scripture by the sole virtue and majesty of his exalted office and power, against all intelligence and erudition" (Luther

1897: 96; Kugel 1986: 22–23)—the latter two being, of course, the hallmarks of recent biblical scholarship. In a real sense, then, it was the modern movement in biblical scholarship that helped to make the Reformers' stance more than that of mere malcontents, just as it was the newly established Protestant denominations that subsequently provided biblical scholarship with its greatest on-going sponsor. (It is less often remarked, but remarkable nonetheless, that their opponents observed the same rules: instead of just sticking to tradition and vehemently invoking the unbroken chain of Church authority in all its force, Catholic scholars themselves argued as learned Hebraists, and their efforts as exegetes are sometimes indistinguishable from those of their Protestant contemporaries.) A knowledge of Hebrew, to whatever ideology's service it was put, passed in the sixteenth century from being the sign of a truly erudite scholar to being simply the *sine qua non* for undertaking serious Old Testament work. Indeed, it was in the sixteenth century that Hebrew entered the mainstream of education, and a solid trilingual foundation—in Latin, Greek, and Hebrew—was now at the heart of humanistic studies in the emerging institutions of higher learning in Europe (see Goshen-Gottstein 1981).

Beyond all these relatively discrete and namable factors responsible for the change in biblical studies in the Renaissance there is of course the far more intractable "shift in consciousness" which was the Renaissance itself. The intractability of such a concept should not cause us to understate its importance. That the printing press, classical studies, Reformist strivings, and so forth had something to do with what happened to biblical studies is certainly undeniable; but surely the spread of modern-style biblical study had not been held back by their absence. After all, the Hebrew text of the Bible had circulated among the Jews of Europe without impediment solely through the efforts of hand-copyists and scribes; comparative linguistic studies, a mastery of Arabic, Aramaic, and other Semitic tongues surely could have been acquired by Christians had the wealth of empires felt the need for it; and so forth. The point is that the change that came about in biblical studies in the Renaissance was but part of the change in consciousness that was the Renaissance as a whole, one of those major settlings in the spiritual continent that causes here a river to shift its course, there a town to be engulfed, but whose vital center lies somewhere beneath the discrete landmarks of ordinary geography. In this century historians have pushed the beginning of the Renaissance back to the twelfth century, perhaps even earlier, and to the extent that their concern is with causes and adumbrations, no doubt there is some merit to their claims.[5] But what is more important to

5. The diffuseness of the Renaissance's beginnings is such that some have even denied its very existence (though of course "Renaissance" is itself a Renaissance term, and its leaders

point out here is that the Renaissance's other extreme is equally fluid, and that in regard to biblical studies, no shift in sensibilities of any comparable magnitude has occurred between the Renaissance and our own day. In this sense most of all, modern biblical criticism is a child of the Renaissance and inhabits the same world, by and large unchanged in its goals and, one might almost say, in the overall cast of its methods.

A Change in the Rules

The overwhelming impression produced by observing the change from medieval to Renaissance exegesis is that in some drastic way the rules of what was and was not acceptable behavior had changed, and that as a result the subject of discourse itself was no longer the same. Again, it would be wrong to imply too swift a change, or indeed to collapse the course of medieval Christian exegesis—the rise of threefold and fourfold exegesis, shifting emphases within the canon of the Hebrew Bible, the role of preaching within the monastic orders, Jewish-Christian scholarly interaction, the resurgence of the *sensus litteralis* in the thirteenth century (on these, see in general Lubac 1959; Smalley 1964; and Froehlich 1977)—into a single whole, the better to oppose it to all that is Renaissance exegesis. (For one aspect of the continuity from late medieval to Renaissance to Reformation religious thought, see Trinkaus 1974; cf. Preus 1969.) Nevertheless it is true that the totality and intensity of innovation in biblical exegesis of, especially, the sixteenth century does set it quite apart from what had preceded it. Something, to put it bluntly, had snapped.

In regard to the Bible, at least, our fuzzy notion "Renaissance humanism" is entirely apt. For like, for example, the name "Impressionism," this phrase too has ballooned beyond the meaning intended in its first use to suggest something still more fundamental about its referent.[6] As far as exegesis is concerned, it well sums up the new focus on the human (as opposed to the divine) side of biblical texts. Of course the polysemous manipulations of the great divine *Auctor*, He who arranges each sentence and even word so as to carry a multitude of significances and point backward and forward to other parts of the Sacred Writ, were still the object of scholarly study. But alongside this was a growing interest in the bearers of

were quite aware of their age as pathbreaking and revolutionary). See in general Kristeller 1979.

6. Properly speaking, "Renaissance humanism" now designates first and foremost a broad set of intellectual concerns and methods. Its sense, however, was initially quite narrow—the "humanist profession" was exercised by a small circle of literary scholars and writers—and had little to do with the concerns now generally connected with "humanism." See briefly Kristeller 1979: 21–32; Kristeller 1974: 367–70; Gray 1968.

that Divine Word, the actual human beings connected with different biblical texts: if Moses or Isaiah had penned this phrase, what could *he*, speaking in this particular historical circumstance and addressing himself, in the rough sonorities of the world's most ancient tongue, to the particular audience he had before him, have intended those listeners to understand? This implied, to a certain extent, an identification between the exegete and the human transmitters of the Divine Word, so that one of the most striking features of Christian biblical scholarship in the sixteenth century was the imaginative comparison between past and present. Luther was hardly unique in his well-known penchant for explaining biblical texts with reference to his own tribulations and/or to the events of his day, an approach predicated on the assumption of a basic comparability and communality between human beings living in the biblical period and those of the sixteenth century. An art historian might well point to similar developments in the representation of biblical figures or scenes by European painters and sculptors of a somewhat earlier period, such as Claus Sluter's magnificent *Well of Moses* (Dijon, France, early fifteenth century), whose prophets (carved, it is said, with the aid of authentic Jewish models imported for the purpose) are no longer the disembodied messengers of God's word, but real people, Jews, an Isaiah absorbed in intense, but utterly human, spirituality, or a Jeremiah musing behind a (now-lost) pair of gilded spectacles.

Now here is the point: *all* of the major trends of modern biblical scholarship, and many of its conclusions, existed in latency as soon as the rules of acceptable assumptions and procedures began to change in the fifteenth and sixteenth centuries: all that remained was to ask, one by one, the questions permitted by the new outlook and by the increasing freedom from established tradition and Church dogma. And indeed, some of the questions were absurdly obvious! How were these books actually written, and by whom? Why should Moses, if he were the author of the Pentateuch, have penned most of it in the third person (even describing himself, in the well-known instance of Num 12:3, in the paradoxical "Now the man Moses was extremely humble, more so than any man on the face of the earth"), then, speaking in the third person in Deuteronomy, begin as it were to quote himself and so switch to an extended first person for much of that book? And how indeed could he have penned the account of his own death and the Israelites' subsequent mourning? Why should David be held to be the author of the Psalter if so many of the Psalms are patently attributed to other men? The problem of narrative doublets, or of apparent contradictions within or between books, has required extended analysis and discussion before today's sophisticated set of conclusions could be arrived at; but the basic problem, *and its answer*—that behind these texts stand different versions and sources—were foreseeable almost as soon as such questions and answers became permissible. And so it is with other concerns of contemporary scholarship, discussions of the institutions of Israelite society, questions about the historicity of biblical figures and narrative details, about the exclusive nature of early Israelite monotheism, the relationship of biblical Israel to its neighbors, and so on. Indeed, it is noteworthy that adumbrations of many of these questions have subsequently been found here and there in the Middle Ages among Jewish and Christian exegetes (for some of the Jewish examples see briefly Sarna 1980)—noteworthy, but not for the reason usually cited. For what is remarkable is not the "insight" itself—which often was all too obvious—but the way in which that dangerous foreign body was then instantly sealed off by the commentator's own efficient immune system, in the elegant apologetics of Augustine or in Abraham ibn Ezra's curt warning, "Let him who understands keep still." Here truly is something remarkable. Why were not these passing insights the springboard to a fullscale reevaluation and new understanding of the Bible back then? Why was not the claim that parts of the Pentateuch had been written by Joshua or the latter prophets or in the days of Jehosaphat (see ibn Ezra *ad* Gen 36:31) the spark that set off a fullscale inquiry into the sources of the Pentateuch? Why did not disbelief in the Davidic authorship of the Psalter, enunciated openly by ibn Gikatilla and others (see Simon 1982: 239), have the same effect on medieval biblical scholarship that it would have eight centuries later? Why, in other words, did not Wellhausen flourish in eleventh-century Spain? The answer to these questions is long, and might, on another occasion, be interesting to pursue; but in the present context our point is simply that, with the rise of Renaissance biblical scholarship, such questions now ceased to be sealed off. They were on the contrary fostered and investigated by a new cadre of scholars pursuing the age-old task of understanding Christendom's sacred book, a cadre that set about, in short order, revolutionizing Western Europe's understanding the Bible.

Biblical Scholarship and Protestantism

It was mentioned that this nascent movement of biblical scholarship was nourished by the Protestant Reformation, and that much of its manpower, then as now, came from the Protestant denominations. This is, as I have implied, hardly an incidental detail in trying to understand its overall stance as a discipline—and yet I daresay the extent of this movement's Protestant character is still today largely ignored. But biblical criticism is Protestantism's child not only in the relatively limited sense already seen—that to displace the power of the Pope it was convenient for a time to enthrone Scripture as the sole authority, demonstrating en route that "Popish" exegesis is wrong, unfaithful to the Hebrew, and so forth. Far more fundamentally, biblical criticism is Protestant in its very attitude toward the text. For the Protestant movement as a whole was predicated on the unmediated encounter between man and God—unmediated, that is, by the saints or semidivine intercessors, by professional clergy, eventually even by the church itself. One was a Christian as a result of conviction; one sought forgiveness and salvation directly from God and found guidance through personal revelation and, most particularly, through the careful study of the corpus of divine revelation, namely, Scripture. The encounter between man and text was the precise parallel of the encounter between man and God. It too was to be entirely unmediated. The explanations put forward of old, hallowed by tradition and the Church's stamp of approval, could no longer be relied upon to bring one to a proper understanding of God's word. Between the open pages of the Book and the individual intently poised above them there would intervene absolutely nothing: it was the Spirit within, the potential to be graced with revelation afresh, that would be the exegete's ultimate guide. The continuation of the passage from Luther cited above (1897: 96) is still apposite: "Scripture is to be understood only by the Spirit in which Scripture was written, because the Spirit is never to be found more present and lively than in the sacred writings themselves." There was no reason to attribute to the Church hierarchy a monopoly on, or even privileged portion of, that Spirit, especially when so much of the Bible seemed now to speak in a way utterly different from that understood by scholastic exegetes or the Fathers of the Church. Indeed, was not the fact that Jerome's *Hebraica veritas* was here and there in error, and that after Jerome virtually all of the Church's great expositors and commentators had been utterly ignorant of Hebrew (and even Greek), proof enough of the unreliability of their understanding?

And so, to understand the Word of God properly, it was now necessary to read it with fresh eyes, uncorrupted by the errors of the past. At first, as we have seen briefly, Jewish tradition presented itself as a new, uncorrupted source of "native" learning—and, compared to the allegorical, anagogical, or tropological readings of medieval Christianity, the Jewish concern with the Letter (though how foolish such a characterization was should be apparent to all nowadays), plus its wealth of marginalia, bits of background information about this or that biblical personage, made it a far more compatible body of exegesis. It was, by reason of being Jewish, considered infinitely closer to the source of the original, and on the other hand it could easily be dispensed with when necessary, written off as merely Jewish fancy or superstition, if not the result of a thoroughly "purblind," "legalistic," or "eternally contemned" approach. But soon enough, even Jewish mediation was done away with. Andreas Masius remarks, without much apparent dissatisfaction, on "what ignorance of their own language the Jews today are cast in, and how they have not the slightest discernment about it" (1574: 185). Johannes Buxtorf similarly believed that knowledge of the methods and system of biblical composition "began to be neglected shortly after the time of the Prophets, and thence, with the ancient wisdom of the Hebrews more and more on the decline, alas finally was cast into a shameful oblivion amongst them" (1629: 627). Such sentiments were increasingly echoed in the seventeenth and eighteenth centuries, until eventually Jewish exegesis, and even Jewish philology, chronology, and the like were banished from Protestant Bible study. For reasons perhaps connected with the tenuousness of various Protestant sects' stance as a "New Judaism" and as a return to the religion of the Bible, a line was drawn between the "Former Jews" and those of today, or between "Israel" of the Bible and later "Hebrews." These latter had increasingly little of interest to teach about the former, for the separation between them came ultimately to deprive rabbinic (and, *a fortiori*, medieval Jewish) writings of the authority of tradition.

So—conveniently, one might say—there was no tradition; there was only the inspired reading, the Spirit within man perceiving the Spirit within the words. Yet it is interesting that Luther in the above citation had mentioned mental as well as spiritual gifts: the blind exercise of the Pope's "right of interpreting Sacred Scripture" was counterpointed to "all intelligence and erudition." For in the encounter between man and text, learning would also be important. It was necessary for Christians to arm themselves with knowledge, first of the Bible itself, then of its languages, its background history (thus the ever popular Josephus's *Antiquities*), and anything else that might prove useful. Detailed philological commentaries flourished, polyglot Bibles, and soon dictionaries, concordances, and other study aids became valued tools for informed Christendom. Home Bible study flourished. By the end of the eighteenth century this library had swelled to include all manner of textual and philological tools and detailed historical-critical monographs, as well as the first general "Introductions" to the Old and New Testaments.

One of the first critical questions to be raised, as mentioned, was that of authorship: How much of the Pentateuch was written by Moses? Which Psalms were *not* written by David? Such questions obviously touched on the texts' authority: a divine revelation granted to the true prophet Moses was fine—but what gave authority to anonymous additions, expansions, nay, the work of imposters? The pursuit of the authentically Mosaic, Davidic, etc. thus acquired a certain nervous urgency, and ultimately led, as is well known, to the birth of Source Criticism. What is less often appreciated is the extent to which, even with Moses, David and others increasingly out of the picture in the nineteenth century, scholars continued to think in terms of known individuals—various later prophets, or Ezra and Nehemiah—as candidates for the true authorship of these biblical books, as if to salvage something of the writers' credentials; or still later spoke of J, E, D, and P as of inspired individuals, seeking to flesh out behind these evocative initials (like those of the heroes of so many nineteenth-century novels) the figures of real people, authors, the better to grapple with each's original meaning and purpose, as well as the real events and circumstances to which his words were addressed.

At the same time, since biblical books themselves were composites and shaped by later editors possessed of their own theological or political designs, the Bible could hardly be considered an adequate account of what really happened. But "what really happened" had, through a complicated evolution that I have only touched upon briefly, come to assume an altogether unprecedented place on the modern biblicist's agenda: for as the Bible became less and less "Scripture" in the sense it had once been, that is, less and less the great repository of all divine teaching that, read aright, would unfold history, theology, and the end of days in its infinitely elaborate manner of exposition—as this Bible receded (albeit slowly), the actual deeds recounted within it came to occupy a correspondingly greater importance. What really *did* happen? This question, whose focus, for example, in the seventeenth and eighteenth centuries was still largely the miracles recounted in Old and New Testament narratives, later on was extended to include nothing less than the entire history of Israel. And if the biblical narratives could no longer be turned to as simple, factual accounts of "what really happened," it became necessary both to explain their purpose as Scripture and to provide the world with an adequate history of what *did* happen. The latter concern resulted in a profusion of works at the end of the nineteenth century all bearing the title "History of Israel" (or slight variants thereupon) in various languages. E. Renan's preface to his own entry into this genre, *Histoire du peuple d'Israel* (1893), well expresses the common spirit of these undertakings, the piecing together of a true account from the imperfect biblical evidence:

> The most stalwart efforts of modern criticism and philosophy have been needed in order to catch a glimpse of the truth in these ancient texts, in which everything seems designed to throw us off the track. Old epic tales, in their own way sincere, a bit of theocratic touching-up, and priestly modifications all jumble together, sometimes in a single paragraph, so that the most intense examination is required to distinguish them. . . . In the historical portions of the Bible, the different redactions so overlap, and the scissors of the compilers have snipped in so capricious a manner, that it is sometimes necessary to give up any

> hope of performing on these strange assemblages any definitive act of sorting. . . . Nevertheless, the critical art has on occasion wrested from these challenges to our wisdom some astonishing victories.

Biblical Bedrock

At the risk of stating the obvious, I might point out here why it was that the way the Bible had been studied in centuries gone by was now conceived as totally irrelevant to the modern movement. That previous sort of Bible study was rejected not because it had been carried out in confessional surroundings and for confessional purposes—such continued to be the case in the new movement as well—but because that old kind of biblical exegesis, the essence of popery, was no longer considered methodologically sound, indeed, it was derided as apologetic, fantastic, and most of all benighted by traditions that had remained too long unquestioned, bolstered by medieval *auctoritas* in the face of common sense or advancing science. The great divine teachings of the Bible had to spring from its very words, not from Church tradition or fanciful interpretation. Now this attitude toward the past, although it can be identified at the very start of the modern movement, hardly ceased when it encountered difficulties (which happened right away: such fundamental notions as the Trinity could no longer, by the new canons of scholarship, be given a biblical locus). On the contrary, it has persisted to our own century. Let me quote from a well-known scholar of the turn of our century, C. A. Briggs, professor of Bible at Union Theological Seminary in New York, in his own Old Testament introduction (1901: 531, emphasis added):

> Ancient Jerusalem lies buried beneath the rubbish of more than eighteen centuries. It is covered over by the blood-stained dust of myriads of warriors, who have battled heroically under its walls and in its towers and streets. Its valleys are filled with the débris of palaces, churches, and temples. But the Holy Place of three great religions is still there, and thither countless multitudes turn in holy reverence and pious pilgrimage. In recent times this rubbish has in a measure been explored; and by digging to the rock-bed and the ancient foundations bearing the marks of the Phoenician workmen, the ancient city of the holy times has been recovered, and may now be constructed in our minds by the artist and the historian with essential accuracy. Just so the Holy Scripture, as given by divine inspiration to holy prophets, lies buried beneath the rubbish of centuries. It is covered over with the débris of the traditional interpretations of the multitudinous schools and sects. The intellectual and moral conflicts which have raged about it have been vastly more costly than all the battles of armed men. For this conflict has never ceased. This battle has taxed and strained all the highest energies of our race. It has been a struggle in

> the midst of nations and of families, and has torn many a man's inmost soul with agony and groanings.
>
> The valleys of biblical truth have been filled up with the débris of human dogmas, ecclesiastical institutions, liturgical formulas, priestly ceremonies, and casuistic practices. Historical criticism is digging through this mass of rubbish. Historical criticism is searching for the rock-bed of the Divine Word, *in order to recover the real Bible*. Historical criticism is sifting all this rubbish. It will gather out every precious stone. Nothing will escape its keen eye.

What I find engaging about this citation is its frank equation of the whole history of biblical exegesis with garbage, so much "débris" to be swept out of the way in order to get at the bedrock of Scriptural truth. But the analogy between archeological exploration and biblical study was hardly *only* that, and was hardly this author's alone. One might describe it more accurately as the controlling metaphor of several generations of modern scholars, those for whom textual and actual digging jointly held the promise of recovering some great, long-lost biblical edifice just below the surface, an edifice that, once fully unearthed and dusted off, would emerge as the authentic and unsullied word of God, the "real Bible," as Briggs calls it, in all its primal splendor.

I hope that this sounds to most of us a bit quaint nowadays. For though our century has not been devoid of archeological or textological thrills—indeed, I would not hesitate to describe ours as the most dramatic, and continually impressive, period ever for scholarship in both departments—nevertheless the great message of biblical scholarship since at least the turn of the century has been that this controlling metaphor, and the conceptions and aspirations that underlie it, are hopelessly naïve. Biblical bedrock has proven to be an elusive item, and far less adamantine than had been imagined. Moreover, we have been shown time and again that the process of paring books down to their original units or to the supposed *ipsissima verba* of this or that historical figure hardly yields the sort of purified sacred corpus that Briggs had hoped for, the "rock-bed of divine truth." For the more precisely we have been able to understand this or that passage within its original boundaries and context, the more have its peculiarities been explainable with reference solely to the aetiological interest of ancient Israelite historiography, to the sociopolitical institution of prophecy in the Judaean state, and so forth. Indeed, what we have come to see is that biblical scholarship, far from peeling off layers of debris from atop a long-buried, pristine building, has accomplished something rather different. It has revealed to us that a building in plain sight, whose dimensions had been familiar to us for two millennia, was actually put together over the course of the preceding millennium from building blocks many of which were originally hewn for quite another purpose; that it was assembled in different stages by different hands; and—here is the most important point—that the architects who finally put it together and made of it a usable edifice were something like collagists or the "junk sculpture" artists of the 1960s, whose creative eye could turn the front bumper of a Buick into a giant lady's smile, and combine that with other finds of metal and of plastic into a mammoth countenance worthy of our reverence.

And so we now live in a time when, as never before in the history of the modern movement, we are increasingly unsure about the overriding relevance of "original meaning" and "what really happened," and for the same reason increasingly interested in, and respectful of, editorial activity, *verba* that are not *ipsissima*, the reasons for this or that collocation, the final shape of this or that book, indeed, even that old embodiment of irrelevance, "precritical" biblical interpretation. For one thing that the discoveries at Qumran and elsewhere have taught us is that some of these precritical interpretations have ancient, nay, biblical roots themselves, and that in the second or third century B.C.E. the process of misreading ancient texts (with a junk sculptor's eye) was already well underway.

I mention Qumran, but certainly that is only one aspect of this latest turn in biblical scholarship. Textual criticism, and particularly the text-critical use of the Old Greek, has likewise highlighted both the manner and the extent to which interpretive traditions or readings have shaped the very words of our text, just as the whole domain of redaction history has done for larger textual units; and textual criticism has likewise demonstrated some of the indeterminancy of our concept of "the text," as well as the ambiguous yield of the search for a text's "most original form." The explosion of interest in the apocrypha and pseudepigrapha of the Hebrew Bible has similarly given prominence (and again, in some places, an address well within the biblical period) to the process of interpreting Israel's literary heritage, and to the extent to which this interpretive process was an element in the social and even political history of postexilic Judah. Indeed, the whole area of "inner-biblical exegesis," in which later biblical texts patently seek to interpret, expand, or apply earlier materials, has begun to be explored with renewed vigor, and it is no longer merely a question of Chronicles or Daniel, but of Isaiah and Deuteronomy and Genesis too.

The upshot of all this, and indeed of the whole general course of biblical studies in this century, has been, as noted, not only a greater respect for those final architects whose quirky vision helped to assemble these diverse fragments into an entity that made sense and was usable, but also a decrease in some of the energy and urgency that characterized the quest for "original meaning" in an earlier day. Indeed, the whole bifurcation into original text and later accretion, true meaning and later interpretation, and even "biblical" and "postbiblical" (a cousin of "Israelite" vs. "Jewish"), has become far more difficult in our day: as an approach it simply does not correspond to our own historical sensibilities and flies in the face of the not inconsiderable data and conclusions of scholars working in various parts of our field over the last few decades. (What such a bifurcation does correspond to, of course, is the old Protestant view of things, fueled by not a little anti-Semitism from the seventeenth to the twentieth century, especially in Germany but hardly limited to that place.)

But I have undertaken this quick tour in order to arrive at a practical matter and to suggest, finally, that the way that we teach the Bible in our universities ought to begin to reflect more directly the change in sensibilities as well as the data to which I have alluded. I daresay this is the case with many a Bible course taught in the university, whether for beginners or advanced students, whether working principally in Hebrew or in English: for is not our whole approach still largely shaped by the original Renaissance/Reformation quest? Indeed, though the context of secular university instruction is *eo ipso* secular, are not our Bible courses still somehow less than courses *in the Bible*, that is, the sorts of things, all things, that could be studied with scholarly rigor about the history of this or that given biblical text even within the biblical period? Are they not in fact exactly the sort of courses you would want to give to a young Protestant clergyman in order to prepare him or her to preach on a given biblical lesson strictly according to Luther's above-cited program, that is, in keeping with the latest findings of "all intelligence and erudition," of course devoid of all popery and Church-transmitted interpretation, and most of all stripped down to the divine essential, the primitive core in which the Spirit is "most present and lively," the very words themselves whispered from the mouth of God to the true prophet's ear?

What I am saying is that our whole notion of how to teach the Bible in a university is still lopsided and fundamentally confessional in character: the things that we do teach are certainly valuable, but they are far less than what ought to be taught, and they are presented with an unspoken order of priorities that translates perfectly the Protestant program. Let me put all of this in rather more concrete terms by talking about a course familiar to all, "Introduction to the Hebrew Bible" (or Old Testament, or Bible).

There are a great many different sorts of courses that go by this name. Some of them might more accurately be described as courses in the history of ancient Israel as glimpsed through its own literary creations, but sharpened by our knowledge of the same events through other texts and comparative data. This is a fine sort of course to teach, but it is hardly an adequate treatment of the Bible, any more than teaching the history of ancient Greece would be regarded as an adequate treatment of Homer or Hesiod or

Plato. Such a course is in fact a concretization of the project of the nineteenth-century historians that I mentioned earlier, who somehow came to believe that the events themselves were the whole point of biblical narrative and, judging the Bible to be an inadequate (because primitive and one-sided) narration of them, sought to write a better Bible, that is, a new history of Israel, on their own.

There are other sorts of introduction courses, ones that seek to read the Bible, or parts of it, in some more systematic way—but here again, the focus is first and foremost on the moment and milieu of origination, when the spirit was "most present and lively." And so such courses read the Abrahamic covenant in Genesis 15 (parenthesizing vv 13–16, of course) in terms of the ancient Near Eastern institution of covenant, and having thus explained things, move on. The exodus from Egypt is similarly discussed principally in terms of its historicity—what really happened—that is, who was the pharaoh of Exodus, which tribes really participated, the accounts found in various sources, how many plagues there really were, possible routes through the Sinai desert, and so forth; then, exit Exodus. Similarly the Psalms are presented in terms of Gunkel's psalm types (or some later modification thereof) and reinserted into their putative original *Sitz im Leben*; even the choice of psalms (itself a matter of nearly unbreakable convention) is tilted toward the earliest datable material, although the original reason for this tilt (an attempt to get at the "authentically Davidic" psalms) has long since passed from the scene. And so on and so forth, with Isaiah and Jeremiah, Amos and Hosea, Proverbs and Job and Ecclesiastes.

Please do not mistake my message. I believe that all the foregoing is quite relevant to an introductory Bible course and ought to maintain its place. But I think that the course I have described is both incomplete and misoriented, and that both of these circumstances are directly attributable to the facts of the little history I have traced above. I should perhaps also add that behind my criticism lurks not the slightest smidgin of religious apologetic, nor any neo-conservative desire to "reverse" the inroads of modern scholarship (whatever that might involve!), nor yet even an attempt to harmonize modern and traditional approaches to Scripture. All I am trying to do is to rethink a Bible course from the ground up, one that would try to present all the material rigorously and above all historically, but without slanting things to conform to any particular confessional orientation.

I should call such a course "The Hebrew Bible in the Making," a title that translates not only the irrefutable contention that the Bible came into its present form in stages, but one that implicitly substitutes for the archeological, pristinification approach that other metaphor, the architectonic, junk-sculpture one. Such a course would aim, simply, at telling the story of how the Bible came to be, and more precisely how it came to be read, from the earliest beginnings of its constituent texts to the time when these came together as מקרא or תורה or τα βιβλία (indeed, the late Latin feminine singular *Biblia*), that is, the sacred book of early Judaism and early Christianity.

It seems to me that this Bible, that is, the finished product, must be included, indeed, must be the logical end point of such a course, not because the so-called "canonization of the Bible" is such a momentous event (indeed, it is no event at all, but a process), but because the time of the institutionalization of a fixed body of Scripture in early Judaism and Christianity was also the time when a peculiar way of reading these ancient texts was institutionalized, and that the two together "made" the Bible for Judaism and Christianity for a very long time. This way of reading (or set of ways) had, as noted, deep biblical roots, but, once set loose in postexilic Judah, it had developed a life of its own, and by, say, the first century of the common era, had come to understand the ancient texts (as well as to augment and rearrange them) in such a way as to make them look in some cases strikingly different from what they had seemed when first uttered, indeed, to change their very essence (this is the junk-sculpture effect). Institutionalized in this changed form, they continued to be read and expounded in basically the same manner for the next thousand years, and more. So "The Bible," by which I mean not only the final form of these texts, but the way in which, in this form, they were read by Jews and Christians, is indeed the last stage of this building process, and one might even describe this assembling and reunderstanding of ancient texts as a second moment of authorship.

Such, then, is the course I have in mind, a tracing of the construction of this edifice from its earliest building blocks until its completed form. This course certainly begins its treatment of Genesis 15, for example, with a discussion of the ancient Near Eastern institution of covenant and why, at a certain point, it was important for ancient Israelites to know that their reputed ancestors had been the recipients of such divine grants. But it will also talk about how Israel's thinking about its ancestors and such traditions as Genesis 15 began to change under new historical circumstances; about how the reference to Abraham in Josh 24:2–4 reflects one such change, and how this passage eventually was "read back" into our Genesis passage (evidence of this collocation is to be found as early as Jdt 5:6–8)—indeed, it might go on to trace the whole story of Abraham's transformation from faceless founder and aetiological front man to early Judaism's Abraham the Tested One (known from Jubilees and elsewhere), Abraham the Astrologer, the priomordial Convert, the one saved from the Chaldeans' fiery furnace (that is, אור כשדים, the "fire" of the Chaldeans), and on to the New Testament's Man of Faith. This catalogue may appear overly ambitious, but surely the idea behind it is not: that it is not sufficient simply to address the moment of origin, the event itself or the earliest text recounting it, as if to say, "Anything after this is degeneration and irrelevant fantasy." Clearly it is not irrelevant, because there is an enormous gap within the history of biblical Israel between the Abraham of the world of ancient Near Eastern covenants and the Abraham of a book called The Bible, the book canonized by early Judaism and Christianity; and the teacher of a course in The Bible will certainly not have done his or her job unless the whole journey from the former to the latter is undertaken. In fact—and this is the whole point of my remarks—the only reason why such a teacher might ever have been persuaded to ignore this gap in the first place and to treat persons, events, oracles, and narratives only in terms of their original significance is if some unspoken theological preconception compelled him to do so, as if he believed that the moment of a text's origin corresponded to the moment of divine inspiration or divine-human interaction. *That* is what privileged it, the "original meaning" was the meaning meant by God, or meant by a narrator fresh from the real encounter between God and Abraham—whereas everything else was merely human and uninteresting. I daresay this is not what most biblical scholars say or probably believe nowadays, but they have unconsciously accepted the program and priorities of the founders of their discipline. So similarly, the words of the *real* Isaiah are what count and what is interesting, and the "rest" is somehow less than that, somehow secondary. And indeed, is not the scheme I have just presented merely a projection back onto the Bible itself of the original Protestant discrimination between the Divine Word of Scripture on the one hand and the merely human words of Church interpreters and dogmatists on the other? Only now Scripture itself is sorted out between divine and human, original (= divine) meaning and event and circumstances vs. later accretions and retellings and interpretations.

Once one abandons this order of priorities, there is no period in the history of Israel that is privileged above another, and all must be taken into account when tracing the history of the construction of the Bible. So, as to the other items I mentioned, this same operation practiced on Genesis 15 would have to be repeated: the Exodus narrative would be examined not only in its original significance and historical setting, but with regard to how it was played up, and played down, in various biblical and extrabiblical accounts and ultimately given new, symbolic significance, not only in Second Isaiah but by early Jewish and Christian commentators as well. Similarly the Psalms would of necessity be dealt with not only in terms of their original, largely cultic, *Sitz im Leben* and function. The apparent expansion of the uses of psalmody even within the biblical period would have to be given equal attention, and with it the development of the Psalter as a book; the psalm headings would be examined for what they show about some of the assumptions of early Scriptural exegesis, that is, how certain psalms were actually approached and read by their earliest interpreters; the figure of David the psalmist/prophet, as reflected in, for example, 11 Q Ps[a] might shed further light on this same subject, as would of course the history of interpretations of specific psalms and passages as reflected in, for example, the apocrypha and pseudepigrapha, in rabbinic texts or the Gospel narratives, or indeed the use of the psalms in early Jewish and Christian worship.

I sense at this point various sorts of disgruntled reactions that my remarks may inspire. The first is the most obvious and the most easily disposed of. It says: "Look, you define my task as teaching the Bible, but that's not how I see it. I am interested in teaching the literature (and, along with it, the history) of ancient Israel, in this case, say, the putative collected speeches of a certain Isaiah of Jerusalem. They could have been dug out of the ground, but I have dug them out of the Bible instead. You can argue about what I choose to label as authentically Isaianic, but surely you cannot quibble with the enterprise."

And I cannot. This seems to me to be a perfectly valid undertaking. And please note that in the introductory course I have been describing, just such an act of digging out Isaiah of Jerusalem and reconstructing not only his corpus but his historical circumstances, the coventions and sociology of eighth-century prophecy, and so forth all have a crucial role. Rather, the point of my remarks is this: that, first of all, performing only that operation is doing considerably less than what one who teaches the Bible, or even just the "history and literature of ancient Israel," can or ought to do; that, second of all, the fact that such a course be taught is one thing, but that a department should teach only such courses, that a department's very "Introduction to the Hebrew Bible" consists merely of the same exercise carried on throughout the Hebrew Bible, is quite another; and that, finally, a greater awareness of the historical context of modern biblical scholarship ought to make one wonder if our fondness for precisely this form of scholarly inquiry has not been shaped, as I have suggested, by confessional, rather than purely scholarly, considerations.

A second, more subtle reaction might be that this talk has been a very long tail attached to a very small dog—that in fact everything that I have had to say is really nothing more than the program of canonical criticism, and indeed this blending of ancient and modern insights had been around for quite a while even before it was put into programmatic form by such outstanding scholars as Brevard Childs. I should hardly seek to deny the connection, but let me add that the movement called canonical criticism (and that title covers several distinct undertakings) is essentially a theologically inspired project, indeed, a Protestant embracing of tradition, albeit of somewhat limited dimension. But while this movement seeks to validate the actual form of the Bible in the first, or third, century, finding in its "canonical shape" a more supple and less constricting (because no longer bound by the tyranny of "original intention") set of texts, it does so the better to undertake the ever-renewed Protestant act of interpreting afresh, or (which is the same thing) picking and choosing among extant interpretations, ancient-or-modern-it-makes-no-difference. Whereas the aim of the course described above is quite different and purely historical: to trace the growth of the Bible from its earliest origins in the life and thought-world of ancient Israel to its institutionalization in the life and thought-world of early Judaism and Christianity.

A third disgruntled reaction is of somewhat opposite tendency. It says, essentially: "You ask too much; this will never do as an introductory course, it is too demanding." I do not believe it is too demanding for *students*. In fact, I should confess at once that this course description is not entirely theoretical: I have been teaching such a course for several years now. Last time around it was taken by some three hundred and fifty only normally discontent undergraduates, and so could not be described as available only to future specialists or those possessed of extraordinary training and interests. More to the point is the objection that relatively few people who teach the Hebrew Bible in universities have the kind of professional training necessary to teach much about The Bible, that is, the canonized, interpreted, end product, as opposed to its constituent parts in their original environment. This *is* a valid objection, though perhaps not as widespread a problem as it might seem at first. For certainly any seminarian or graduate student who ever took a course in the New Testament and its historical environment has become acquainted with a good part of the picture, just as those with some exposure to rabbinic exegesis are likewise not on unfamiliar ground. What is more, to the extent that some biblicists are also Qumranologists and/or specialists in the apocrypha and pseudepigrapha, they are more than a little equipped to take on the task outlined. Nevertheless the objection stands, and stands therefore in the way of many who might otherwise be tempted to construe the task of teaching the Hebrew Bible in the terms outlined. It is not, however, an all-or-nothing proposition, and any course that moves from the exclusivist time-of-origination approach even one step in the direction of The Bible will have, to my mind, improved itself. Certainly a concerned instructor desirous of working toward this end can, even without formal graduate training in the fields mentioned, avail him- or herself of a variety of available tools without too much difficulty. But ultimately, the question with which I should like to close is not this personal and practical one, to which a whole gamut of personal and practical answers may be provided, but a rather long-winded theoretical one, the one to which this entire presentation has been pitched: Is there not something biased and rather wrongheaded in the way we currently conceive of the task of teaching the Bible, a wrongheadedness whose origins are all too obviously located in the religious polemics of the sixteenth century and which, having been institutionalized by the modern scholarly movement and passed on from teacher to pupil for generations, now stands more clearly than ever in contradiction both to what we know about the Bible's earliest origins and to what we have come to glimpse of the origins of biblical interpretations (and radical rereading) within the biblical period itself?

Bibliography

Briggs, C. A.
1901 *General Introduction to the Study of Holy Scripture*. New York: Scribners.

Buxtorf, J.
1629 *Thesaurus grammaticus linguae sanctae hebraeae*. Basel.

Ebeling, G.
1964 "Sola Scriptura" und das Problem der Tradition. Pp. 91–143 in his *Wort Gottes und Tradition*. Göttingen: Vandenhoeck und Ruprecht.

Froehlich, K.
1977 "Always to Keep to the Literal Sense in Holy Scripture Means to Kill One's Soul": The State of Biblical Hermeneutics at the Beginning of the Fifteenth Century. Pp. 20–48 in *The Literary Uses of Typology*, ed. E. R. Miner. Princeton: Princeton University.

Goshen-Gottstein, M.
1975 Christianity, Judaism, and Modern Bible Study. Pp. 69–88 in *Congress Volume: Edinburgh 1974*. Supplements to Vetus Testamentum 28. Leiden: Brill.
1981 Humanism and the Flowering of Jewish Studies—from the Christian to the Jewish Renaissance. *Newsletter of the World Union of Jewish Studies* 19 (August): 1–8.

Grabois, A.
1975 The Hebraica Veritas and Christian Intellectual Relations in the Twelfth Century. *Speculum* 50: 613–34.

Gray, H. H.
1968 Renaissance Humanism: The Pursuit of Eloquence. Pp. 199–212 in *Renaissance Essays*, ed. P. O. Kristeller and P. P. Wiener. New York: Harper and Row.

Hailperin, H.
1963 *Rashi and the Christian Scholars*. Pittsburgh: University of Pittsburgh.

Kristeller, P.
1974 The Role of Religion in Renaissance Humanism and Platonism. Pp. 367–70 in *The Pursuit of Holiness in Late Medieval and Renaissance Religion*, ed. C. Trinkaus and H. O. Oberman. Leiden: Brill.
1979 *Renaissance Thought and Its Sources*. New York: Harper and Row.

Kugel, J. L.
1986 Biblical Studies and Jewish Studies. *Association for Jewish Studies Newsletter* 36: 21–24.
de Lubac, H.
1959 *Exégèse médiéval: les quatre sens de l'Écriture*. Paris: Aubier.
Luther, M.
1897 Assertio Omnium Articulorum M. Lutheri per Bullam Leonis X, Novissimam Damnatorum. In his *Werke*, vol. 7. Weimar: H. Böhlau.
Masius, A.
1574 *Iosuae imperatoris historia*. Antwerp: Christoph Plantin.
Münster, S.
1534–35 *Hebraica Biblia latina*. Basel.
Pellican, C.
1504 *De modo legendi et intelligendi Hebraeum*. Strasbourg.
Pfürtner, S. H.
1977 Das Reformatorische "Sola Scriptura"—Theologischer Auslegungsgrund des Thomas von Aquin? Pp. 48–80 in *Sola Scriptura?*, ed. C.-H. Ratschow. Marburg: Elwert.
Preus, J.
1969 *From Shadow to Promise: Old Testament Interpretation from Augustine to the Young Luther*. Cambridge: Belknap Press of Harvard University.
Renan, E.
1893 *Histoire du peuple d'Israël*. Paris: Calmann-Levy.
Reuchlin, J.
1506 *De Rudimentis Hebraicis*. Pforzheim.
Roth, C.
1959 *The Jews in the Renaissance*. Philadelphia: Jewish Publication Society.
Sarna, N.
1980 היבטים לא מצויים של פרשנות התנ״ך בימי הביניים in הגות ומעשה: ספר זכרון לשמעון ראבשזיבורץ Haifa: Haifa University.
Simon, U.
1982 ארבע גישות לספר תהילים. Ramat Gan: Bar Ilan University.
Smalley, B.
1964 *The Study of the Bible in the Middle Ages*. 2d ed. Notre Dame: Notre Dame University.
Trinkaus, C.
1974 The Religious Thought of the Italian Humanists. Pp. 339–66 in *The Pursuit of Holiness in Late Medieval and Renaissance Religion*, ed. C. Trinkaus and H. O. Oberman. Leiden: Brill.
Weil, G.
1963 *Elie Levita*. Leiden: Brill.

"Sectually Explicit" Literature from Qumran

Carol A. Newsom
Emory University

The Dead Sea Scrolls: A Sectarian Library?

For nearly forty years there has been an almost universal consensus that the scrolls found in the eleven caves around Khirbet Qumran form the remains of a sectarian library belonging to the community whose headquarters were located at nearby Qumran. By an assumption that is nearly as widely held, this community has been regarded as an Essene fellowship. In the last few years, however, there have been suggestions that the "sectarian library of Qumran" was neither a library nor particularly sectarian. Hence it has become necessary to reconsider the question whether one can in fact identify "sectually explicit" literature among the Dead Sea Scrolls and, if so, what such texts indicate about the nature of the scrolls as a whole.

One of the most radical challenges has come from Norman Golb. In a recent article entitled "Who Hid the Dead Sea Scrolls?" (1985: 68–82) Golb challenges three of the fundamental assumptions of what can be called the prevailing consensus about the Dead Sea Scrolls. He denies that the evidence is adequate to connect the Dead Sea Scrolls with the reports of Essenes given by Philo, Josephus, and Pliny; he denies the connection between the site of Khirbet Qumran and the caves in which the scrolls were found; and, finally, he rejects the notion that the scrolls themselves should be understood as constituting a community library, that is, an intentional collection of manuscripts belonging to a single community.

On what grounds does Golb challenge these widely held views? He suggests that the hypothesis that these writings constitute the library of an Essene sectarian community "resulted primarily from the sequence in which the finds were made" (1985: 69). The fact that the manuscripts in Cave 1 were found first and that some of these manuscripts showed affinities with Essenism allowed the nearby site to be identified as an Essene community center and led scholars to attribute discoveries in other caves to this hypothetical Essene community. In the process the substantial diversity of the contents of the other caves was not recognized and their contents were erroneously attributed to this same Essene community. In Golb's view a different sequence of discovery that did not begin with Qumran Cave 1 would have resulted in a different, better hypothesis—that after the fall of Galilee to the Romans and even during the initial months of the siege of Jerusalem, the manuscripts found in the eleven caves were brought by a variety of individuals from Jerusalem, individuals who reflected great diversity of religious practice and belief, certainly not all members of a sectarian organization. The manuscripts that they brought were stored in a number of caves and only by merest chance have been mistaken as the remains of a sectarian library.

I do not intend to review each of Golb's arguments. Since my interest is in whether the manuscripts from the caves can be viewed as a sectarian library, there are two matters in particular that I think may be set aside. First is the issue of whether or not the community described in the Serek ha-Yaḥad should properly be termed "Essene." To be sure, the word "Essene" does not appear in the documents form Qumran. Indeed, it is not clear what its Hebrew or Aramaic equivalent would be. The description of the sectarian organization found in the Serek ha-Yaḥad, though strongly evocative of the descriptions of the Essenes given by Josephus and Philo, also differs significantly from them (see Vermes 1977: 125–30). Even though there is good warrant for describing the community as at least "Essene-like," it is probably better scholarly practice not to use the terms Qumran and Essene as though they were interchangeable. Purists might argue that the proper expression to use is "Yaḥad," drawn from the community's own terminology. The question with which I am more concerned, however, is whether the community referred to in the Serek ha-Yaḥad should be considered responsible for the collection of manuscripts found in the eleven caves.

The other issue that I do not intend to consider here in any detail is Golb's rejection of the connection between the ruins of Khirbet Qumran and the caves and scrolls. Golb rather disingenuously obscures the connections between the pottery found in the caves and the pottery found in the ruins of the nearby site. He suggests, rather lamely it seems to me, that when the Jerusalemites "had brought the bundles or sackfuls of texts from the capital to the desert caves for hiding" that "the Jewish inhabitants of the site and surrounding area might well have contributed to the sequestration by supplying storage vessels" (1985: 80). The relationship of the site to the caves and their documents is an important issue, bearing on the interpretation of the scrolls. A positive correlation between the ruins and the scrolls strongly supports the hypothesis that the scrolls form the remains of a community library. Even if it could be shown that the ruins have nothing to do with the manuscripts found in the caves, however, one would still have to ask whether the scrolls represent an intentional collection or an accidental congeries. Consequently, it seems worthwhile to consider the manuscripts without presuppositions as to their relationship with the ruins of Khirbet Qumran.

If Golb's hypothesis were correct, and the scrolls were deposited by a diverse group of unrelated individuals, one might reasonably expect the caves to contain a random hodge-podge of a broad spectrum of Jewish literature. According to the view that the caves contain a sectarian library, one would not necessarily be forced to claim that everything in the caves is of sectarian *authorship*—that is a different question altogether. But one should expect to see some evidence, just from examining the content and distribution of the manuscripts themselves, that they in some way represent an intentional collection.

One way of obtaining such information is to chart the number of nonbiblical manuscripts that exist in multiple copies, noting especially those that are found in more than one cave. If the manuscripts that occur in multiple copies can be shown to have a distinctive profile (in terms of content, idiom, style, etc.) and to have affinities with the Serek ha-Yaḥad, then one has good grounds for the hypothesis that the community referred to in that text was the agent responsible for the collection of texts found in the eleven caves.

Table 1 indicates the number of copies and the distribution of texts that occur in multiple copies. It should be obvious at a glance that the distribution is not a random one, such as Golb's hypothesis should produce. While it will be necessary to discuss the criteria for determining the provenance of a text in more detail below, I will anticipate the results of that discussion here. Texts that can be securely identified as products of the sectarian community known as the "Yaḥad" include the following: the pesharim (both continuous and thematic), the Serek ha-Yaḥad, the Damascus Document, the Hodayot, the Ṭeharot (see Milik 1972: 126–30; Kobelski 1981: 37–42), and the Berakot (Milik 1972: 130–37). To this group one should probably add the War Scroll (at least in its final form), and the Songs of the Maśkil (see discussion below). The Miqṣat Maᶜaśe ha-Torah are also of Qumran provenance, according to Qimron and Strugnell (1985: 401). The books of Enoch and Jubilees probably antedate the establishment of the Yaḥad but have strong theological affinities with the sectarian documents, Jubilees even being alluded to in the Damascus Document. The large number of calendrical texts from Cave 4 may or may not be Qumran compositions but are perhaps, like Jubilees, sources for Qumran literature. Milik (1976: 61) reports

TABLE 1. *Distribution of Qumran Texts Existing in Multiple Copies*

Text	*Cave Number : Number of Copies*							*Total*
Calendars				4:20		6:1		21
Pesharim[a]	1:3			4:11				14
Serek ha-Yaḥad	1:1			4:10	5:1			12
Sabbath Songs[b]				4:8			11:1	9
Enoch[c]	1:2			4:7				9
Damascus Document[d]				4:5	5:1	6:1		7
Hodayot	1:1			4:6				7
Milḥamah	1:1			4:6				7
Jubilees	1:2	2:2	3:1	4:1			11:1	7
Miqṣat Maᶜaśe ha-Torah				4:6				6
Ṭeharot				4:6				6
Berakot				4:5				5
New Jerusalem	1:1	2:1		4:1	5:1		11:1	5
Visions of Amram				4:5				5
Prayers for the Feasts	1:1			4:3				4
Words of the Heavenly Luminaries				4:3				3
Songs of the Sage (Maśkil)				4:2				2
Temple Scroll[e]				4 (disputed)			11:2	2

[a]There are no duplicates of any individual pesher. I am treating the pesharim as a distinct type of composition for purposes of tabulation. For the identification of the pesharim see Horgan 1979.

[b]One copy of the Sabbath Songs was discovered at Masada.

[c]Four copies of astronomical texts related to Enoch were discovered in Cave 4.

[d]Two copies of the Damascus Document were recovered from the Cairo Geniza.

[e]The identification of Temple Scroll fragments among the manuscripts of Cave 4 is discussed by Stegemann, 1988.

Sources: This table has been compiled from the official and preliminary publications of texts and from reports of forthcoming publications; see, in particular, Fitzmyer 1975; Milik 1972; Milik 1976: 61; and Qimron and Strugnell 1985. The identification of certain fragmentary texts is not always certain, and the figures in the table could vary slightly.

that one copy of the Serek ha-Yaḥad (4Q260) contains portions of the calendar. Qimron and Strugnell (1985: 400) also state that one manuscript of the Miqṣat Maᶜaśe ha-Torah begins with a copy of the calendar. Similarly, whether or not the Visions of Amram can be shown to be of sectarian authorship, its articulation of a light/darkness dualism that involves angelic and human beings is very close to the ideas found in the Milḥamah and in the Serek ha-Yaḥad. The provenance of the Songs of the Sabbath Sacrifice will be discussed further below. Whether or not it is a composition of the Qumran community, this text shares with the texts of sectarian authorship an adherence to the solar calendar and a preoccupation with priesthood and angelology. The New Jerusalem texts (Aramaic descriptions of a heavenly city in terms dependent on the style of Ezekiel's temple visions) are not well understood. I hesitate to venture a judgment on their authorship or relationship to the theology of the Qumran community. The Prayers for the Feasts and the Words of the Heavenly Luminaries give no particular evidence of sectarian authorship or special affinity with theological themes characteristic of the Qumran community. The provenance of the Temple Scroll has been sharply debated (Levine 1978: 5–23; Schiffman 1980: 143–58; Yadin 1980: 153–69). Although Yadin claimed that several fragmentary manuscripts of the Temple Scroll were found in Cave 4, the interpretation of these fragments has been challenged by John Strugnell and Hartmut Stegemann, who believe them to be expanded pentateuchal texts but not copies of the Temple Scroll (see Stegemann, 1988). According to their conclusion the Temple Scroll is attested only in two copies, both from Cave 11.

What appears from this simple count is that most of the nonbiblical texts that exist in two or more copies and the great majority of those found in more than one of the caves are either products of the Qumran community or are closely related to central aspects of its theology and praxis. It is not the order of discovery but the pattern of multiple copies that suggests that the scrolls do not simply represent a random collection of texts. Among the texts that exist in multiple copies—and only among those—one finds descriptions of a sectarian organization that it is reasonable to identify as the social agent responsible for the collection and preservation of the group of manuscripts of which these texts form a part. The hypothesis that the scrolls from the Dead Sea caves represent a sectarian library remains the best one available. Like Golb's hypothesis it also can account for the wide variety of the texts, both biblical and nonbiblical. But it succeeds better than Golb's in explaining why certain texts and not others are present in multiple copies.[1]

1. Two other questions might be raised about the distribution of texts. The first is the absence of duplicate texts from caves 7–10. While it is not impossible that manuscripts from certain of these caves might be independent of the sectarian library, one has to reckon with the fact that very little manuscript of any sort was found in them. Only if they contained much more material would the absence of texts found in the other caves be of significance. The other question concerns the still unpublished material from Cave 4. Will it change the picture developed here? While I do not have access to all of the unpublished materials, Prof. John Strugnell has shared with me information about the texts for which he is responsible. In the conspectus for the first volume of texts that he will be publishing from Cave 4, there are indeed several examples of apocryphal narratives and psalms that exist in two copies and that are almost certainly nonsectarian in origin. But the two texts that exist in substantial numbers of copies are either of sectarian origin or are closely related to the theological issues characteristic

What Does It Mean to Call a Text "Sectarian"?

Even if one concludes that the scrolls represent the remains of a sectarian library, what does that conclusion have to say about the provenance of the individual texts? Dupont-Sommer represents one point of view that has been quite influential. His governing assumption is that if a nonbiblical document was found in one of the Qumran caves, then it is presumed to be of sectarian (specifically, Essene) composition. Even concerning the Targum of Job from Cave 11 (a document that gives few internal clues as to its provenance) he says "its presence in the Essene library suggests that it was written by an Essene" (1973: 306). In a less explicit fashion a similar view has informed the highly influential books of Geza Vermes, *The Dead Sea Scrolls in English* (1975) and *The Dead Sea Scrolls: Qumran in Perspective* (1977), and may be said to have been characteristic of most scholars of the Dead Sea Scrolls. For the past several years, however, there has been increasing reluctance on the part of Qumran scholars to make such a blanket assumption. An appreciation of the diversity of the texts has led to a growing concern to distinguish sectarian from nonsectarian texts, and attempts have been made to establish the criteria that will allow this distinction to be made. In a lecture on apocalyptic literature at Qumran, given in Uppsala before the International Colloquium on Apocalypticism, Hartmut Stegemann outlined criteria for distinguishing "specifische Qumrantexte." Such texts, he suggested, may be recognized as those that ascribe an authoritative function to the figure of the Teacher of Righteousness; or that reflect the particular rule of the Qumran community; or whose formal or terminological connections *necessarily* associate them with such texts (1983: 511).[2]

Before one begins to sort through the great pile of manuscript, however, it is best to think for a moment about the kind of judgment one is trying to make. What does it mean to attempt to distinguish between sectarian and nonsectarian texts? The terms require some definition. There are at least three different things that one might mean by referring to a scroll as

---

of the theology of the Yaḥad. These are a pseudo-Ezekiel document concerned with calendrical calculations (seven or eight copies) and the Miqṣat Maᶜaśe ha-Torah (six copies), which Qimron and Strugnell have suggested may be a letter outlining the basis for the separation of the Yaḥad from other parts of the Jewish community (1985: 400–407).

2. Stegemann would include as specifically Qumranic the pesharim, the Damascus Document, the Serek ha-Yaḥad, the Hodayot, the thematic midrashim 4Q Florilegium and 11Q Melchizedek, as well as other texts. Stegemann regards the Milḥamah as a pre-Qumran text edited and adapted by the community. Some texts may be excluded as non-Qumran compositions (noncanonical hymns in several Psalm manuscripts, the Words of the Heavenly Luminaries, the Genesis Apocryphon, the Temple Scroll, and many fragmentary compositions of various genres). There remains, however, a large "gray zone" of works whose provenance is difficult to determine.

sectarian. First, one might mean that it had been written by a member of the Qumran community, and, indeed, in most discussions of this sort the terms sectarian or "specifically Qumranic" clearly are used to mean texts written by members of the Qumran community. But that is not the only way that the terms sectarian and nonsectarian might be used. A second possibility is that one might assert that it was the way a particular text was read that made it a sectarian text, no matter who had written it. While this criterion would include almost all of those texts written by members of the community, it might also include a number of others besides—adopted texts, one might say. Finally, one might use the term sectarian not as shorthand for facts of authorship or community use but as a way of describing content or rhetorical stance, that is, those texts that speak specifically of the unique structures of the community and the history of its separation from a larger community, and/or that develop its distinctive tenets in a self-consciously polemical fashion. This last use of the term "sectarian text" might well not include everything actually written by members of the community. Each usage points to a question worth asking. To consider only authorship is to oversimplify. It remains to be seen, though, how these are three distinct questions.

Use and Readership of Texts

Consider first what it would mean to think about the terms sectarian and nonsectarian as referring to patterns of text use within the community. One might argue that the criterion of use (rather than authorship) corresponds more closely to the ancient sense of what are "our writings" as opposed to "not ours" or "theirs." As is well known, attribution of a text to a particular author is virtually ignored in ancient Israel (the special case of pseudepigrapha being an exception). It is difficult to imagine a member of the Qumran community puzzling over the question of whether a member of the community did or did not write the War Scroll or the Songs of the Sabbath Sacrifice or another of the texts that falls into the gray area, insofar as authorship is concerned. The large number of copies of these two texts, and, in the case of the War Scroll, the apparent existence of variant textual traditions suggest that these documents were of particular interest to the community. Whether or not these texts were written by members of the Qumran community, it is plausible that they may have influenced the self-understanding of the community as deeply as the pesharim or the Hodayot.

In one sense, to focus on the use of texts within the community rather than on their authorship would be to revive a slightly more sophisticated form of Dupont-Sommer's thesis. The presence of a document among the Dead Sea Scrolls would not be an indication of Qumran authorship but of Qumran readership and appropriation. In a rough fashion the number of copies of a document might be taken as indicating the frequency of its use or some measure of its importance in the community. Such an approach would seem not only to be consistent with ancient values but also to receive support from modern theorists. Recent discussions of the nature of texts and the reading process in literary criticism have made the point that it is not adequate simply to define a text by reference to its authorship. In a very significant sense a text is created through the reading process. (See the various perspectives represented by Jauss 1982 and Fish 1980.) A text written by someone not a member of the sectarian community may nevertheless become a sectarian text through the type of reading it is given in a sectarian setting.

The problems with this approach, however, become evident when one considers the best documented case we have for understanding how texts were read at Qumran. Through the evidence preserved in the pesharim, we know how certain biblical books were read at Qumran. They were read as referring specifically to the history and fate of the sect and its enemies. If one understands a text not as the utterance of an author but as the product of the reading of an individual or reading community, then one would have to say that the biblical texts found at Qumran were sectarian texts. It does indeed take a strong effort of the imagination for modern scholars to set aside their own reading conventions and to appreciate fully how a member of the sectarian community did read scripture. The claim that the biblical texts found at Qumran are sectarian texts has a certain heuristic value. At the same time one cannot help but feel that such a conclusion obscures more than it clarifies. The fact that such sectarian interpretation was not simply a matter of unconscious assumption but of self-conscious effort, the results of which were embodied in special compositions, should warn us against wholly collapsing the categories of text and reading.

Moreover, we really know very little about the interpretation of most texts at Qumran. While the pesharim do give an indication of how biblical texts were read and understood, there is no positive ground for thinking that other texts were read in such a manner.[3] It is because the biblical texts have

3. A rather interesting attempt to read a nonbiblical text as it might have been read at Qumran is the interpretation of the Wiles of the Wicked Woman as an allegory of the enemies of the sect (see, for example, Carmignac: 1965 and Burgmann 1974). To be sure the scholars who advance this interpretation consider the text to be written by members of the Qumran community and consider their interpretation to be an explanation of the author's intentions. Quite rightly, their view has not been widely accepted, for they do not make their case on those terms. Their interpretation becomes much more provocative if understood as an attempt to read the text as it might have been read at Qumran, whatever its meaning for readers in other contexts. But there are problems even so, since we do not know whether nonbiblical texts were interpreted in a manner analogous to the biblical exegesis found in the pesharim.

a peculiar authority that they are read in this fashion—other texts that did not have such authority might well have been read according to very different conventions.

While there are some texts that appear to be of non-Qumran authorship but became very influential in the Qumran community (for example, Jubilees), for the most part we simply lack information about the use or lack of use that a text received in the life of the community. Even the presence of a large number of copies of the text may be difficult to interpret. Milik (1976: 7), for instance, has tried to make a case from the date and condition of the Enoch manuscripts that the text ceased to be of much significance for the Qumran community fairly early in its history.

For both practical and theoretical reasons it does not seem advantageous to use the term sectarian to designate texts that had a particular status or use within the community, irrespective of their authorship. But posing the question of the way in which particular texts were used and interpreted within the community is extremely important, even though the information available to us is often limited.

Authorship of Texts

Most scholars who raise the question of distinguishing sectarian from nonsectarian Dead Sea scrolls would explain that what they are interested in *is* the question of authorship. Was a text *composed* at Qumran (or by a member of the Qumran community) or merely *copied and preserved* by the Qumran community? Just because the ancient Semitic world was not particularly interested in the question of authorship does not mean that it is not an important question for scholarship. The problem, of course, is that since the ancient writers did not explicitly assert authorship, the assignment of authorship has to be deduced from internal criteria—historical or social allusions, distinctive vocabulary, particular theological ideas, etc. It certainly seems reasonable to assume that writings by members of a sectarian community would tend to bear distinctive traits of content, vocabulary, and style—and many undoubtedly do. But *must* all documents written by members of a sect be so marked? I have a scholarly friend who humorously dismisses the question of distinguishing sectarian from nonsectarian literature from the Qumran caves by saying that it is like what former Chief Justice Berger said about pornography: I may not be able to define it, but I know it when I see it. My friend, I would suggest, is conflating the categories of content/style and authorship. If sectarian is assumed to mean Qumran authorship and if it could be shown that members of the Qumran community wrote material that was not readily identifiable by details of content and style, then the adequacy of my friend's appealingly simple non-definition would be put in question. To put the matter another way, is it certain that all psalms or prayers written by a member of a sect would be discernibly different from those written by a nonmember? For some important categories of writing (for example, prayers and certain liturgical texts) stereotypical, traditional language might well have been the norm for the sectarian as well as the nonsectarian author.

An example of this problem is the curious document form Cave 4 that Baillet (1982: 81–105) called a "Marriage Ritual." Whatever the nature of the text (its interpretation as a marriage ritual has been questioned; see Baumgarten 1983: 125–35), my interest is in the grounds Baillet finds for calling it Essene (or, as I would prefer, Qumranic). There is no reference to the name of the sectarian community or to the Righteous Teacher, no reference to organizational features of the community or its distinctive institutional structure, no reference to distinctive theological ideas or use of distinctive idiom. By the criteria that Stegemann and others have proposed such a text would not attract attention as possibly of sectarian authorship. What Baillet noticed, however, was that one fragment (4Q502 16) apparently cites a part of the Serek ha-Yaḥad. Although the fragment is small, Baillet's judgment about its overlap with 1QS iv 4–6 seems well founded.[4] Because it cites a clearly sectarian text, one would be justified in concluding that this "marriage" text is also of sectarian authorship (or at the very least updated for use by a member of the sect). The existence of such a text is thus a reminder that much that does not strike us as sectarian in content may nevertheless have been written by a member of the sect.

The opposite problem exists, too. Where a text makes explicit references to the organizational features of the group or to its history, one may be able to conclude quite confidently that it was written by a member of the community. But what about texts that lack such clear markers of origin but do employ a diction, style, and theological slant that has significant overlap with what one finds in the core group of texts that are of sectarian authorship? It is possible to describe the similarities and differences of content or idiom, but much more difficult to move convincingly from such descriptions to claims about authorship.[5] In such cases perhaps it would be

4. Baillet does not discuss the relationship between the paleography of 4Q502 and that of the copies of the Serek ha-Yaḥad from Cave 4 that Milik is to publish. One assumes, however, that the possibility that the fragment belongs to a copy of the Serek ha-Yaḥad was investigated. Although Baillet does not discuss at length his reasons for assigning the fragment in question to 4Q502, he does say in his general introduction that some of the fragments of 4Q502 might belong to 4Q503 (Daily Prayers). Even if that were the case with the fragment that cites the Serek ha-Yaḥad, the issue with which I am concerned would be the same. Like the Marriage Ritual, the Daily Prayers are not marked by the features that one usually points to as characteristic of texts of Qumran authorship.

5. In fact the entire notion of authorship and the production of a text within a single community may become problematic categories. A case in point is the War Scroll. The

better for heuristic reasons to reverse Dupont-Somer's presumption and to regard such texts as of non-Qumran origin. One does not "lose" the text for Qumran—the readership of the text within the community is still assumed. But one is forced to consider what other place of origin such a text might have had in Second Temple Judaism.

Even if one cannot be certain that documents composed by members of the sect will contain a distinctive content, there may be some features that are clearly *incompatible* with sectarian authorship. In documents that are demonstrably of Qumran authorship the tetragrammaton is always avoided, except in quotations from scripture. This practice is not unique to Qumran, of course, but is arguably the norm for Jewish writings after the third century B.C.E. (Stegemann 1978: 216; cf. Skehan 1980: 14–44). It means, though, that any text containing the tetragrammaton in free and original composition can be presumed to be of non-Qumran authorship. See, for example, the collection of noncanonical psalms recently published by Schuller (1986: 38–41).

Calendrical assumptions might provide another criterion. While adherence to the solar calendar is reflected in texts written by the Qumran community, it is widely agreed that not every text that reflects the solar calendar is necessarily of Qumran provenance. Since the calendar was a polemical issue for the sect, however, a text that reflected different calendrical assumptions could be excluded from the list of documents written in the Qumran community. An example of such a text is 4Q507–509, the Prayers for the Feasts. The text, of which 1Q34–34*bis* is an additional copy, has been construed as a Qumran sectarian composition, apparently on the basis of the reference to the renewal of the covenant (1Q34*bis* 3 ii 6). While the language is suggestive, the adjoining reference to separating the covenanted ones 'from all the peoples' (*mkl hᶜmym*) makes one wonder if the reference might not be to Israel as a whole. None of the rest of the preserved fragments contains language that points clearly to Qumran authorship.

The impasse can be breached by examining the order in which the feasts appear in the cycle of prayers. One of the copies, 4Q509, is written on the recto of a papyrus scroll, the verso of which contains a copy of the War

---

different recensions of the book that exist and the complexities of its structure have suggested to many scholars that the work has a complicated textual history. Some have argued that the work derives in whole (Rost 1955: 205–6) or in part (von der Osten Saken 1969: 88–91, 105) from a period before the emergence of the Qumran community. Because we possess so little of the literature from the period, it is extremely difficult to judge whether terms such as *grl*, *mᶜdy tᶜwdwt*, the pair *bny ᵓwr/bny ḥwšk*, etc., were distinct idioms developed in a relatively closed intellectual environment or whether they were rather broadly shared terms used in sectarian and nonsectarian settings for discussing predestinarian and dualistic ideas.

Scroll (4Q496) and a copy of the Words of the Heavenly Luminaries (4Q505). One of the fragments (4Q496 3 = 4Q509 3) contains on the verso a portion of text from the beginning of the War Scroll (= 1QM i 4–9). The recto contains part of the prayer for the autumn New Year.[6] The simplest explanation for this state of affairs is that fragment 4Q496 3 = 4Q509 3 comes from the beginning of the scroll and preserves material from near the beginning of both compositions.

The question next to be asked is whether a calendrical sequence beginning with the New Year in Tishri is consistent with the calendrical practices of the Qumran community. It appears that it is not. Judging from what Milik (1957: 24–25) has published on the priestly courses from Qumran, their calendar reckoning begins not with Tishri but with Nisan (see also Talmon 1965: 172). Although it is not difficult to see how such a collection of traditional prayers for the feasts might have been valued and used at Qumran, it seems most unlikely that a cycle of prayers *composed* at Qumran would begin with the fall New Year if the rest of the sect's cultic organization began its reckoning with Nisan. Consequently, one seems warranted in concluding that the Prayers for the Feasts were not written by a member of the Qumran community.

The question "What kinds of texts did members of the Qumran community actually compose?" is an extremely important one. To the extent that we can answer it, the question not only provides valuable information about the life and values of the sect but also opens new perspectives on Second Temple Judaism in general. Every text whose composition cannot be placed at Qumran must have originated elsewhere. It appears, however, that the matter of distinguishing texts of Qumran authorship is not so simple as "knowing it when we see it." Some texts that are not characterized by the style and idiom that we associate, for example, with the Serek ha-Yaḥad or the pesharim may be of Qumran authorship, while others that share important features of that style and idiom may not be, or may have a compositional history that begins in another environment.

Rhetorical Function of Texts

Because the issue of authorship seems to be a more subtle matter than first appears, it might be better to reserve the term "sectarian text" for another purpose than as a synonym for "Qumran authorship." Of the three alternative meanings for the term sectarian that I discussed above (authorship, use, and rhetorical purpose) the third and most restrictive category seems the most useful. A sectarian text would be one that calls upon its

6. Fragment 4Q509 3 overlaps 1Q34bis 2 + 1, which contains the end of the prayer for the New Year and the beginning of the prayer for the Day of Expiation.

readers to understand themselves as set apart within the larger religious community of Israel and as preserving the true values of Israel against the failures of the larger community. A text may do this in a variety of ways. There may be overtly polemical rhetoric of an "us vs. them" sort. Or there may be references to the community's history, or teaching about the institutional structure of the community. Liturgies that serve to constitute the community as set apart from the larger community would also be sectarian. While particular theological ideas and values may be almost always present in such sectarian documents, they do not of themselves make a document sectarian. Some self-conscious reference to separation from the larger religious community would be necessary to identify the text as sectarian. By focusing on questions of content and rhetorical purpose one restores attention to differences that are obscured when the issue is seen primarily as one of authorship or use. After all, the Temple Scroll, whoever wrote it, does not present itself as a sectarian document. The Serek ha-Yaḥad does.

I certainly do not mean to diminish the significance of questions of authorship and use. It is important to attempt to discover whether members of the sectarian community wrote a text like that of the Temple Scroll and to know, whether or not they wrote it, why they read it, and how they understood it. But it must not be overlooked that the means by which the text claims its authority and achieves its persuasiveness are not those by which the Serek ha-Yaḥad or the Damascus Document achieve theirs.

A Test Case—The Songs of the Sabbath Sacrifice

My interest in the issue of what it means to call something a sectarian text stems directly from my work in editing the Songs of the Sabbath Sacrifice (Newsom 1985). It represents one of those texts from the Dead Sea Scrolls whose provenance seems particularly hard to determine. I would like to reexamine that question in the following pages. Certain evidence that I had previously neglected needs to be included in the discussion. In addition, more self-conscious division of the issue into separate questions of use, authorship, and sectarian rhetoric helps to clarify the relationship between the evidence one has and the assumptions one invokes in interpreting that evidence.

The Sabbath Songs are a liturgical cycle of thirteen related compositions, one song for each of the first thirteen Sabbaths of the year. Although there is some reference to the human community and its priesthood, by far the greatest portion of the text is concerned with the angelic priesthood, the praises offered by the angels, the heavenly temple, the chariot of God, and the sacrifices offered in the heavenly temple. Ten copies are extant, eight of which come from Qumran Cave 4, one from Qumran Cave 11, and one from Masada. Two other compositions from Qumran have phraseology so similar to some of the most distinctive language of the Sabbath Songs that one must assume some pattern of influence among the texts. These other documents are the Songs of the Maśkil (4Q510 and 4Q511; published in Baillet 1982: 215–62) and the Berakot texts from Cave 4 (discussed and excerpted but not yet fully published in Milik 1972: 95–144).

If one examines the Sabbath Songs with respect to content and rhetorical purpose, there is nothing clearly sectarian about them. That is to say, they do not appear to be concerned with defining and maintaining the boundaries between a religious subgroup and a dominant religious community. The songs are nonpolemical. The only contrast between one religious group and another is between the angelic priesthood and the human priesthood (see 4Q400 2 6–8). Although the human community is referred to self-deprecatingly, it appears that the angelic priesthood provides a model and projected self-image for the human speakers/hearers of the text. Deterministic language and references to the eschatological war in heaven do occur, but the references are not explicitly related to the fates of any particular human group (see 4Q402 4). The solar calendar is assumed by the date headings for each of the songs, but there is no indication in the text that the use of such a calendar is regarded as in any way distinctive or exceptional. That is to say, the calendar is not made the subject of polemic. One must remember, however, that a religious sect may have other needs as a community that do not have to do explicitly with defining the boundaries between itself and the larger religious community from which it has separated. The lack of sectarian self-consciousness in the content of the songs cannot of itself exclude Qumran as the place of origin of these compositions.

Are there references to sectarian community institutional structures or history? While nothing of the sort occurs in the body of the songs, it is very significant that the heading *lmśkyl* occurs at the beginning of each composition, for Maśkil does appear to be the name for a sectarian office in texts of Qumran authorship (1QS and 1QSb; cf. CD; Vermes 1975: 22–25). The terse heading *lmśkyl* is not without ambiguity, both with respect to the sense of the preposition ('to'?, 'by'?, 'for'?) and the noun ('sage' or 'the Maśkil'?). But one does have to reckon here with the possibility that the heading served to identify the text as belonging to the provenance of that sectarian leader who had responsibility for community instruction (1QS iii 13) and for certain liturgical tasks (1QS ix 26–x 5; 1QSb). Whether one is dealing with a text composed within the community or adopted by it, the similarity between the angelological and liturgical knowledge attributed to the Maśkil in 1QS/1QSb and the content of the Sabbath Songs makes it seem likely that in the context of the Qumran community *lmśkyl* was construed with reference to this sectarian office.

It is also necessary to assess what can be known or guessed about the use of the text within the Qumran community. The number of copies found at Qumran suggests that it was a text of considerable importance. Of course, we do not have independent evidence to indicate how the text was used. I assume that it was used "as directed," that is, read in sections over the course of the first thirteen Sabbaths of the year. If the text could be shown to be of Qumran *authorship*, then the assumption would be almost certainly true. But if one concludes that the text was not of Qumran authorship, then it would be less certain. While the text may well have been adopted for actual liturgical practice, there would be some chance that the text was not put into actual use but consulted only as a study text for the speculations on the heavenly world that it contained.[7]

There is another measure for the use of a text besides the number of copies extant, and that is the evidence for its influence on other texts. As I mentioned above, there are two documents from Qumran that may show the influence of the Sabbath Songs. One, which I have discussed in greater detail in my edition of the Sabbath Songs, is 4QBerakot. This text, which makes explicit reference to the sectarian community (4Q286 10 ii 1: *ᶜṣt hyḥd* 'the council of the Community'), Milik interprets as the liturgy that the Qumran community used for covenant renewal on the day of Pentecost (1972: 136). The points of similarity between the Sabbath Songs and 4QBerakot concern the very peculiar terms used for the description of the heavenly temple, the chariot throne, and the angelic attendants. Since the description of such heavenly realia forms one of the principal subjects of the Sabbath Songs, whereas it appears to be more peripheral in the Berakot, it seems likely that the author of the Berakot has been influenced by the Sabbath Songs rather than the other way around. The other text that shows strong terminological and formal similarities with the Sabbath Songs, the Songs of the Maśkil (4Q510–511), is almost certainly of Qumran authorship (see below). Although it is not possible to examine all the evidence here, the Songs of the Maśkil appear to be literarily dependent upon both the Hodayot and the Songs of the Sabbath Sacrifice.

To sum up so far, the Sabbath Songs seem to have been influential within the Qumran community, judging both from the number of copies extant and from their influence on other Qumran compositions. While the Sabbath Songs do not reflect a significant degree of sectarian self-consciousness, they may well have formed part of the literature of instruction

7. This possibility was suggested to me by H. Stegemann. In my own opinion, however, I think that the liturgical use is more likely. We do know that the Qumran Maśkil was associated with other liturgical utterances (1QSb; 1QS ix–x). Elsewhere I have described the way in which liturgical recitation of these songs would have served the needs of the Qumran community (Newsom 1985: 59–72).

or liturgical praxis associated with the figure of the Maśkil. The question that remains is whether there is enough evidence to justify a judgment as to their authorship.[8]

The lack of explicit sectarian polemic is, as I have suggested above, indecisive. There are, however, two other pieces of information that are important. The first is the presence of a copy of the text at Masada. Previously, I had expressed my agreement with Yadin's suggestion that the text might have been carried there by a member of the Qumran community after the destruction of Khirbet Qumran (Newsom 1985: 74 n. 5). And so it might. I must admit, though, that the suggestion has something of the flavor of the theory of epicycles introduced to save the ptolemaic cosmology from erosion by apparently contradictory empirical observations. The possibilities are more various. While the text might have belonged to a former member of the Qumran community or to a member of the "New Covenant" who lived in a city or village (see the Damascus Document), the presence of the Sabbath Songs at Masada requires one to reckon with the possibility that the text was known and used in circles quite distinct from the Qumran community. The implications of that possibility for the authorship of the text and the direction of its dissemination are quite ambiguous, however. Does one have a document from a nonsectarian source adopted at Qumran because it was congenial to the community's interests or a document composed at Qumran but congenial to a wider readership because of its lack of explicitly sectarian rhetoric? The mere fact of its presence at Masada does not allow one to decide.

There remains one piece of evidence that I did not consider in my previous discussion of the provenance of the text, evidence that I think may be sufficient to tip the balance toward the conclusion that the Sabbath Songs were *not* composed by a member of the Qumran community. As I noted above, in texts whose Qumran authorship seems reasonably certain, there is no use of the tetragrammaton except in direct scripture quotations. It is also the case, however, that the word *ʾĕlōhîm* is avoided. The term *ʾĕlōhîm* is, indeed, rare in most of the nonbiblical texts of the Dead Sea Scrolls from whatever sources they derive (see the discussions of Stegemann 1978 and

8. For purposes of comparison with the following discussion, in my edition of the Sabbath Songs I summarized the question of the provenance of the text as follows (1985: 4): "To conclude, there is no internal evidence which can establish beyond question the provenance of the Sabbath Shirot. The absence of specifically sectarian references in the body of the Shirot, however, need not indicate a pre-Qumran origin for the Sabbath Songs. Strong points of relationship with the clearly Qumran 4QBerakot, the technical significance of the heading *lmśkyl*, plus additional points of verbal similarity with other Qumran documents are adequate to support the working hypothesis adopted here, that the scroll of the Sabbath Shirot is a product of the Qumran community."

Skehan 1980).[9] While the Sabbath Songs also avoid the tetragrammaton, they differ sharply from the pattern of usage in the texts of Qumran authorship in their frequent use of *ᵓĕlōhîm*. Of all words, names and terms for God would be among the most likely to be governed by convention and not left to the whim and preference of individual writers within a religious community. Consequently, the deviant use of *ᵓĕlōhîm* seems to point toward non-Qumran authorship of the Sabbath Songs.

But the picture becomes clouded again when the relationship between the Sabbath Songs and the Songs of the Maśkil is considered. These mysterious texts share a number of similarities with the Sabbath Songs. There is an apparently similar use of *lmśkyl* as a heading; the individual compositions are referred to as songs (*šyr*) in both; there is a similarity in the imperative calls to praise that open the songs; certain terminology for describing praise is attested only in these two documents, out of the corpus of the Dead Sea Scrolls (for example, *tšbwḥh/tšbwḥwt*). One fragment (4Q511 44) uses terms for the heavens and the cherubim that are almost identical to those of the Sabbath Songs. One of the most interesting points of comparison occurs in 4Q511 35, where the speaker describes God's act of setting apart priests for himself. It is not entirely clear whether the priests are human or angelic. In either case, however, the passage is quite similar to the description of the consecration of the angelic priesthood in the first Sabbath Song (4Q400 1 i), a topic of utmost importance in the Sabbath Songs. The most distinctive point of similarity between the Sabbath Songs and the Songs of the Maśkil, however, is the striking preference for the divine epithet *ᵓĕlōhîm* in both texts. At the same time, the Songs of the Maśkil appear to be much more closely related to the language and idiom of the clearly sectarian documents of Qumran authorship than are the Sabbath Songs. Baillet documents extensive similarities with the diction of the Hodayot. Predestinarian and dualistic language similar to that of the documents of Qumran authorship is found (*bqṣ mmšl*[*t*] *ršᶜh wtᶜwdwt tᶜnywt bny ᵓw*[*r*] [4Q510 1 6–7]; *bgwrl ršᶜ* [4Q510 2 1]; [*g*]*wrl ršyt byᶜqwb wnḥlt ᵓl*[*why*]*m* [4Q511 2 i 5]; *gwrl ᵓlwhym* [4Q511 2 i 8]). And though the terminology is rather different, there is a close parallel between the claims to insight into human nature in the Songs of the Maśkil (4Q511 63 iii 2–3) and that claimed for the Maśkil in the Serek ha-Yaḥad (1QS iii 13–15). While highly suggestive, these features alone would not constitute definitive evidence for Qumran authorship.[10] What seems to

9. The occurrences in 1QS viii 14 and 1QM x 4, 7 are all in the context of quotations from scripture. The only exception appears to be 1QSb iv 25 (*ᵓlwhy ṣbᵓ*[*wt*]). In his unpublished notes on the Sabbath Songs Stegemann had already observed the uncharacteristic use of *ᵓĕlōhîm* as grounds for doubting that the Sabbath Songs were composed at Qumran.

10. In *Gott und Belial* Peter von der Osten Saken (1969) has argued convincingly that not all dualistic terms are necessarily sectarian. In his analysis of 1QM i he has attempted to show

make the case for Qumran authorship in the Songs of the Maśkil is Baillet's claim that one passage refers explicitly to the sect: *tkn lmwʿdy šnh* [*wm*]*mšlt yḥd lḣṫḣl̊k̊*[*b*]*gwrl* [*ʾlwhym*]*l̊p̊ẙ kbwd̊*[*w*] (4Q511 2 i 9–10). Although the passage is damaged, it is difficult to see how one could construe the crucial phrase other than as Baillet reads it ("du go]uvernement de (la) Communauté").[11]

How should this rather complex evidence be assessed? One could assume that both texts originated in a non-Qumran priestly milieu that favored the divine epithet *ʾĕlōhîm* and that had a strong interest in the heavenly and demonic realms and in powerful and esoteric knowledge. That approach would fail to explain, however, why only one text (the Songs of the Maśkil) had been rewritten within the Qumran community to incorporate a more explicitly sectarian perspective. Alternatively, if one assumed that both texts originated within the Qumran community, one would have to explain why only these two texts freely use the divine epithet *ʾĕlōhîm*. A case might be made that the use of *ʾĕlōhîm* is an example of privileged speech associated with the figure of the Maśkil. The difficulty is that, in addition to being a rather *ad hoc* explanation for which there is virtually no positive evidence,[12] one would still lack an explanation for the difference between the more strongly sectarian rhetoric of the Songs of the Maśkil and the apparently nonsectarian orientation of the Sabbath Songs. The most plausible explanation seems to be that the Sabbath Songs alone originated outside of and probably prior to the emergence of the Qumran community.[13] Appropriated by the Qumran sect, this document became an important text in the community for the reasons that I have discussed in my edition of the Sabbath Songs. At some point, probably during the first century B.C.E., the Songs of the Maśkil were composed, under the strong influence both of the Hodayot and the Sabbath Songs. That the normally avoided divine epithet *ʾĕlōhîm* should be used in this sectarian composition is not as surprising as it

how the Qumran community drew on an existing vocabulary and literature in the development of its own sectarian terminology.

11. There are other examples of unarticulated *yḥd* that refer to the community. Cf. 1QS iii 2, 12; ix 6; xi 8; 1QSa i 26; 1QSb iv 26. So long as *mmšlt* is understood to be in construct and not used absolutely (as it is in Ben Sira 7:4), one can scarcely construe *yḥd* as other than a noun.

12. It is perhaps relevant that the one free (that is, nonquotational) use of *ʾĕlōhîm* in a text of Qumran authorship occurs in a blessing spoken by the Maśkil (1QSb iv 25). Elsewhere in that text, however, *ʾādôn* and *ʾēl* are used to refer to God.

13. It is not possible to consider here what the original *Sitz im Leben* of the Sabbath Songs may have been, if it was composed outside of the Qumran Community. The adherence to the solar calendar and the preoccupation with the priesthood and its angelic representatives have significant affinities with the traditions associated with Levi in the Aramaic Testament of Levi and in Jubilees. But the liturgical form of the document assumes a rather well-organized community.

might first appear. According to the Songs of the Maśkil; the description of the "splendor of His beauty" (4Q510 1 4) serves a quasi-magical purpose, "to frighten and ter[rify] all the spirits of the angels of destruction . . ." (4Q510 1 4–5). The Songs of the Maśkil are conceived of as words of power. In such a context the use of a normally restricted divine name is readily explicable.

Is Songs of the Sabbath Sacrifice, then, a sectarian text? In terms of its rhetoric, no, it is not. In terms of its authorship, it appears most likely not to have been composed within the Qumran sect. But in terms of its use—that is, the way in which it was read and employed within the Qumran community (whether as a document for study or for guiding worship), the number of copies found in the caves, and the apparent influence that it had on other texts of the community—there are good grounds for thinking that the Songs of the Sabbath Sacrifice functioned as an adopted or naturalized text within the sectarian perspective of the Qumran community.

The problem with "sectually explicit" literature from the Qumran caves is that it is often not sectually explicit enough. The question of determining what is sectarian or nonsectarian literature from the Qumran library cannot be a matter merely of dividing the manuscripts into two separate piles with appropriate labels. The questions of content/rhetoric, of authorship, and of use must each be posed for the document in question. With certain texts, such as the Milḥamah or the Sabbath Songs, the answer to the question "Is it sectarian?" cannot be answered either with a simple yes or no. Despite the need for nuance in assessing the relation of particular texts to the life of the Qumran community and for being sensitive to the possibility of diverse origins, there remain good reasons for assuming that the documents recovered from the eleven caves near Khirbet Qumran are indeed the remains of the library of the sect described in the Serek ha-Yaḥad.

Bibliography

Baillet, M.
1982 *Qumrân Grotte 4: III (4Q482–4Q520)*. Discoveries in the Judaean Desert 7. Oxford: Clarendon.

Baumgarten, J.
1983 4Q502, Marriage or Golden Age Ritual? *Journal of Jewish Studies* 34: 125–35.

Burgmann, H.
1974 The Wicked Woman: Der Makkabäer Simon? *Revue de Qumran* 8: 323–59.

Carmignac, J.
1965 Poèm allégorique sur la secte rivale. *Revue de Qumran* 5: 361–74.

Dupont-Sommer, A.
1973 *The Essene Writings from Qumran*. Gloucester, MA: Peter Smith.

Fish, S.
1980 *Is There a Text in This Class?: The Authority of Interpretive Communities*. Cambridge: Harvard University.

Fitzmyer, J.
1975 *The Dead Sea Scrolls: Major Publications and Tools for Study*. Sources for Biblical Study 8. Missoula, MT: Scholars Press.

Golb, N.
1985 Who Hid the Dead Sea Scrolls? *Biblical Archaeologist* 48: 68–82.

Horgan, M.
1979 *Pesharim: Qumran Interpretations of Biblical Books*. Catholic Biblical Quarterly Monograph Series 8. Washington: Catholic Biblical Association.

Jauss, H.
1982 *Toward an Aesthetic of Reception*. Theory and History of Literature 2. Minneapolis: University of Minnesota.

Kobelski, P.
1981 *Melchizedek and Melchireša*ᶜ. Catholic Biblical Quarterly Monograph Series 10. Washington: Catholic Biblical Association.

Levine, B.
1978 The Temple Scroll: Aspects of Its Historical Provenance and Literary Character. *Bulletin of the American Schools of Oriental Research* 232: 5–23.

Milik, J.
1957 Le travail d'édition des manuscrits du désert de Juda. Pp. 17–26 in *Volume du Congrès: Strasbourg 1956*. Supplement to Vetus Testamentum 4. Leiden: Brill.
1972 Milkî-ṣedeq et Milkî-rešaᶜ dans les anciens écrits juifs et chrétiens. *Journal of Jewish Studies* 23: 95–144.
1976 *The Books of Enoch*. With the collaboration of M. Black. Oxford: Clarendon.

Newsom, C.
1985 *Songs of the Sabbath Sacrifice: A Critical Edition*. Harvard Semitic Studies 27. Atlanta: Scholars Press.

von der Osten Saken, P.
1969 *Gott und Belial*. Studien zur Umwelt des Neuen Testaments 6. Göttingen: Vandenhoeck and Ruprecht.

Qimron, E., and J. Strugnell
1985 An Unpublished Halakhic Letter from Qumran. Pp. 400–407 in *Biblical Archaeology Today: Proceedings of the International Congress on Biblical Archaeology, Jerusalem, April 1984*. Jerusalem: Israel Exploration Society.

Rost, L.
1955 Zum Buch der Kriege der Söhne des Lichts gegen die Söhne der Finsternis. *Theologische Literaturzeitung* 80: 205–6.

Schiffman, L.
1980 The Temple Scroll in Literary and Philological Perspective. Pp. 143–58 in *Approaches to Ancient Judaism*, vol. 2, ed. W. S. Green. Chico, CA: Scholars Press.

Schuller, E.
1986 *Non-Canonical Psalms from Qumran: A Pseudepigraphical Collection.* Harvard Semitic Studies 28. Atlanta: Scholars Press.

Skehan, P.
1980 The Divine Name at Qumran, in the Masada Scroll, and in the Septuagint. *Bulletin of the International Organization for Septuagint and Cognate Studies* 13: 14–44.

Stegemann, H.
1978 Religionsgeschichtliche Erwägungen zu den Gottesbezeichnungen in der Qumrantexten. Pp. 195–217 in *Qumrân: sa piété, sa théologie et son milieu,* ed. M. Delcor. Bibliotheca Ephemeridum Theologicarum Lovaniensium 46. Leuven: University Press.
1983 Die Bedeutung der Qumranfunde für die Erforschung der Apokalyptik. Pp. 495–530 in *Apocalypticism in the Mediterranean World and the Near East,* ed. D. Hellholm. Tübingen: J. C. B. Mohr (Paul Siebeck).
1988 The Origins of the Temple Scroll. Pp. 235–56 in *Congress Volume: Jerusalem 1986,* ed. J. A. Emerton. Supplements to Vetus Testamentum 40. Leiden: Brill.

Talmon, S.
1965 The Calendar Reckoning of the Sect from the Judean Desert. Pp. 162–99 in *Aspects of the Dead Sea Scrolls.* Scripta Hierosolymitana 4. Jerusalem: Magnes.

Vermes, G.
1975 *The Dead Sea Scrolls in English.* 2d edition. Harmondsworth, Eng.: Penguin.
1977 *The Dead Sea Scrolls: Qumran in Perspective.* With the collaboration of P. Vermes. Cleveland: Collins and World.

Yadin, Y.
1980 Is the Temple Scroll a Sectarian Document? Pp. 153–69 in *Humanizing America's Iconic Book: SBL Centennial Addresses 1980,* ed. G. Tucker and D. Knight. Chico, CA: Scholars Press.

Eden Sketches

William H. Propp
University of California, San Diego

Gen 2:4b–3:24, the Yahwistic (Steck 1970: 20–40) story of the Garden of Eden, is doubtless the best studied passage in the Hebrew Bible.[1] The basic plot, which tells of the rupture of the harmony of God, humanity, and nature, is fairly clear; nevertheless, many details are not well understood. My aim here is to further our comprehension of eleven problematical features of the text.

1. What is the function of Gen 2:4a, *ʾēlle(h) tôlĕdôt haššāmayim wĕhāʾāreṣ bĕhibbārĕʾām*, which precedes the opening of the J story? It is from the P source, according to the classical formulation of the Documentary Hypothesis (for example, Driver 1891: 9), but does it necessarily summarize the prior priestly creation account (so Driver 1891: 6–7 n.)? All other *tôlĕdōt* notations precede the material to which they refer (Gen 5:1; 6:9; 10:1; 11:10, 27; 25:12, 19; 36:1 [9]; 37:2), rather than summarize, and indeed we expect *ze(h)*, *zō(ʾ)t*, and *ʾēlle(h)* (as opposed to backreferencing *hûʾ*, *hîʾ*, *hēm*, and *hēnnâ*) to introduce new matter (GKC §136 a–b [p. 442]). Accordingly, Cross (1973: 302) and Friedman (1981: 81) correctly conclude that Gen 2:4a is a priestly introduction to the Yahwistic account. Furthermore, Friedman (1981) has demonstrated the existence of two strata of P (already raised as a possibility by Cross 1973: 304–5), the later of which, to which the *tôlĕdōt* references belong, is the work of the exilic redactor of JE and P. Gen 2:4a, then, is not really an introduction so much as a seam. J contains no account of the creation of heaven and earth, so *bĕhibbārĕʾām* must refer to Genesis 1, especially since only that narrative uses the verb *bārāʾ* (Gen 1:1, 21, 27; 2:3). In other words, the verse must be translated 'These are the generations of the heaven and the earth after their creation.'[2] The infinitive construct

1. It has now become *de rigeur* to include in essays on this topic a footnote commenting on the vastness of its bibliography. For a survey of scholarship see Westermann 1984: 178–81, 186–89.

2. Elsewhere *tôlĕdōt* refers, as expected, to human generations. 'The *generations* of the heaven and the earth' is therefore anomalous. Perhaps it is a heritage of the poetic traditions of

preceded by *bĕ-* usually expresses an action taking place slightly before that of the main clause, though, of course, it can connote simultaneity.[3] Elsewhere the redactor uses a *tôlĕdōt* notice to push the narrative forward; note particularly Gen 25:19, where the 'generations of Isaac' prove to be the story of Jacob and Esau (despite the brief genealogy of Isaac in 25:19b), and Gen 37:2, which prefaces the story of Joseph with 'these are the generations of Jacob'. Ever since the Torah left the redactor's stylus, traditionalist readers have understood Gen 2:4 (both halves) to mean that Genesis 2 gives more information on the events of Genesis 1, as was the editor's intent.

2. How are we to understand the opening words of Gen 2:4b, *bĕyôm ʿăśôt yahwe(h) ʾĕlōhîm ʾereṣ wĕšāmayim*? Since *bĕ-*, *kĕ-* or *bĕyôm* plus infinitive construct may connote simultaneity, the expected translation is 'when Yahweh Elohim made earth and sky'. Such a sentence would introduce a cosmogony, whether *ʾereṣ wĕšāmayim* refer simply to the earth and sky, that is, the framework of the universe, or are a merismus for 'everything'. The problem is that, contrary to the reader's expectation, no cosmogony follows. The negative subordinate clauses[4] in vv 5–6 presuppose the existence of heaven and earth, water and soil. In the light of these verses, the reader or listener immediately revises his or her understanding of *bĕyôm ʿăśôt* to connote, not simultaneity, but sequence. In other words, J begins *in medias res* with 'after Yahweh Elohim had made earth and heaven'. J's "creation story" is thus not of the same type as P's (Gen 1–2:3), which truly seeks to account for everything (except God and chaos). Instead, it presupposes the basic elements of the Cosmos. This silence regarding cosmic origins is conceivably a reaction to the old combat myth;[5] compare the manner in

theogony; on Near Eastern theogonies see Cross 1976: 329–38. The Bible hints of theogony in Ps 90:2 and Job 38:8–9, while Kselman (1971) has explored the possibility that such a tradition lies behind Genesis 1. In the context of P, however, the prime referent of 'generations' must be organic life, or, more specifically, human life.

3. We ordinarily translate *bĕ-* and *kĕ-* plus infinitive construct as 'when'. Likewise, *bĕyôm* often is to be rendered 'when' rather than the more specific 'on the day' (cf. Akkadian *enūma*). English 'when' has precisely the same temporal ambiguity as these Hebrew constructions. Compare "when you get to the store, buy some bread" ("after" can be substituted for "when") with "when the truck arrived I was home" ("while" can be substituted). The former sentence features sequence, the latter simultaneity. A Hebrew example of the latter type is Num 10:35, "When the ark travelled Moses would say. . . ." For an example of the former type, compare Gen 2:17 *bĕyôm ʾăkolkā . . . tāmût*, 'you will die when you eat', which could be rendered 'you will die once you have eaten' or even 'after you eat you will die'.

4. The disjunctive *wāw* (Lambdin 1971: 263–64) indicates that these concessive clauses are subordinate to vv 7ff., which begin with *wāw* consecutive. As is often noted, negative subordinate clauses also begin Enūma Eliš; Gen 1:2, while not grammatically negative, uses such terms as *tōhû*, *bōhû*, and *ḥōšek*, all connoting absence of a positive quality.

5. As in Babylon and Ugarit, so in Israel was it said that in mythic time the warrior god (in Israel, Yahweh) had battled the personified Sea or a sea monster. The relevant biblical

which P seemingly refutes the myth by depersonalizing the Cosmos and depicting an orderly unfolding of God's work. Alternatively, the Yahwist may simply not have cared to speculate about the Beginning.

3. Why is the deity called Yahweh-Elohim? The double name probably does not reflect combination of sources, as older commentators were wont to assume (cf. the criticisms of L'hour 1974: 534–56). Yahweh-Elohim might be a primitive sentence name meaning either 'Elohim creates' (Freedman 1960: 156) or 'he creates [or, created] the gods' (Brownlee 1977: 39–40); to the latter the Ugaritic epithet *qnyt ʾilm* 'creatress of the gods' (Athiratu) is comparable and possibly *yahwe(h) ṣĕbāʾôt* 'he creates armies (?)'. I think it more likely, however, that it is a true compound divine name, minus the conjunction attested in Ugaritic names such as *kṯr wḫss*, *qdš wʾamrr*, or *nkl wʾib*; compare Sefire *ʾl wʿlyn*, which in Hebrew becomes *ʾēl ʿelyôn* (Fitzmeyer 1967: 37–38).[6] Note, too, that a compound name may be broken up in poetry, divided between members of a bicolon,[7] and hence in poetry Yahweh parallels El(ohim). I suspect that the Yahwist's use of the double name is less an archaism than a polemical formulation. The biblical writers were faced with a problem, inasmuch as their deity was referred to as both Yahweh and Elohim. The sources E and P record that the name Yahweh was a Mosaic innovation whose equivalence to Elohim was established just before the Exodus (Exod 3:14, 6:3). Presumably the tradition protests so much because, in fact, the god(s) of Israel's ancestors were different from Yahweh; certainly this could be said of the El of the Canaanites. Texts such as Psalm 82 and Deut 32:8–9 may reflect a distinction, even in later Israel, between Yahweh and the old creator god El-Elyon. The Yahwist, too, has to deal with the equation of Yahweh and Elohim, but he makes their identity all the firmer by using the dual name Yahweh-Elohim in his description of the Beginning; perhaps the older credentials of El as primordial creator god (Cross 1973: 15–20) influenced his choice. He makes it clear, however, that humans did not use the name Yahweh until the time of Enosh (Gen 4:26). Until his time only the narrator calls the deity Yahweh, while the name is absent from the dialogue.[8] The association with Enosh may in turn reflect a tradition that

---

passages are 2 Sam 22:16 (= Ps 18:16), Isa 11:15, 41:5, 50:2, Jer 5:22, Nah 1:4, Hab 3:10, Ps 29:3, 74:13–15, 77:17, 89:10–11, 93:1–4, 104:7, Prov 8:27–29, Job 7:12, 9:13, 26:12–13.

6. In the Sefire inscription the relation between *ʾl* and *ʿlyn* is a little unclear; the context suggests that they may be different beings, but the biblical use of *ʿelyôn* makes it more likely that we have a double name *à la* Ugaritic.

7. For example, the normal Ugaritic pair *kṯr wḫss* may be written asyndetically as *[k]ṯr ḫss* in *Ug* 5.7.71, or be entirely broken in *CTA* 6.6.48–49, 17.5.10–11. Similarly, *qdš wʾamrr* is called *qdš ʾamrr* in *CTA* 3.6.11 and the name is split between cola in *CTA* 4.1.16–17. *Nkl wʾib*, too, is divided in *CTA* 24.17–18.

8. It is true that in the MT Eve says 'Yahweh' in Gen 4:1, but the LXX reflects the expected 'Elohim', as in the dialogue in Genesis 2–3 and 4:25. The LXX is probably original, in

Yahwism was indeed as old as humanity; there was apparently a legend identifying Enosh ('Human') as first man, since his place in the priestly genealogy of the Cainites corresponds to Adam's position in J (Hallo and Simpson 1971: 32). Having made his point about the identity of Yahweh and Elohim, the Yahwist virtually abandons the latter name after Enosh.

4. What are the roles of the Tree of Life and the Tree of Knowing Good and Bad?[9] The fruit of the Tree of Life, we learn, imparts immortality (Gen 3:22), while the latter's fruit makes one wise like a god (Gen 2:7, 3:22). Taken together, they confer divinity. Only the latter is forbidden to humanity (2:17). Does Man, then, at first eat of the Tree of Life? In that case, why does Yahweh so fear in 3:22 lest the man and woman live forever that he is forced to expel the humans from the garden? A rational, indeed too rational, explanation is that, like the apples of the Norse gods and the herb of Gilgamesh, the fruit of life must be taken regularly to be effective (Obbinck 1928). The problem is that Yahweh's words, 'lest he reach out and take from the Tree of Life too and eat and live forever', are most naturally interpreted as meaning that, like the fruit of knowledge, the fruit of life works once and forever. We are forced to conclude from 3:22 that Man never tasted of the Tree of Life, though it was allowed, and that he is yet mortal. Man from the beginning had permission to taste immorality, but, being young and healthy, he had not yet done so. We may compare Gilgamesh, whose tragedy is not the loss of immortality, but the loss of access to it.

If the story is so simply to be understood, why have many modern scholars (Westermann 1984: 187) been quick to divide the trees with the

---

light of Gen 4:26, though that verse refers specifically to the origin of prayer, not at issue in Gen 4:1.

9. For ancient parallels to the Tree of Life see Wallace 1985: 103–15, and for the syntax of *ʿēṣ haddaʿat ṭôb wārāʿ* see GKC §115d (p. 354). Wallace (1985: 116–30) clearly summarizes the arguments in favor of the three interpretations of 'knowing good and bad': the intellectual capabilities of an adult (as contrasted with the very young and very old); sexual experience; and omniscience (taking 'good and bad' as a merismus). Wallace prefers the last understanding, but in fact the other two views, especially the first, are also persuasive. Wallace accordingly notes (p. 129) that the phrase could be polyvalent. Indeed we need not expect each biblical author to use the phrase in the same way. I believe that the Yahwist's story plays with the different meanings of 'knowing good and bad'. It is said to be a characteristic of gods (cf. 2 Sam 14:17, 20), that is, omniscience, but its first manifestation is awareness of nudity, typical of the adult but not of the child or childlike (cf. Deut 1:38, 2 Sam 19:36, Isa 7:15). That the phallic snake brings about the transition strongly suggests an association with physical as well as intellectual or social maturation. Note that Isa 11:1–9, which shares other motifs with Genesis 2–3 describes a special shoot, the personified king, which presides over a paradise in the mountain of Yahweh; the plant is said to possess "the spirit of Yahweh, a spirit of wisdom and understanding, a spirit of counsel and heroism, a spirit of knowledge and fear of Yahweh" (v 2); this may be Isaiah's own understanding of 'knowing good and bad', a phrase he also uses in 7:15 to denote maturity.

documentarian hatchet? Of course, the text does not explain everything to the reader. The Yahwist did not wish to mystify his audience, but he expected it to focus only on one issue at a time, and this differs slightly from Western modes of narration. Specifically, the Eden story ends as an etiology of death, but begins as an etiology of wisdom. A tree is the agent of both, though in one case its fruit must be eaten, in the other case not. To impose a measure of consistency on these themes, the author plants both trees in the garden (2:9); thereafter he concentrates first on one, then the other. It is wrong to claim that the two trees are literary doublets because the themes of wisdom and life are incompatible, for they are similarly opposed in the Mesopotamian tales of Gilgamesh and Adapa (*ANET* 72–99, 503–7; 101). Rather, the humans had a choice between wisdom and life; they elected the former, though Yahweh had intended them for the latter.

Note that the Tree of Knowing Good and Bad functions both in the world of the story and in the world of the reader, but primarily in the former. On the other hand, the Tree of Life has almost no role in the story but has its pathos with respect to the world of the reader (Trilling 1965: 56–60), who pauses to confront his or her own mortality and learns that far in the imaginary east is a Tree of Life. One might attempt a journey, but the directions are baffling (Gen 2:10–14), and the way is barred by monsters (Gen 3:24). We could imagine a tale of an Israelite Gilgamesh making the long journey only to be turned back almost in sight of the Tree of Life.

5. Why is Woman created from Man's rib (along with its meat)? Kramer (1963: 149) seeks an explanation in Sumerian paronomasia (TI = 'rib, life' = *Ḥawwâ*), while Goedicke (1985) looks to Egyptian homophony (*imw* 'clay', *imw* 'rib'); but until ancient texts about the creation of Woman out of a rib are discovered, such theories are not provable. That man and woman were originally of one body is, of course, a widespread etiology of human sexual intercourse, whereby men and women try to restore their primordial unity.[10] The Bible also stresses the social aspect of marriage by the use of the phrase 'bone and flesh', that is, kin (Steck 1970: 94–95), and the psychological aspect by the use of *ʿeṣem*, implying that a spouse is another 'self'.

Of course, the problem with the extraction of a rib from the Man is that it is not a promising explanation for sexual union (Gen 2:24), for the genitals are not near the ribs. Gen 2:24 would fit better in an androgyne myth, and so some render *ṣēlāʿ* as 'side', reading Genesis 2–3 as the story of the separation of a primordial hermaphrodite. This is farfetched, for the

10. The oldest certain example is found in Plato's *Symposium* 190, but the notion also occurs in Jewish sources (Ginzberg 1925: 5.88–89). For an Indian example see Carnoy (1917: 294; for Amerindian parallels see Métraux 1946: 367, and Grubb 1914: 115. The observation of Siamese twins in humans and animals no doubt contributed to the creation of these myths.

allusion to 'bone' in 2:23 shows that the Woman is fashioned from the Man's rib. If the narrator believed that *hāʾādām* was a hermaphrodite that Yahweh split in Gen 2:21, he would have ceased using the term *ʾādām* to refer to the man after Gen 2:21 and would have written **wayyibqaᶜ ʾet-hāʾādām wayyaᶜăśēhû lĕʾîš ûl(ĕ)ʾiššâ* or the like. Quite the contrary, the *ṣēlāᶜ* is clearly extracted from the Man's body, and so he recognizes the Woman as 'one of my bones and some of my flesh' (*ᶜeṣem mēᶜăṣāmay ûbāśār mibbĕśārî*). Thus man preempts woman's most awesome attribute—the creation of new life from her abdomen (Philips 1984: 32). The motif of the removal of a child from a male's body is also found in the myths of Sumer, Hatti, Greece, and many other cultures.[11]

Yet Gen 2:24 does sound like the conclusion of a myth of the splitting of a primordial pair joined like Siamese twins, though of opposite sex. The protasis of a cuneiform omen text is suggestive: *šumma sinništu tuʾāmē ūlidma ina* TI(*ṣēlī*)*šunu* DIB.DIB(*tiṣbutū*)*ma*, 'if a woman gives birth to twins and they are joined at their rib/side' (*CT* 3:23, 27:1). In light of the antifemale bias of the Eden story, perhaps the author (or his source) revised an androgyne myth of equal beings joined front-to-front, leaving behind two vestiges of the older version: the etiology of sexual union and the use of a rib. Of course, this remains as speculative as the suggestions of Kramer or Goedicke until such a myth is uncovered.

6. Does Gen 2:25 belong, as in the MT, with chap. 2, or, as in the recent Jewish Publication Society translation, with chap. 3? In fact it points in both directions, that is, it is a seam, yet I think its affinity strongest with chap. 3. The only connection with Genesis 2 is the absence of shame in nudity, admittedly apropos after an explanation of the origin of sexual intercourse. It seems, however, that the author's main point has little to do with sex, but rather is that the humans still have the unselfconsciousness of animals. After all, in Gen 3:10 the Man's claim that it is unseemly for Yahweh to behold him naked is not due to sexual shame, and the same is true of the only other story in J where nudity plays a role, Gen 9:20–27. We might also note that the repetition of *š(ĕ)nêhem* and *ᶜărûmmîm / ᶜêrummīm* constitutes an inclusio for 2:25–3:7 (Trible 1978: 105). If this is true, however, what do we make of the syntax of Gen 3:1? The opening *wĕhannāḥāš hāyâ* is cited as a classic example of the use of disjunction to separate narrative segments. If, however, we read Gen 2:25 with 3:1, an attractive interpretation emerges. The paronomasia of *ᶜărûmmîm* (2:25) and *ᶜārûm* (3:1) suggests that we read these two verses as follows: 'Now the two of them

11. The births of Abu, Nintulla, Ninsutu, Ninkasi, Nazi, Azimua, Ninti, and Enshag from Enki's body (*ANET* 40–41), Kumarbis from Anus's (*ANET* 120), and the births of Athena from Zeus's brow and Dionysus from his thigh all parallel the extraction of Woman from Man.

were *ᶜărûmmîm* [naked], though they were not embarrassed, but the serpent was the most *ᶜārûm* [sly] of all the beasts of the field.' In other words, the humans were no match for the serpent. Note that the ambiguity of the consonants *ᶜrm* works in two directions, for the humans acquire cunning in the course of the story, while the serpent is the quintessentially nude animal, being hairless and periodically shedding its skin. Similar motifs occur in the story of the trickster Jacob, a smooth or slippery (*ḥālāq*) man who dons and doffs deceptive skin (Gen 27:11).

7. Why does the Man claim to be naked in Gen 3:10? He is not (Gen 3:7). The Man responds to Yahweh's *ˀayyekkâ* (Gen 3:9) with a double lie: 'I heard your sound in the garden and feared, since I am naked, and I hid.' The first lie concerns his motive—he in fact hid in fear of punishment, not out of modesty. The second lie concerns his state, and it ironically invalidates his first lie—he is not naked, but clothed in leaves. Man's new found wisdom now expresses itself in cunning, but he is less experienced than the serpent, who had not actually lied to the Woman in Gen 3:1, 4–5. Yahweh immediately realizes that the Man knows more than he should, and the jig is up.

8. What is the significance of the loss of the serpent's legs (Gen 3:14)? The implication is that the serpent had originally been legged, that is, a lizard.[12] I have purposely avoided translating *nāḥāš* as 'snake', but have used instead the more ambiguous 'serpent' (< *serpo* 'creep'), which etymologically includes both snakes and lizards. Indeed, were it not for tradition, I would have preferred to render *nāḥāš* as 'reptile'. In other words, the Eden narrative probably contains the "Just So Story" of how the lizard lost its legs, or, more precisely, how the reptile class became differentiated. It is barely possible that inspection of snake skeletons, which preserve vestigial legs, abetted such speculations. Puzzlement over serpentine locomotion is also expressed in Prov 30:19.

It may seem frivolous to speculate as to the species of the snake. The wordplay in Gen 3:15 involving the root(s) *šwp*, however, brings to mind the *šĕpîpōn*, a species (conventionally, the horned viper) said to attack the heels of horses in Gen 49:17, just as the serpent of Eden attacks the heels of humans.

12. This seems more likely than the rabbinic hypothesis that the serpent had stood upright like a man (*Gen. Rab.* 19:1). Note that the serpent (MT *tannîm*) of Ezek 32:1–8 has legs (v 2). It is probable that the cousin of the Genesis serpent, the "earth lion" of Gilgamesh, is a lizard; this is in fact the Greek etymology of "chameleon." According to my consultation with the herpetologist Steven Anderson, most lizard species shed their skins, though few as completely as the snakes. It may be more than coincidence that in Ethiopic *ˀarwē* 'beast' can mean 'serpent', since *ˀarwē* may originally have meant 'lion' as in Hebrew *ˀărî*/*ˀaryē(h)*. In fact, often when referring to a serpent *ˀarwē* is followed by *medr* 'earth'. Note, too that Akkadian *nēšu* 'lion' is probably cognate to Hebrew *nāḥāš*. See Mowinckel 1963.

9. What is the meaning of *Ḥawwâ* 'Eve'? The Yahwist connects it with *ḥyy* 'to live', and the LXX *Zōē* follows this line of interpretation. Due to their inveterate suspicion of biblical etymologies, however, scholars have sought long and hard to explain Eve's Hebrew name in other ways (Kapelrud 1977; Williams 1977). Some suggest derivation from the Hurrian goddess Hebat, the ethnicon *Ḥiwwî* (Hivite) or *ḥawwâ* 'settlement'. The most popular guess, as old as the Talmud, *Bereshit Rabbah*, and Clement of Alexandria (Williams 1977: 358–62), is a connection with the root *ḥwy*, which yields in old Aramaic (Sefire A.30) *ḥwh*, in later Aramaic *ḥewyāʾ* (and related forms), and in Arabic *ḥayya*, all meaning 'snake'.[13] No such Hebrew word is attested, however; perhaps the verb *hištaḥăwâ* derives from a root *ḥwy* 'to coil', but the evidence is not conclusive (see Emerton 1977, Davies 1979, and Kreuzer 1985). It is indeed possible that an old version of the story described interactions between a man and a serpent who stole immortality and that tradition turned 'Serpent' into the name of a woman, but this is at present undemonstrable. It is more profitable to consider the Yahwist's own understanding of the name, probably as a feminine *qaṭṭāl nomen agentis* of the root *ḥyy/ḥwy* 'live'.[14] 'Life-maker', as Rashi notes, is a fitting title for the mother of all humanity and like 'Man' (*ʾĀdām*) appropriately generic for a myth of origins. The presence of a *wāw* in the root is admittedly anomalous and arguably due to derivation from 'Serpent', but, in fact, the Phoenician verb 'to live' does contain a *wāw*, and Ugaritic uses both *ḥyy* and *ḥwy*; note, too, that the similarly shaped root *hyy* interchanges with *hwy* in both Hebrew and Semitic. A rather good parallel to the Yahwist's understanding of *Ḥawwâ* is Talmudic *ḥayyâ* 'lying-in woman, midwife'.[15] Interestingly, the

13. There are two candidates, I believe unrecognized, for Ugaritic cognates: *ḥwt* (parallel to buffalo; perhaps a decorative motif in *CTA* 4.1.43) and *ḥw* (*UT* 1001.1.6), which, as it is followed by *bṯnm* 'snakes', is probably a type of serpent; cf. Hebrew *śēʿîr ʿizzîm*, etc. Arabic *ḥawā* 'gather' and *taḥawwā* 'coil' provide a probable etymology, unless the derived form was influenced by the noun *ḥayya* 'snake'. Nevertheless, since this verbal root is not attested in this sense in Northwest Semitic, speakers in Syria-Palestine probably linked 'snake' to the root *ḥyy/ḥwy* 'to live' and, more precisely, to Hebrew *ḥayyâ* and Aramaic *ḥēwāʾ* 'animal'. Semantic interchanges between generic and specific terms are fairly common; cf. Hebrew *ʾaryē(h)* 'lion' and Ethiopic *ʾarwē* 'animal'; Hebrew *ʿēnāb* 'grape' and Akkadian *inbu* 'fruit'. Sometimes this shift can even be between very different species; for instance, Hebrew *nāḥāš* 'serpent' and *zĕʾēb* 'wolf' are probably cognate to Akkadian *nēšu* 'lion' and *zību* 'vulture'.

14. On the *qaṭṭāl* pattern for final weaks in Semitic see Barth 1894: 51, but, as he notes, we have no examples from biblical Hebrew. We can resort to reconstruction of what such a form might look like, however. If we have in the Niphal participle m. *nibne(h)*, f. *nibnâ*, so might the root *ḥwy* produce m. **ḥawwe(h)*, f. **ḥawwâ*.

15. There may be some connection with Exod 1:19 *kî ḥāyôt* (revocalize **ḥayyôt*?) *hēnnâ* in the context of birth and midwifery. I find no evidence, though it would be possible, that the Talmudic use of *ḥayyâ* has been influenced by Exod 1:19. A similar usage may also be attested in Gen 18:10, 14; 2 Kgs 4:16, 17 *ʿēt ḥayyâ*, which perhaps is to be rendered 'time of childbirth', despite Gen 17:21.

name seems to appear as Punic *ḥwt*, an epithet of the goddess Tanit (Lidzbarski 1902–15: 1.30).[16]

10. Why does Yahweh make the couple leather garments? In 3:21 he seeks a more permanent solution to the problem of nudity than fig leaves by making leather cloaks for the Man and his wife. Most view this as a work of mercy (for example, Steck 1970: 116), which of course it is, but note that in the Near East garments of skin were worn by such outcasts and wanderers as Elijah (2 Kgs 1:8), Gilgamesh (*ANET* 88), and John the Baptist (Mark 1:6); perhaps, too, the exile of Jacob is presaged in his donning skins (Gen 27:16). In Gen 3:21 the leather garments are hence an implicit threat of exile. Of course, they also reflect the author's theory that at first humans went naked, then wore ready materials such as leaves, and then animal skins procurable through hunting. The textiles of the author's day were a consequence of the later development of agriculture and herding.

11. Finally, what does the serpent represent? As Joines (1974, 1975) has shown, the serpent in the Bible is a symbol of rejuvenation, wisdom, and chaos. In its latter associations it often appears as a monstrous adversary to Yahweh in primordial times, and so it is no coincidence that in the Yahwist's demythologized version the enemy is a serpent, though divested of most of its supernatural attributes (McKenzie 1954). One might simply say that the serpent has associations with life and death, since it is ostensibly immortal, on the one hand, yet secretes poison, lives underground, and is akin to the monsters of primordial chaos, on the other. Not surprisingly, in the Near East as in Greece, the serpent is a symbol of healing (cf. Num 21:4–9) and magic, in turn facets of wisdom.[17] We might describe the serpent as quintessentially ambiguous.

For instance, in Genesis 2–3 the serpent's chief trait is wisdom, but the word used is the morally ambivalent *ᶜārûm*,[18] rather than the positive *ḥākām*, for his wisdom leads to harm, both for himself and others. Though the

16. Here, too, 'Life-maker' is a possible interpretation, but Lidzbarski (1902–15: 1.30) connects the title with the terms for snake discussed above. This is suggestive in light of Cross's attempt (1973: 32–33) to derive the name Tanit from *tannîn* 'serpent'.

17. The Israelites may well have associated *nāḥāš* with *nāḥaš* 'to divine', and certainly did with *nĕḥōšet* 'copper', since the copper serpent was called *nĕhuštān* (2 Kgs 18:4). Perhaps the metallic sheen of some reptiles, especially snakes, contributed to this association.

18. Arabic *ᶜarima* means, it is true, 'to be vicious', but the Hebrew usage of the root is not always negative, and in Aramaic it generally has a positive sense. It can carry a connotation of malice (Exod 21:14; Ps 83:4; Job 5:12–13, 15:5), or a connotation of prudence (Prov 1:4; 8:5, 12; 12:16, 23; 13:16; 14:8, 15, 18; 15:5; 19:25; 22:3; 27:12; see Alonso-Schökel 1962); it may even be neutral shrewdness in Josh 9:4 and 1 Sam 23:22, though these two examples might be grouped under malice. Overall, the best translation for *ᶜārûm* is 'sharp'. Of course, the word was also chosen for Genesis 2–3 because of the paronomasia with 'naked', but this alone does not account for its appearance, as the Yahwist was under no obligation to pun.

theme of eternal life is present, the rejuvenation of the snake is not at issue. One suspects that the Yahwist was familiar with a version of the widely attested tale wherein the snake (or the crab or the bird [cf. Ps 103:5]) achieves immortality, that is, the ability to change its skin (Frazer 1919: 1.66–77), for in this story the humans are given new skins (Gen 3:21).[19] The existence of such a story would explain the craftiness of the serpent, for in the current story there is no possible benefit to himself in his actions (Frazer 1919: 1.49–52).

The Yahwist in fact provides the serpent with no motive for his actions other than cleverness for its own sake. He is a mischief maker by very nature, even if he suffers as a consequence. All the serpent ultimately gains is the joy of thwarting Yahweh and the humans by the exercise of his wits. The serpent is thus in some respects the best biblical analogue to the Trickster archetype, which Radin (1956: ix–x) describes as,

> at one and the same time creator and destroyer, giver and negator, he who dupes others and is always duped himself. He wills nothing consciously. At all times he is constrained to behave as he does from impulses over which he has no control. He knows neither good nor evil yet he is responsible for both. He possesses no values, moral or social, is at the mercy of his passions and appetites, yet through his actions all values come into being. . . . Trickster himself is, not infrequently, identified with specific animals, such as raven, coyote, hare, spider.

The Trickster is often said to be one of the oldest beings on earth, if not a deity, and the originator of many evils of human existence such as death, theft, rape, lying, and irresponsibility (Radin 1956: 147, 164). Kerényi (Radin 1956: 189) describes him as an "enemy of boundaries." He may also be a creature of intense, indeed exaggerated, sexuality, having, in some of his Amerindian incarnations, a long, snakelike penis, which is eventually curtailed (Radin 1956: 19–20, 38–39, 129). He is the object of amusement mingled with awe (Radin 1956: x). In some regions he is regarded as a demoted, mischief-making deity (Radin 1956: 164–65), and with the influence of Christianity he comes to be identified with the Devil (Radin 1956: 147–49). He seems to stand for, among other things, the impulses toward mischief and sexuality that humans learn to repress in the course of maturation and socialization.

Much of this could be said of the serpent of Eden.[20] He grants humanity civilization, but robs it of immortality and consigns it to the hard life of the

19. That the rabbis responded unconsciously to this allusion is shown by the midrash that the garments were of snakeskin (*Pirqê dĕ-Rabbî ʾElîʿezer* 20; *Targum pseudo-Jonathan*).

20. For a discussion of other Trickster tales in Genesis see Niditch 1987. On the deceptions Jacob practices and suffers see Friedman 1986.

farmer. Though sly, he is eventually caught and made to suffer, in a sense curtailed, by the god whom he has outwitted. He is later identified with the expelled angel Lucifer-Satan. There are plain sexual overtones to the story (Coppens 1948; McKenzie 1954; Engnell 1955; Gordis 1957), which even pre-Freudian Late Antiquity recognized, speculating that the serpent lusted for and in some versions seduced Eve (see Ginzberg 1925: 5.133–34). To us, the serpent is an obvious phallic symbol (note its special relation with Woman and women) who leads Man and Woman to maturity.

There are differences, too, between Trickster and the serpent. The latter is not humorous, nor is he is particularly impulsive, save that he has no evident motive for tempting the Woman. The Trickster of America is the protagonist of a picaresque cycle of adventures, many both funny and scatological, whereas we know of no other adventures of the serpent, and, in any case, he is not the main character in Genesis 2–3.

Of course, one can say a good deal in defense of the serpent. The plot of Genesis 2–3 might be summarized as follows: God withholds a desideratum from Man, misleadingly threatening death should Man try to attain it. An intelligent serpent tells one of the humans that there will be no death, but that God is simply afraid of competition. The humans follow the serpent's advice and indeed benefit, and the serpent has succeeded in foiling God's plan. As the sly beast had predicted, the humans' fear of divine punishment had been exaggerated. They do not immediately die, but by a reinterpretation of God's threat they lose access to immortality. All three suffer for the episode, but the serpent has succeeded in, as it were, stealing wisdom from Heaven and bestowing it upon humanity. Since the collusion of serpent and humans has been so effective, Yahweh replaces their former amity with enmity (Gen 3:15; cf. a similar dissolution of a threatening alliance in Genesis 11).[21] The serpent thus need not be viewed as a villain. Perhaps the ambivalence of the serpent arises in the mixed feelings with which we recall the loss of childhood dependence and innocence.

Such a retelling, with the Suffering Serpent as benefactor of humanity, is obviously reminiscent of the myth of Prometheus, as Ehrenzweig (1921) briefly notes. Some Gnostics, likewise sensitive to this reading, went so far as to describe the serpent as divinely inspired (Kaestli 1982), and, in keeping with the Gnostic glorification of the feminine, Eve too turned out to be a heroine. Even the Christian tradition, though identifying the serpent as Satan, conceded the beneficial effects of the *felix culpa* that elicited the incarnation of Christ (Phillips 1984: 78–95).

21. Note that in the restoration of paradisiacal conditions described in Isaiah 11, where natural enemies like the wolf and the lamb, the leopard and the kid, etc., live in harmony, the child is safe with the serpent (v 8).

The Yahwist seemingly has no sympathy for the serpent, yet he uses a literary genre that, in other societies, would lead us to at least grudgingly admire the villain. This tells us something about the Yahwist's, and perhaps Israel's, view of humanity.

Some ancient myths assigned mortals a lowly place in the universe. We were created as an afterthought or as drudges to the gods (and, logically, their human representatives). The Bible accorded humanity a loftier status, but there was a commensurate loss of a certain type of heroism. The world of myth was full of struggle against the divine Establishment. The psychological reasons for this were sundry: resentment toward parents, resentment toward priests, resentment toward human limitation in the face of nature's limitless power. The attempt to rise above these limitations was the essence of heroism. When the gods were angered and the attempt failed, there was pathos. In contrast, Israel accorded less nobility to struggle against the will of Yahweh. The Bible is of course filled with tales of rebellion against God, but in general little nobility accrues to the rebels, who are merely sinners. Admittedly, Abraham, Jacob, Moses, Jeremiah, and Job have their moments of tension with Yahweh, but they return to orthodoxy. By stressing the quasi-divine essence of humanity (Genesis 1–3, Ps 8:6), Israel alleviated some of its need to break beyond the bounds of human limitation. As in extra-biblical myths, humanity may try to storm heaven and may suffer the consequences (Genesis 2–3, 11:1–9), but the Yahwist had little sympathy for *hybris*.

Bibliography

Alonso-Schökel, L.

1962 Motivos Sapienciales y de Alianza en Gn 2–3. *Biblica* 43: 295–315.

ANET J. B. Pritchard (ed.), *Ancient Near Eastern Texts Relating to the Old Testament*. 3d. ed. Princeton: Princeton University, 1969.

Barth, J.

1894 *Die Nominalbildung in den semitischen Sprachen*. 2d. ed. Leipzig: Hinrichs.

Brownlee, W. H.

1977 The Ineffable Name of God. *Bulletin of the American Schools of Oriental Research* 226: 39–46.

Carnoy, A. J.

1917 Iranian Mythology. Pp. 253–368 in *The Mythology of All Races*, vol. 11. Boston: Jones.

Coppens, J.

1948 *La connaissance du bien et du mal et le péché du paradis*. Analecta lovaniensia biblica et orientalia II/3. Gembloux: Duculot.

Cross, F. M.
1973 *Canaanite Myth and Hebrew Epic*. Cambridge: Harvard University.
1976 The "Olden Gods" in Ancient Near Eastern Creation Myths. Pp. 329–38 in *Magnalia Dei: In Memoriam G. E. Wright*, ed. F. M. Cross, W. Lemke, and P. D. Miller. Garden City: Doubleday.

CT *Cuneiform Texts from Babylonian Tablets in the British Museum*. London: British Museum, 1896– .

CTA A. Herdner (ed.), *Corpus des tablettes en cunéiformes alphabétiques*. 2 vols. Paris: Geuthner, 1963.

Davies, G. I.
1979 A Note on the Etymology of *hištaḥᵃwāh*. *Vetus Testamentum* 29: 493–95.

Driver, S. R.
1891 *An Introduction to the Literature of the Old Testament*. Edinburgh: Clark.

Ehrenzweig, A.
1921 Zusatz (to "Genesis 2–4" by N. Rhodokanakis). *Zeitschrift für die alttestamentliche Wissenschaft* 39: 82–83.

Emerton, J. A.
1971 The Etymology of *hištaḥᵃwāh*. *Oudtestamentische Studiën* 20: 41–55.

Engnell, I.
1955 "Knowledge" and "Life" in the Creation Story. Pp. 103–19 in *Wisdom in Israel and in the Ancient Near East: Presented to H. H. Rowley*, ed. M. Noth and D. W. Thomas. Supplements to Vetus Testamentum 3. Leiden: Brill.

Fitzmeyer, J. A.
1967 *The Aramaic Inscriptions of Sefire*. Biblica et orientalia 19. Rome: Pontifical Biblical Institute.

Frazer, J. G.
1919 *Folk-lore in the Old Testament*. 3 vols. London: Macmillan.

Freedman, D. N.
1960 The Name of the God of Moses. *Journal of Biblical Literature* 79: 151–56.

Friedman, R. E.
1981 *Exile and Biblical Narrative*. Harvard Semitic Monographs 22. Chico: Scholars Press.
1986 Deception for Deception. *Bible Review* 2: 22–31, 68.

GKC E. Kautzsch and A. E. Cowley (eds.), *Gesenius' Hebrew Grammar*. 2d English ed. Oxford: Clarendon, 1910.

Ginzberg, L.
1925 *The Legends of the Jews*. 7 vols. Philadelphia: Jewish Publication Society.

Goedicke, H.
1985 Adam's Rib. Pp. 73–76 in *Biblical and Related Studies Presented to Samuel Iwry*, ed. A. Kort and S. Morschauser. Winona Lake: Eisenbrauns.

Gordis,R.
1957 The Knowledge of Good and Evil in the Old Testament and the Qumran Scrolls. *Journal of Biblical Literature* 76: 123–38.

Grubb, W. B.
1914 *An Unknown People in an Unknown Land*. 4th ed. London: Seely, Service.

Hallo, W. W., and W. K. Simpson
1971 *The Ancient Near East: A History*. New York: Harcourt Brace Jovanovich.
Joines, K. R.
1974 *Serpent Symbolism in the Old Testament*. Haddonfield, NJ: Haddonfield House.
1975 The Serpent in Genesis 3. *Zeitschrift für die alttestamentliche Wissenschaft* 87: 1–11.
Kaestli, J.-D.
1982 L'interprétation du serpent de Genèse 3 dans quelques textes gnostiques et la question de la gnose "ophite." Pp. 116–30 in *Gnosticisme et monde hellénistique: Acts du colloque de Louvain-la-Neuve (11–14 mars 1980)*, ed. J. Ries. De l'institut orientaliste de Louvain 27. Louvain-la-Neuve: Institut orientaliste de l'université catholique de Louvain.
Kapelrud, A. S.
1977 Ḥawwāh. Pp. 794–98 in *Theologisches Wörterbuch zum Alten Testament*, ed. G. J. Botterweck and H. Ringgren, vol. 2. Stuttgart: Kohlhammer.
Kramer, S. N.
1963 *The Sumerians*. Chicago: University of Chicago.
Kreuzer, S.
1985 Zur Bedeutung und Etymologie von *hištaḥ*^{a}*wāh/yšt*ḥ*wy*. *Vetus Testamentum* 35: 39–60.
Kselman, J.
1971 The Poetic Background of Certain Priestly Traditions. Ph.D. diss., Harvard University.
Lambdin, T. O.
1971 *Introduction to Biblical Hebrew*. New York: Scribner.
L'hour, J.
1974 Jahweh Elohim. *Revue biblique* 81: 524–56.
Lidzbarski, B. C. M.
1902–15 *Ephemeris für semitische Epigraphik*. 3 vols. Giessen: Töpelmann.
McKenzie, J. L.
1954 The Literary Characteristics of Genesis 2–3. *Theological Studies* 15: 541–72.
Métraux, A.
1946 Ethnography of the Chaco. *Smithsonian Institution Bureau of American Ethnology Bulletin* 143: 1.197–370 (= Handbook of South American Indians 1).
Mowinckel, S.
1963 *Šaḥal*. Pp. 95–103 in *Hebrew and Semitic Studies Presented to G. R. Driver*, ed. D. W. Thomas and W. D. Hardy. Oxford: Clarendon.
Niditch, S.
1987 *Underdogs and Tricksters*. San Francisco: Harper and Row.
Obbink, H. T.
1928 The Tree of Life in Eden. *Zeitschrift für die alttestamentliche Wissenschaft* 46: 105–12.
Phillips, J. A.
1984 *Eve*. San Francisco: Harper and Row.

Radin, P.
1956 *The Trickster*. New York: Philosophical Library.

Steck, O. H.
1970 *Die Paradieserzählung*. Biblische Studien 60. Neukirchen-Vluyn: Neukirchener Verlag.

Trible, P.
1978 *God and the Rhetoric of Sexuality*. Philadelphia: Fortress.

Trilling, W.
1964 *Denn Staub bist du*. Leipzig: St. Benno-Verlag.

Ug C. F. A. Schaeffer (ed.), *Ugaritica*. 7 vols. Paris: Geuthner, 1939–78.

UT C. H. Gordon, *Ugaritic Textbook*. Rome: Pontifical Biblical Institute, 1965.

Wallace, H. N.
1985 *The Eden Narrative*. Harvard Semitic Monographs 32. Missoula: Scholars Press.

Westermann, C.
1984 *Genesis 1–11*. Minneapolis: Augsburg.

Williams, A. J.
1977 The Relationship of Genesis 3:20 to the Serpent. *Zeitschrift für die alttestamentliche Wissenschaft* 89: 357–74.

People and High Priesthood in Early Maccabean Times

James C. VanderKam
North Carolina State University

I. Qumran Beginnings

A. Modern Datings and the Qumran Texts

Although some of the earlier proposals regarding Qumran origins spanned a wide range of years in late antiquity—from the second century B.C. to Qaraite times—the most widely accepted hypotheses today involve a rather narrow time-range (see Cross 1980: 109–60). Two external factors—archeology and paleography—have been very helpful in defining the general limits with which one should be working. Roland de Vaux was able to date his period I*a* at Qumran only in relation to I*b*, since coins of the latter indicated that its buildings were occupied under the reign of Alexander Jannaeus (103–76 B.C.) and had possibly been constructed during the time of John Hyrcanus (134–104 B.C.): "This construction marks the concluding date of Period I*a*. It is possible that this would have commenced under one of the predecessors of John Hyrcanus, but we cannot push it back very far because the modest nature of the buildings and the scarcity of archeological material attest the fact that this first installation was of short duration" (de Vaux 1973: 5). F. M. Cross has reached similar conclusions on paleographical grounds. He has divided Judean scripts of the period 200 B.C. to A.D. 70 into three phases: Archaic (200–150 B.C.), Hasmonean (150–30 B.C.), and Herodian (30 B.C.–A.D. 70). There are no sectarian documents copied in a script belonging to the Archaic Period, while copies of the Manual of Discipline and the Damascus Document (which mentions the death of the Teacher of Righteousness) come from the first third or so of the first century. "In short, paleographical analysis of the texts now sets limits within which we must look for the events which gave rise to the sectarian movement: the upper limit, while not certain, is suitably drawn about 150 B.C.; the lower limit, which I should regard as definitively fixed, falls not far from 100 B.C.; in other terms from the priesthood of Jonathan (160–142 B.C.) to the reign of Alexander Jannaeus (103–76 B.C.)" (Cross 1980: 121–22; see 118–22).

If one examines the literary evidence for this period, similar conclusions can be reached. It is likely that the Teacher of Righteousness was instrumental in defining the group at a very early stage in its existence. He seems not to have been the one who founded it, since CD 1:5–11 speaks of a twenty-year period of groping like blind men before God raised up a teacher of righteousness for them. But he was obviously pivotal in giving a precise orientation to the members who preceded him. According to 4QPs[a] frgs. 1–10, iii:15–16, God chose the Teacher of Righteousness (only the definite article of הצדק is preserved) "to stand, f[or] he had established him to build a community of [ ] for him" (my translation; cf. Horgan 1979: 198 and supplement 54; see also CD 1:11: להדריכם בדרך לבו [Rabin 1958: 3]). Now this teacher was a priest; in fact, he is called "the priest." For example, in the passage from 4QPs[a] just cited (1:15) one reads: "its interpretation concerns the priest, the Teacher of [Righteousness]." Hartmut Stegemann has used instances of this sort to argue that the Teacher was the acting high priest in the period for which the sources seem to mention no reigning high priest—ca. 159–152 B.C. He maintains that the titular use of הכוהן for this man entails this conclusion (Stegemann 1971: 102, 212–14; cf. Murphy-O'Connor 1976). Moreover, the Teacher is brought into direct connection with the archenemy of the sect—the Wicked Priest (הכוהן הרשע, who is also called 'the priest'—in the familiar episode in 1QpHab 11:4–8 in which the Wicked Priest is said to have come to the place of the Teacher's exile on the Day of Atonement in order to devour the Teacher and his group. 4QPs[a] frgs. 1–10, iv:8 similarly connects the two priests and claims that the Wicked Priest tried to kill the Teacher. It has been argued that the Wicked Priest was himself a high priest; indeed, his pejorative title may be a play on הכוהן הראש—an attested title for the high priest (Ezra 7:5; see for references Stegemann 1971: 102 n. 330).

It seems quite possible, then, that a priestly conflict, which may even have involved holders of the high-priestly office, was a decisive factor in the decision to establish a community on the shores of the Dead Sea. It should also be remembered that there is frequent reference in the Qumran literature to the sons of Zadok who were part of the community. That is, there were other priests who were members and they belonged to the highest ranking family among the priests. There are, of course, other indications that priestly differences separated the Qumran sectaries from their countrymen in Jerusalem. The religious calendar may be cited in this context. The 364-day solar calendar, which is attested in 1 Enoch 72–82, Jubilees, and the Temple Scroll, is explicit in 11QPs[a] DavComp 11 6–7 (regarding the *tāmîd* offering: ". . . for all the days of the year, 364; and for the *qorbān* of the

Sabbaths, 52 songs" [Sanders 1965: 92]). It hardly needs to be stressed anymore that differences in cultic calendar would make the distinctions between people readily visible to all and make communal life difficult (Talmon 1958: 163–64). The calendar involved not only a different number of days and thus differing dates for many festivals but also, it appears, some festivals that were new (the system of firstfruits festivals in the Temple Scroll, which is also reflected briefly in Jubilees 32, for instance [Yadin 1977: 1.81–99]).

B. Origins according to Related Texts

It is very likely, then, that at some time near the middle of the second century B.C. some sorts of priestly controversies resulted in the physical separation of what was a small group, including some priests, to Qumran. But, as noted above, this was not, in the estimation of these sectaries, the beginning of their community. The twenty-year period in CD 1 has already been mentioned; to it can be added an intriguing set of references in several documents that the Qumran group copied and apparently admired. A set of passages in 1 Enoch and Jubilees speaks of a revival or reform movement or movements in pre-Maccabean times. The vagueness of the descriptions in them makes it difficult to determine whether each of these sections is referring to the same group and if that group was historically related to the one that later fled to Qumran; but at the very least all of them locate the rise of a new movement to roughly the same period.

The Apocalypse of Weeks (1 Enoch 93:1–10, 91:11–17), which may be the most ancient Jewish apocalypse that includes a historical survey (see Dexinger 1977: 137–40; VanderKam 1984: 521–23), says the following about the pivotal seventh week in the drama of sacred history:

> And after this in the seventh week an apostate generation will arise, and many (will be) its deeds, but all its deeds (will be) apostasy. And at its end the chosen righteous from the eternal plant of righteousness will be chosen, to whom will be given sevenfold teaching concerning his whole creation (93:9–10 [Knibb 1978]).

The Animal Apocalypse (1 Enoch 85–90) speaks in a similar fashion about the immediate pre-Maccabean years (just before the removal of Onias III; Milik 1976: 43):

> And small lambs were born from those white sheep, and they began to open their eyes, and to see, and to cry to the sheep. But the sheep did not cry to them and did not listen to what they said to them, but were extremely deaf, and their eyes were extremely and excessively blinded (90:6–7 [Knibb 1978]).

And Jubilees 23 (VanderKam 1977: 207–85; Nickelsburg 1981: 77), which attaches one of the book's rare apocalyptic sections to a notice about Abraham's relatively modest age (175 years) at his death, speaks thus about a new movement:

> And in those days the children will begin to study the laws,
> And to seek the commandments,
> And to return to the path of righteousness.
> And the days will begin to grow many and increase amongst those children of men,
> Till their days draw nigh to one thousand years,
> And to a greater number of years than (before) was the number of days (23:6–7 [Charles 1902]).

Though one can infer from each of these texts that they are depicting in symbolic terms the beginnings of a new group in pre-Maccabean times, only the Damascus Document furnishes chronological data. In CD 1:5–10 one learns that some 390 years after Nebuchadnezzar had taken Judah,

> He visited them; and He caused to grow forth from Israel and Aaron "a root of cultivation, to possess His land" and to wax fat in the goodness of His soil. And they considered their trespass and they knew that they were guilty men; but they "were like the blind and like them that grope *their* way" for twenty years (Rabin 1958: 2).

The meaning of these numbers (390 and 20) of years has been debated at length (Ginzberg 1976: 257–60), but if they were intended by the author to be historically accurate and if in fact they are, then the writer of the Damascus Document would be dating the inception of this 'root of cultivation' (שורש מטעת) to ca. 196 B.C. and the arrival of a teacher of righteousness to ca. 176 B.C.

The minimum that emerges from texts of this sort is that a new movement or series of them appeared in the Jewish community in pre-Maccabean times. The importance at Qumran of the Damascus Document, 1 Enoch, and Jubilees and the favorable terms in which the members of the new bodies are described in these compositions suggest that the sectaries saw themselves as in some sense their heirs. Like the covenanters, these people, who are called "elect ones," "lambs," "children," and "root of cultivation," seem to have opposed aspects of the mainline community. But there is no indication in any of these texts that the individuals in question separated themselves geographically from the remainder of the Jewish population. It is reasonable to suppose that the differences that divided these people from their fellow religionists did not entail their physical removal from the company of their opponents. And, as noted above, the archeological and paleographical evidence that is available leads one to think that the exile to the shores of the Dead Sea did not take place until some time near the mid-second century—perhaps about a generation after the rise of the new group or groups.

II. Causes for the Separation

The next and obvious question is: What caused a body of people that may have included high-ranking priests to remove itself from the temple in Jerusalem? One cannot argue that issues such as calendrical differences were *per se* the decisive factor because it is now apparent that the 364-day solar calendar was known and defended well before the schism that produced the first settlement at Qumran. It is described in some detail in the Astronomical Book of 1 Enoch (chaps. 72–82), which apparently dates from no later than the third century B.C. (Milik 1976: 7–11), and Jubilees, which was also written before the founding of the Qumran community (VanderKam 1977: 207–85), defends it stoutly. So, as least some of the ideological and practical differences between these Jewish groups long antedated the mid-second-century exodus to Qumran. The immediate cause or causes that triggered the geographical separation of the earliest Qumran residents will have to be sought in another direction.

A. Source Problems

This brings one back to the issue of priestly politics and disputes in the relevant period. Is there information available about the priesthood then that will shed some additional light on the problem of Qumran origins? One could and should, of course, look at the Qumran literature for such data. After all, the first group that went to Qumran was probably very small, judging by the buildings that belong to phase I*a*, and it seems that their contemporaries did not note the fact of their exodus (not, at least, in the literature that has survived). But the Qumran library has proved frustrating for those who approach it with modern historical questions because there is in it no work that is aimed at giving the kinds of information that contemporary historians need in order to reconstruct the origin of the group. It may be that texts yet to be published (for example, the letter from the Teacher of Righteousness to the Wicked Priest [Qimron and Strugnell 1985]) will offer new and historically useful information, but it is unlikely, given what has been published, that a document from this library will provide direct answers to historical questions about the earliest days of the community.

Methodologically, it makes more sense to turn to works that deal with this period and purport to give historical information. The major sources are, naturally, 1–2 Maccabees and the writings of Josephus, especially his *Antiquities*. These compositions may seem no more promising than the Qumran texts for answering the particular historical question that is under consideration. One problem with them is that they were written later and probably never mention the exodus to Qumran. The attention of their authors was focused on the great events that transpired in connection with the temple and the Maccabean family, not on the sundry dissident groups who may not have found the Hasmonean contribution to Judaism quite so splendid as they did. In fact, in contemporary research on the Scrolls, the two leading candidates for the post of the Wicked Priest are the first two Maccabean high priests—Jonathan and Simon. These two, far from being considered wicked priests in 1 Maccabees and Josephus's *Antiquities*, are heroes of the stories. Consequently, one must recognize that the very documents that are available for this period and seem to be the only ones likely to yield more information about priestly problems in the mid-second century are written from a point of view that is drastically different than what one finds in the Qumran texts. That is, one is reduced to using pro-Maccabean propaganda in the hope of clarifying the historical conditions amid which an anti-Hasmonean group left Jerusalem and its temple.

Scholars have, of course, been well aware of this problem but have scoured these sources nevertheless, perhaps largely because there is no choice in the matter. And they have proved to be very helpful. But I doubt that the full amount of relevant information that they contain has been wrung from them yet, and, as an example, I wish to investigate an aspect of the high priesthood in early Maccabean times that is pertinent to the subject of Qumran origins but has not received adequate attention. The remainder of this paper will focus on the ways in which the first Maccabean high priests attained their supreme office and what relevance this might have for the decision by some to emigrate to Qumran. Even the pro-Maccabean sources retain traces of very unusual happenings around the top office in the land—abnormal procedures that may well have offended strong traditionalists such as those who formed the Dead Sea community.

B. *The Accession of the First Maccabean High Priests*

The sources leave one with no doubt that strange, unprecedented conditions obtained for the high priesthood beginning with the deposition of Onias III in 175 B.C. Jason, a brother of Onias, bribed the new and financially strapped king—Antiochus IV—and received the high priesthood from him (2 Macc 4:7–10). Three years later, he was outbid by another priest Menelaus (2 Macc 4:23–26) who, with varying degrees of success, held the office for some ten years (2 Macc 13:1–8). At that point a certain Alcimus received royal appointment as high priest, a position that he held until his death three years later in 159 B.C. (2 Macc 14:3–13; 1 Macc 9:54–57). It is well known that the sources mention no high priest for the next seven years, but in 152 Jonathan, the second Maccabean commander, accepted Alexander Balas's offer of the high priesthood (1 Macc 10:1–21). The office then remained in the hands of the Hasmonean family for more than one hundred years.

One would think that the period when Jason, Menelaus, and Alcimus ruled (175–159) would be the most propitious time for conservatives to become offended and leave. However, as we have seen, the archeological and paleographical evidence from Qumran suggests that this may be too early a time for the community to have separated itself. This leaves the intersacerdotium (159–152), the reign of Jonathan (152–142), and the tenure of Simon (142–134) as the most likely era for the exodus. What was happening then that may have induced a preexisting body of people to move to the desolate shores of the Dead Sea? Probably we shall never know all that went into the decision, but one facet of the early Maccabean high priesthood that deserves attention in this setting is its military nature—something that had not characterized the office before the Maccabean brothers assumed control of it. The combination of military power with the high priesthood probably made opposition foolish and useless and, one would think, utterly changed the nature of power struggles within the priestly class. This new feature of the high priesthood should now be investigated in some detail.

1. *Unusual Features.* A striking implication that may be drawn from the strongly pro-Hasmonean accounts in 1 Maccabees about the accession of Jonathan and Simon to the high-priestly dignity is that their appointments seem to have diverged sharply from traditional practice. The meager surviving evidence indicates that the office had, before 175 B.C., been passed from father to son in the Zadokite line (Exod 29:30, Lev 6:22 [Hebrew 6:15], 16:32, 1 Chr 5:29–41, Neh 12:10–11; cf. 11QT 15:15–16) or, in exceptional cases when this was not possible or not feasible, to another member of the previous high priest's immediate family (*Antiquities* 12:43–44, 157–58). The same genealogical principle prevailed once more at the death of Simon and thereafter until the Roman period. The information in 1 Maccabees shows that both of the first Maccabean high priests violated this standard. Jonathan received his appointment from the pretender Alexander Balas (1 Macc 10:20–21), who was garnering support for his successful bid to wrench the Seleucid throne from Demetrius I. Jonathan's predecessors had also gained royal nomination for the position, since the high priest was a kind of Seleucid official in Judea (Bickerman 1979: 36–38; Goldstein 1976: 75–76), but, besides the fact that Jonathan belonged to the priestly clan of Joarib (1 Macc 2:1–5), which had not produced the genealogical line of high

priests, he clearly did not inherit the position. What little can be gleaned about his accession from the terse account in 1 Maccabees proves that he received the office as pre-payment for military support of Alexander, who billed himself as the son of Antiochus IV (1 Macc 10:1). The two contenders for the throne—the incumbent Demetrius I and Alexander—needed military help and enlisted Jonathan's aid toward this end. Something of the nature of Jonathan's obligations can be deduced from the writer's comment: "Jonathan put on the sacred vestments in the seventh month of the year 160, on the festival of Tabernacles. He also raised troops and manufactured large quantities of arms" (1 Macc 10:21 [Goldstein's translation, as are all citations, from 1 Maccabees]). Strictly priestly or genealogical considerations were irrelevant or decidedly secondary. In a sense, the royal appointment of Jonathan reversed the circumstances of two of his hellenizing predecessors, Jason and Menelaus: whereas they had had to bribe the sovereign in order to receive the position (2 Macc 4:7–10, 23–25), the monarch himself bribed Jonathan with the office. Perhaps it is not terribly surprising that Jonathan ended his days, not in service at the altar, but as a casualty of war to another rival for the Seleucid throne.

Simon, Jonathan's older brother and successor, also gained the high priesthood under curious circumstances. Jonathan was lured into captivity by the Seleucid general Tryphon and thus presumably rendered incapable of executing his sacerdotal functions (1 Macc 12:39–48). Once he was removed from the scene, Simon was, at some point in 142 (Goldstein 1976: 171), appointed high priest. Jonathan did have sons from whose ranks tradition dictated that his successor should come, but if one of them was considered for the office the sources do not mention the fact. Indeed, Simon himself delivered these sons as hostages to Tryphon in the vain hope of securing Jonathan's release. According to 1 Macc 13:16–24, he took this dangerous step against his better judgment because he feared the wrath of the people if he declined to make the attempt to save Jonathan.

Perhaps difficult and even unprecedented circumstances explain some unusual aspects of Simon's appointment, but the most puzzling feature of the entire affair is the assertion of 1 Maccabees that he received the supreme office in the land neither by automatic genealogical succession, installation by Jewish officials, nor in the first place by royal appointment; rather he received it from *the people* (ὁ λαός [1 Macc 14:35]; Greek citations from 1 Maccabees are from Kappler 1936). A natural question to ask is whether it is possible to determine from the surviving evidence who these people were and what legal or *de facto* authority they possessed (or someone thought they possessed) to take so momentous a step. In the following pages an effort will be made to identify the people who engaged in this remarkable act through a study of those passages in 1 Maccabees that describe Simon's rise and through an analysis of how the author uses the term ὁ λαός in these and other pericopes.

2. 1 Macc 14:27b–45. The logical starting point for the inquiry is the document in 1 Macc 14:27b–45 in which one encounters the claim that is under consideration, namely, that initially Simon owed his appointment as high priest to the people. Verses 25–26 provide an editorial introduction to what follows: "When the People [ὁ δῆμος] learned of these achievements, they said, 'How shall we show gratitude to Simon and his sons? He arose with his brothers and his family and fought off the enemies of Israel, and they gained freedom for our people [or: and they (Israel) established a thanksgiving to him (that is, Simon), for (their) freedom (so Sievers 1981: 316–17 n. 4)]!' They drew up a document and set it up on stone slabs on Mt. Zion." The document itself—vv 27b–49—is then quoted. It records both the occasion (vv 27b–28) and the content of a decree that was made relative to Simon. The occasion was a "great assembly" in Simon's third year as high priest (140 B.C.); it was attended by priests, people, rulers of the nation, and elders of the country. At that meeting someone announced (ἐγνώρισεν) to those present the material found in vv 29–45—a document that had been composed by an unnamed group or individual. The process of ratification is described in vv 46–49: all the people agreed to it, Simon himself accepted the almost unlimited powers accorded him, and orders were given that the decree itself be placed on bronze tablets in the temple area and that copies be placed in the treasury for Simon and his sons. The decree itself takes a rather standard form (Abel 1949: 255): a whereas-section, which explains the grounds for the honors to be granted, precedes a description of the honors given the hero. In this case, the whereas-section begins in v 29 with the word ἐπεί and extends through v 40; in v 41 one finds, it seems, the beginning of the honors, although the true function of the verse has been obscured by the presence of ὅτι in nearly all witnesses to the text. That is, as the text now reads, vv 41–43 are also parts of the whereas-section. It seems likely, however, that they form the beginning of the second part of the decree (Stern 1965: 132–39; Goldstein 1976: 500–509; Sievers 1981: 309–12).

The decree first summarizes some major Maccabean accomplishments (vv 29–34). Verse 29 quickly mentions the military bravery of Simon and his brothers (Judas is never mentioned by name) on behalf of the sanctuary, law and nation. Jonathan's career is lightly touched upon in v 30 where three of his acts are noted: he gathered the nation, became high priest, and died. Then one reaches the reign of Simon, which is transparently the center of interest (vv 31–40) in the whereas-section. The decree mentions that he took command when Israel's enemies determined to invade (after Jonathan's removal) and notes that he fortified the cities of Judea, Beth-zur, Joppa, and Gazara. These events can be located in the previous chapters (1 Macc 12:53–13:48), although Simon captured Beth-zur in 11:65–66 when Jonathan was still the leader (this passage does not mention his fortifying it; cf. 14:7). After these notices in vv 31–34, the decree states: "The people [ὁ λαός] saw Simon's faithfulness and the glory which he had resolved to win for his nation, and they made him their leader and high priest, because he had done all these things and because of the justice and loyalty which he had maintained toward his nation. He sought in every way to exalt his people [τὸν λαὸν αὐτοῦ]."

The text then turns to Simon's momentous act of driving the residents of the Akra from this bastion and his refortification of the Akra and of Jerusalem itself (vv 36–37; see 1 Macc 13:49–52). Simon's accomplishments led to his confirmation as high priest by Demetrius II and his enlistment as one of the king's friends (vv 38–40; cf. 1 Macc 13:36–40). Here the whereas-section concludes. The honors that then follow include Simon's being leader, high priest forever, governor, the one in charge of the sanctuary, etc. (vv 41–45). His position as high priest, which he had already occupied for at least two years, was confirmed, according to this document, by three parties: Demetrius II (v 38), the Jews and the priests (v 41), and the people who ratified this decree (v 46).

One conclusion of some importance that emerges from a study of the decree is that the accomplishments of Simon are not listed in order, or at least they do not appear in the same order as they do in the preceding narrative. A case in point occurs in vv 35–40 where the removal of the Gentiles from the Akra is related before Demetrius's confirmation of Simon's high priesthood. In 1 Maccabees 13 the two events are reversed. Also, Gazara is listed among the cities that Simon had fortified and in which he settled law-keeping Jews (v 34)—an event that is presented as one of the motives why the people appointed him high priest (v 35). However, in the narrative of 1 Maccabees this event figures in 13:43–48—after Demetrius had confirmed Simon's investiture (13:36–40). This suggests that the military exploits of Simon may be arranged topically rather than in strict chronological order (Stern 1965: 136–37). Other reasons for doubting the order of events in the decree will be presented below.

3. The People. The essential point for the present purposes is that according to the document in 1 Macc 14:27–45, the people (ὁ λαός) were the first to install Simon in the high-priestly office. Chap. 14 provides more information about the sort of group that these people were. From it, it is apparent that the term ὁ λαός can be used in a specific sense that includes neither the entire body of people present at the assembly nor the nation as a whole. It is noteworthy that the writer employs the word δῆμος in v 25 for those who wished to honor Simon on this occasion; it is also found elsewhere for the citizenry of a nation in official documents (in the correspondence with the Romans and Spartans in 1 Maccabees [Goldstein 1976: 500]). The participants in the great assembly that conferred honors upon Simon are identified as priests, people (λαός), rulers of the nation, and elders of the country (v 28). The facts that the people are distinguished from the other groups and occupy second position in the list are perhaps significant. In order to define more exactly who these people were and what authority they had or claimed, it would be helpful if the account about the occasion when they made Simon high priest could be located.

Though the solemn decree in 1 Macc 14:27b–45 unambiguously names the people as the party that was originally responsible for Simon's investiture as high priest, the preceding narratives that deal with Simon contain no passage in which the author explicitly describes the time when the people made their appointment. When one bears in mind the importance of the office—far and away the highest in the land—and the status of Simon in 1 Maccabees (2:65; 5:17, 20–23; 11:59, 64–65; 12:33; etc.), it seems unlikely that the writer would have left the event unrecorded. It is plausible, though, to suppose that he did narrate the occasion but that, for whatever reason(s), he declined to mention the high priesthood at that particular stage in Simon's rise (cf. Goldstein 1976: 476–77). After all, as noted earlier, the manner in which he acquired the office deviated in some respects from the normal procedure. According to the decree of 1 Macc 14:27–45, the people's appointment of Simon preceded royal *confirmation* (ἔστησεν), and 1 Macc 13:36–40 indicates that their action must also have antedated Demetrius's letter to Simon, since in it the king, without comment, calls Simon "high priest" (v 36). 1 Macc 13:41–42 then adds that in the Seleucid year 170 (=142) " . . . the people [ὁ λαός] began to write as the dating formula in bills and contracts, 'In the first year, under Simon, high priest, commander, and chief of the Jews'" (v 42). All of this entails that Simon became high priest at the very beginning of his period of leadership, probably not after every one of the accomplishments listed at the beginning of the decree.

The sequence within the decree itself, if it is chronological in this case, and the order in the preceding narratives strongly favor the thesis that the people appointed Simon as high priest at the meeting described in 1 Macc 13:1–9. It is worthwhile to study the larger context of this pericope because it is crucial for identifying who the people of 1 Macc 13:1–9 were. The preceding chapter relates the events that led to Tryphon's deceptive capture of Jonathan. When Jonathan came to meet this Seleucid general with some 40,000 troops (1 Macc 12:41, 46; cf. *Antiquities* 13:190), Tryphon asked, "Why did you weary all these people [πάντα τὸν λαὸν τοῦτον] when we are not at war" (1 Macc 12:44)? Jonathan was inexplicably duped by Tryphon's reassuring words and dismissed all but one thousand of his men. He was then promptly seized and the one thousand remaining soldiers were executed (vv 46–48). Next Tryphon dispatched units of his troops whose assignment was to take the two thousand soldiers of Jonathan's army who had been left in Galilee, but the Jewish soldiers managed to elude them and return to Judah where they mourned for Jonathan and the one thousand who had perished in Ptolemais (vv 49–52). One then reads the enthusiastic words that the author places on the lips of the Seleucid forces: "They are leaderless and helpless. Now, therefore, let us wage war upon them and wipe out the memory of them from the human race" (1 Macc 12:53b). This is the situation, incidentally, that is mentioned at the beginning of the decree in chap. 14. The anti-Seleucid elements in Judea were thrown into a worse quandary when they heard that Tryphon was assembling a large force " . . . intending to invade the land of Judah and wipe it out" (1 Macc 13:1b; cf. v 12). The story about the meeting in question at which Simon addressed the people then follows immediately.

The context indicates that the people whom Simon rallied at the Jerusalem gathering described in 1 Macc 13:1–9 were those members of the Maccabean forces who had escaped to Judah. As noted above, Jonathan's army had been called the people (1 Macc 12:44), and the crowd of 13:1–9 is also called the people: "Perceiving the terror and dismay of the people [τὸν λαόν], he [Simon] went to Jerusalem and called a meeting of the people [τὸν λαόν]" (13:2). He managed to revive their fainting spirits by recalling the singular contributions that his family had made to their welfare. As the last of them, he, too, was willing to sacrifice himself for the cause of the nation and sanctuary. The people [τοῦ λαοῦ] then took heart from his words and exclaimed, "You are our chief [ἡγούμενος], in the place of your brothers Judas and Jonathan! Fight our war, and we shall perform all your commands" (1 Macc 13:8b–9). It should be added that the title ἡγούμενος specified here is the very one that is given in 14:35 with ἀρχιερέα as an office or honor and that the people had originally bestowed upon Simon. This provides extra support for the thesis that 1 Macc 13:1–9 depicts the occasion when Simon became high priest, though the author fails to mention the title.

It seems the case, then, that the people appointed Simon their leader and high priest at the assembly described in 1 Macc 13:1–9 and that the people there were the remnants of the Maccabean army that had been under Jonathan's command. The language of these people in 1 Macc 13:8b–9 lends added force to the argument that Hasmonean troops were the ones who first gave Simon his offices. Their exclamation echoes the words of Judas's military companions who had, some years before, appointed Jonathan to succeed his fallen brother (Judas's death is related in 1 Macc 9:18):

1 Macc 9:30: Accordingly, we hereby choose you today to replace him as our commander [ἄρχοντα] and chief [ἡγούμενον] to carry on our war.	1 Macc 13:8b–9a: You are our chief [ἡγούμενος], in the place of your brothers Judas and Jonathan! Fight our war. . . .

The context of 1 Macc 9:30 shows that the group that passed along the Maccabean mantle did not consist of all anti-Seleucid Judeans but only of Judas's friends who were in need of a new general (1 Macc 9:28–29). Similarly, it is most likely that the people of 1 Macc 13:1–9 who designated Simon as Jonathan's successor were the Maccabean party and more specifically the Hasmonean army. The people were neither all the residents of Jerusalem nor even all its anti-Seleucid inhabitants. They were Hasmonean soldiers.

These are not the only passages in 1 Maccabees in which the potentially very general term ὁ λαός has the specific meaning 'soldiers'. Before turning to some of them, it should be noted that λαός at times clearly has its familiar inclusive sense (for example, 1 Macc 14:46); but there is a series of cases (besides those mentioned above) in which it must have a more restricted referent. For example, 1 Macc 3:55 says that Judas appointed commanders of thousands, hundreds, fifties, and tens over the people (τοῦ λαοῦ); 5:43 relates that Judas and all the people [πᾶς ὁ λαός], during a military campaign, swam across a river—hardly an exercise for an entire populace of men, women, and children but one that would be quite feasible for an army. Other instances include 5:61, which designates the defeated troops of the subordinate officers Joseph and Azariah 'the people' (ἐν τῷ λαῷ); 6:19–20, which reports that all the people (πάντα τὸν λαόν) laid siege to the citadel; 7:6, in which the high priest Alcimus, in the course of bringing charges against Judas and his band, denounced the people (τοῦ λαοῦ) to the king, etc. (cf. also 7:26, 48; 10:7, 46).

The practice of calling an army 'the people' has a long history both in Greek and Hebrew sources. Homer uses the term frequently in the Iliad "specifically for the army, the soldiers, especially in distinction from their leaders" (Strathmann 1967: 30)—a usage that later disappears from Greek texts. In the Hebrew Bible military units are often labeled העם (Liver 1971: 237–38), and presumably this word appeared in the Hebrew original of 1 Maccabees wherever ὁ λαός in its various forms now stands. Good examples can be found in many biblical battle stories. In Josh 6:3–5 Joshua receives battle instructions from the Lord:

> You shall march around the city, all the men of war going around the city once. Thus shall you do for six days. And seven priests shall bear seven trumpets of rams' horns before the ark; and on the seventh day you shall march around the city seven times, the priests blowing the trumpets. And when they

> make a long blast with the ram's horn, as soon as you hear the sound of the trumpet, then all the people [העם = ὁ λαός in the LXX] shall shout with a great shout; and the wall of the city will fall down flat, and the people [העם = ὁ λαός] shall go up every man straight before him (*RSV*; see also vv 7, 8, 10, 20; 8:1, 5, 10–11, 14, 16, 20; 10:21, 33; 1 Sam 30:21).

2 Sam 1:4 should also be quoted: "'The people [העם] have fled from the battle, and many of the people [העם] also have fallen and are dead'" (*RSV*). This list of passages is merely illustrative, not comprehensive.

If one may, therefore, conclude that the people of 1 Macc 13:1–9 were the remnants of Jonathan's army and that they named Simon high priest in his brothers' stead, then some new light is shed on the great assembly in chap. 14. The people, that is, the Maccabean army, conferred the high priesthood on Simon as part of the general transfer of Jonathan's authority—a procedure that they had effected earlier when Jonathan had succeeded Judas. The situation was more complicated in the present case, though, because Jonathan had acquired the high-priestly office after taking over the leadership of the Maccabean forces. It may be that the appointment of Simon by the people was provisional—perhaps a temporary measure, depending on Jonathan's fate (his death is reported later, in 13:23). There were precedents in the Second Temple period for a brother or another relative of a high priest to assume the office temporarily under special circumstances. For instance, Josephus (*Antiquities* 12:43–44) says that when an earlier high priest named Simon died, he left an infant son. So his brother Eleazar ruled in his place. 2 Macc 4:29 reports that Menelaus, when he had to be away from Jerusalem, left his brother Lysimachus as his substitute. Josephus also records (*Antiquities* 11:306) a case in which a high priest's brother shared the office with him. Then there is the later episode (A.D. 17) in which the brother of another high priest named Simon had to serve as his substitute because the spittle of an Arab had defiled Simon before the Day of Atonement (Jeremias 1969: 153).

If this was the nature of Simon's appointment in 142, it would have required confirmation later from other power groups in order to make it appear fully legitimate. But his soldiers were the first body to recognize him as cultic chief, and they were the ones who began, after Jonathan's death was confirmed (1 Macc 13:25), to write on contracts: "In the first year, under Simon, high priest, commander, and chief of the Jews" (1 Macc 13:42b). By this time, Simon had been recognized as high priest by the Seleucid monarch Demetrius II, as the greeting in his letter to Simon shows (1 Macc 13:36). Confirmation and elaboration of Simon's positions were subsequently given by Jewish authorities as well and approved by the δῆμος (14:25) in the events of chap. 14. At that meeting the high-priestly office was made Simon's in perpetuity—that is, the succession reverted to the traditional genealogical form (Simon was the last surviving son of Mattathias).

If Simon did in fact first gain recognition as high priest at the meeting with Jonathan's terrified soldiers (1 Macc 13:1–9), why did the author of 1 Maccabees fail to mention the office in his account? Simon was undoubtedly his hero, and one would think that he would have been delighted to write that immediately after Jonathan's removal the people made him the heir of all his brother's positions. The writer does not, of course, explain his omission, but some suggestions can be made. He would have wished to avoid giving the impression that there was anything illegal about Simon's assumption of the high priesthood. Since the high priest in Jerusalem was a notable official in the Seleucid realm, it was necessary that the king make the appointment even if his act meant no more than that he set his seal of approval on the result of a legal Jewish process of nomination. It would not have been proper—or at least not traditional—for an army to usurp the king's right to appoint a high priest. This may have been one reason why the author does not name the high priesthood in 1 Macc 13:1–9. Rather, he allows Demetrius II to be the first person in his narrative to address Simon as high priest (1 Macc 13:36). In this way Simon's investiture receives royal legitimation (see also Goldstein 1976: 476–77).

While this and perhaps other factors may have motivated the author not to mention the high priesthood in 1 Macc 13:1–9, he did not remove from his book all traces of Simon's earlier elevation. He used as a source the document now found in 1 Macc 14:29–45 and did not alter it significantly, perhaps because of its official character. It did include a reference to Simon's appointment as high priest by the people, but perhaps it was thought that the note could safely be left at this later point in the book whereas it would have raised uncomfortable questions if it had appeared at the beginning of chap. 13. One possible unintended result of using the word λαός for the group that first made Simon high priest was that to later readers Simon appeared to have been chosen high priest by popular acclaim. Josephus understood it in this sense. He does not reproduce the decree of chap. 14, but in his paraphrase of 1 Macc 13:1–9 he writes: "Thereupon Simon, seeing that the people of Jerusalem [τοὺς Ἱεροσολυμίτας] were dismayed at these happenings . . . , called the people [τὸν δῆμον] together in the temple . . ." (*Antiquities* 13:197, Marcus's translation, as are all citations from *Antiquities*). Later, when summarizing the end of 1 Maccabees 13, he observes: "And Simon, after being chosen high priest by the populace [τοῦ πλήθους] . . ." (*Antiquities* 13:213).

4. Judas and the High Priesthood. With Jonathan and Simon the army—their army—had become a dominant factor in obtaining the high priesthood.

Jonathan gained the office in return for military assistance to Alexander Balas, and Simon was initially named to the position by his army. It is possible that they were not the first to seize upon the advantage that controlling a private army offered in this regard. It is well known that neither 1 Maccabees nor 2 Maccabees claims that Judas, the first Maccabean commander, became the high priest, but Josephus reports that he did take the office. His assertions have not garnered much enthusiasm among modern scholars (see Schürer 1973: 170; Smith 1961: 6), but they ought not to be dismissed too lightly. There are three passages in which the historian advances his claim for Judas. In *Antiquities* 12:414 he writes: "And when he [Alcimus] died, the people [ὁ λαός] gave the high priesthood to Judas. . . ." One immediately encounters the difficulty that 1 Maccabees, which is Josephus's principal source here, places Judas's death before that of Alcimus (Judas's death: 1 Macc 9:18–22; Alcimus's death: 1 Macc 9:56–57). That is a problem, to be sure, but it need not affect the validity of the statement that Judas served as high priest. Josephus again refers to Judas as high priest when he says that a decree from the Roman senate was signed by his emissaries Eupolemus and Jason, "Judas being high priest of the nation . . ." (12:419). And, when he relates the death of Judas, the historian notes that "he had held the high priesthood for three years . . ." (12:434). It is true, as Marcus observed (1943: 216), that Josephus contradicts his own narrative, since in *Antiquities* 20:237 he explains: "Now when Jacimus [=Alcimus] had retained the priesthood three years, he died, and there was none that succeeded him, but the city continued seven years without a high priest." Yet, though one should concede that there are weighty objections to accepting Josephus's claim, it is interesting that he names the *people* as the ones who gave Judas the office. Is this the first military appointment to the high priesthood in the Maccabean family?

One cannot be sure, but the narratives of 1 and 2 Maccabees are not necessarily opposed to what Josephus asserts. In 1 Maccabees it is evident that Judas, after wresting the temple from Seleucid control (4:36–61), never lost it except perhaps momentarily when Antiochus V attacked it (6:51–54) and demolished the wall that encircled it (v 62). Moreover, Alcimus, who did receive royal appointment as high priest (1 Macc 7:5, 9), was unable to assume office at the temple until after Judas's death (1 Macc 9:54–57). In 2 Maccabees one finds similar information. There Alcimus, who is called a former high priest who wanted his position restored (14:3), complains that he has been deprived of his ancestral right—the high priesthood—by Judas (14:6–7). Subsequently, King Demetrius dispatches Nicanor to execute Judas, scatter his men, and install Alcimus as high priest (2 Macc 14:12–13). That is, if Alcimus is to serve as high priest, Judas must be removed. Judas is clearly in Jerusalem in the sequel (for example, 2 Macc 14:22), and later, when Nicanor breaks his friendship with Judas, he assumes that he is to be found in the temple (vv 31–36).

Perhaps it is acceptable to say that Judas functioned as a rival high priest to Alcimus and that he enjoyed control of the temple. Josephus says that the people appointed him high priest—certainly an unofficial though effective act—and this would again mean that the army had appointed him to the position. One must be cautious, however, because, as seen earlier, Josephus does not consistently use λαός where his source does. Nevertheless, it is an intriguing possibility—and not at all an unlikely one—that Judas's army did select him as high priest after the death of Menelaus. His name would not have appeared on official lists of high priests (such as the one in *Antiquities* 20 or in those of 1–2 Maccabees) because Judas lacked royal confirmation—something that clearly would not have stopped him from acting in the capacity of high priest. In placing his elevation after Alcimus's death, Josephus may have assumed that the two could hardly have been high priests at one time and that therefore Judas must have assumed office after the former high priest died. He then tried in places to introduce this conclusion into his chronology for the high priests but did it rather poorly and inconsistently. If Josephus's statement that Judas was high priest is true in some sense, then the military had asserted itself in the high-priestly succession already with the first Maccabean leader.

Two Maccabean brothers did gain the high priesthood through their armies and Judas may have done so as well. One result of this role for the Judean military was that priestly disputes would take on a new form: who could oppose a high priest who had an army behind him? But another was that these high priests were able, through their martial skill and daring, to accumulate immense wealth. This is a prominent motif particularly in 1 Maccabees for the careers of Judas, Jonathan, and Simon. The armies of all three captured an immense amount of booty (Judas: 1 Macc 4:23; 5:3, 35, 51, 68; 7:47 [2 Macc 8:25, 27–28; 30–31]; Jonathan: 1 Macc 9:40; 10:84, 87; 11:48–51, 61; 12:32; and Simon: 1 Macc 5:22; 11:65–66). Jonathan (1 Macc 10:20, 62, 89; 11:58) received rich gifts from Seleucid kings, while he (1 Macc 10:59–60; 11:24) and Simon (1 Macc 13:17–19, 37; 15:26) were able to send them large amounts of money or lavish presents. Simon also sent the Romans a gold shield of one thousand minas (1 Macc 14:24; cf. 15:18). He is said to have supplied cities with food and to have equipped them for defense (1 Macc 14:10); to have made the temple splendid and improved its vessels (1 Macc 14:15); and to have spent large amounts of his own money to arm and pay his soldiers (1 Macc 14:32). It is not surprising, then, to read of his magnificence (1 Macc 14:4), of the splendor of his court (1 Macc 15:32—it even impressed a Seleucid official), and that Ptolemy was supposed to have been wealthy " . . . for he was the son-in-law of the high priest" (1 Macc

16:11–12). Moreover, Simon was authorized to coin money (1 Macc 15:6), though the surviving evidence suggests he never actually did so. In short, the three Maccabean brothers became extremely rich men.

This paper began with questions about the occasion that led some dissatisfied people to absent themselves from Judean society and retire to the shores of the Dead Sea. What made a previously existing group do this at some point near the mid-second century B.C. or slightly later? Clearly we do not know much about this, but it is evident from 1–2 Maccabees and Josephus's *Antiquities* that the high priesthood had entered a new phase of its history: it was thoroughly militarized at that time and was occupied by violent men who had accumulated great wealth, men who could no longer be opposed effectively. It may well be that, as Stegemann (1971) and Murphy-O'Connor (1976) have argued, the Teacher of Righteousness was an acting or actual high priest during the years 159–152 and that when Jonathan was appointed he ousted him from office. Jonathan's army and royal appointment, which was based on his military value, made opposition useless. The continued prominence of the Maccabean armies during the reign of Jonathan (152–142) and at the initial nomination of Simon and throughout his rule (142–134) hardly provided encouraging conditions for the Teacher's group to return and attempt to restore an older order to the high priesthood.

C. *The Qumran Evidence*

Are there echoes of this in the Qumran literature? There may be some references to the wealth of the Maccabean high priests and their military nature in 1QpHab 8:3–17, which quotes and comments upon Hab 2:5–6 and 7–8a. The first biblical lemma refers to a wealthy man who is insatiable and multiplies for himself what does not belong to him. The commentary reads as follows:

> The interpretation of it concerns the Wicked Priest, who was called by the true name at the beginning of his course, but when he ruled in Israel, he became arrogant, abandoned God, and betrayed the statues for the sake of wealth (הון—היין in MT). He stole and amassed the wealth of the men of violence who had rebelled against God, and he took the wealth of peoples to add to himself guilty sin. And the abominable ways he pursued with every sort of unclean impurity (1QpHab 8:8–13 [Horgan 1979: 17]).

In elucidating Hab 2:7–8a, which speaks of one who plundered many nations but who will fall prey to them, the expositor declares:

> The in[terpretation of the passage] concerns the priest, who rebelled [and trans]gressed the statutes of [God, plundering many peoples, but they will pl]under him. . . . (1QpHab 8:16–17 [Horgan 1979: 17–18]).

In the next column, as he interprets the same verse, he adds that this concerns "the last priests of Jerusalem, who amass wealth and profit from the plunder of the peoples; but at the end of days their wealth together with their booty will be given into the hand of the army of the Kittim" (1QpHab 9:4–7 [Horgan 1979: 18]). In col. 12:10 (on Hab 2:17b) the commentator says that the Wicked Priest "stole the wealth of the poor ones" (Horgan 1979: 20)—a designation for the Qumran community, which, whatever its full range of meaning, forms a stark contrast with the wealth of their opponents. One wonders, too, whether the several references in the commentaries to the "violent ones of the covenant" (see especially 1QpHab 2:6; 4QpPs[a] 1–10 ii 14; 1–10 iii 12; 1–10 iv 1–2, cf. 18–19; for a related expression see 1QpHab 8:11 [אנשי חמס]) also intends the Maccabean high priests and their martial partisans.

Certainty is impossible, but through sundry hints and allusions in the different sorts of texts—either from the Qumran library or from other sources that deal with the time of its origins as a home for exiles—one can perceive conditions that would have provided these dissidents no comfort and may have encouraged them to leave the mainline community and stay away for some time.

Bibliography

Abel, F. M.
1949 *Les livres des Maccabées*. Études bibliques. Paris: LeCoffre.

Bickerman, E.
1979 *The God of the Maccabees*. Studies in Judaism in Late Antiquity 32. Leiden: Brill [translation of *Der Gott der Makkabäer* (Berlin: Schocken, 1937)].

Charles, R. H.
1902 *The Book of Jubilees; or, The Little Genesis*. London: Adam and Charles Black.

Cross, F. M.
1980 *The Ancient Library of Qumran & Modern Biblical Studies*. Rev. ed. Grand Rapids: Baker.

Dexinger, F.
1977 *Henochs Zehnwochenapokalypse und offene Probleme der Apokalyptikforschung*. Studia Post-Biblica 29. Leiden: Brill.

Ginzberg, L.
1976 *An Unknown Jewish Sect*. Moreshet Series 1. New York: Jewish Theological Seminary of America [revised and updated translation of *Eine unbekannte jüdische Sekte* (New York: privately printed, 1922)].

Goldstein, J.
1976 *I Maccabees*. Anchor Bible 41. Garden City: Doubleday.

Horgan, M. P.
1979 *Pesharim: Qumran Interpretations of Biblical Books*. Catholic Biblical Quarterly Monograph Series 8. Washington: Catholic Biblical Association of America.

Jeremias, J.
1969 *Jerusalem in the Time of Jesus*. Philadelphia: Fortress [translation of the 3d ed. of *Jerusalem zur Zeit Jesu* (Göttingen: Vandenhoeck und Ruprecht, 1962)].

Kappler, W.
1936 *Septuaginta: Vetus Testamentum Graecum, IX/I Maccabaeorum Liber I*. Göttingen: Vandenhoeck und Ruprecht.

Knibb, M. A.
1978 *The Ethiopic Book of Enoch: A New Edition in the Light of the Aramaic Dead Sea Fragments*. 2 vols. Oxford: Clarendon.

Liver, J.
1971 עם. Cols. 235–39 in אנציקלופדיה מקראית, vol. 6. Jerusalem: Bialik.

Marcus, R.
1937 *Josephus: Jewish Antiquities Books IX–XI*. Loeb Classical Library 326. Cambridge: Harvard University/London: William Heinemann.
1943 *Josephus: Jewish Antiquities Books XII–XIV*. Loeb Classical Library 365. Cambridge: Harvard University/London: William Heinemann.

Milik, J. T.
1976 *The Books of Enoch: Aramaic Fragments of Qumrân Cave 4*. Oxford: Clarendon.

Murphy-O'Connor, J.
1976 Demetrius I and the Teacher of Righteousness. *Revue Biblique* 83: 400–420.

Nickelsburg, G. W. E.
1981 *Jewish Literature between the Bible and the Mishnah*. Philadelphia: Fortress.

Qimron, E., and J. Strugnell
1985 An Unpublished Halakhic Letter from Qumran. Pp. 400–407 in *Biblical Archeology Today: Proceedings of the International Congress on Biblical Archaeology, Jerusalem, April 1984*. Jerusalem: Israel Exploration Society.

Rabin, C.
1958 *The Zadokite Documents*. 2d ed. Oxford: Clarendon.

Sanders, J.
1965 *The Psalms Scroll of Qumrân Cave 11 (11QPs[a])*. Discoveries in the Judaean Desert of Jordan 4. Oxford: Clarendon.

Schürer, E.
1973 *The History of the Jewish People in the Age of Jesus Christ (175 B.C.–A.D. 135)*. Revised and edited by G. Vermes and F. Millar, vol. 1. Edinburgh: T. & T. Clark [translation of *Geschichte des jüdischen Volkes im Zeitalter Jesu Christi* (3 vols.; 3d/4th ed.; Leipzig: J. C. Hinrichs, 1901–9)].

Sievers, J.
1981 The High Priesthood of Simon Maccabeus: An Analysis of 1 Macc 14:25–49. Pp. 309–18 in *Society of Biblical Literature Seminar Papers*, ed. K. H. Richards. Chico: Scholars Press.

Smith, W. F.
1961 A Study of Zadokite High Priesthood within the Graeco-Roman Age: From Simeon the Just to the High Priests Appointed by Herod the Great. Ph.D. diss., Harvard University.

Stegemann, H.
1971 *Die Entstehung der Qumrangemeinde*. Bonn: Rheinische Friedrich-Wilhelms-Universität.

Stern, M.
1965 **תעודות למרד החשמונאים**. Tel Aviv: Hakibbutz Hameuchad.

Strathmann, H.
1965 λαός. Pp. 29–39 in *Theological Dictionary of the New Testament*, ed. G. Kittel, vol. 4. Grand Rapids: Eerdmans.

Talmon, S.
1958 The Calendar Reckoning of the Sect from the Judaean Desert. Pp. 162–99 in *Aspects of the Dead Sea Scrolls*, ed. C. Rabin and Y. Yadin. Scripta Hierosolymitana 4. Jerusalem: Magnes.

VanderKam, J. C.
1977 *Textual and Historical Studies in the Book of Jubilees*. Harvard Semitic Monographs 14. Missoula: Scholars Press.
1984 Studies in the Apocalypse of Weeks (1 Enoch 93:1–10; 91:11–17). *Catholic Biblical Quarterly* 46: 511–23.

de Vaux, R.
1973 *Archeology and the Dead Sea Scrolls*. The Schweich Lectures 1959. London: Oxford [revised edition and translation of *L'archéologie et les manuscrits de la mer Morte* (London: Oxford, 1961)].

Yadin, Y.
1977 **מגילת המקדש**. 3 vols. and a supplement. Jerusalem: Israel Exploration Society/The Institute of Archeology of the Hebrew University/The Shrine of the Book.